GLUT

MASTERING INFORMATION
THROUGH THE AGES

GLUT

MASTERING INFORMATION
THROUGH THE AGES

ALEX WRIGHT

Cornell University Press
Ithaca and London

Hardcover edition originally published by Joseph Henry Press. Paperback edition published with permission. All rights reserved. First printing, Cornell Paperpacks, 2008.

Printed in the United States of America

Library of Congress Cataloging-in-Publication Data

Wright, Alex, 1966–
   Glut : mastering information through the ages / by Alex Wright.
     p. cm.
   Includes bibliographical references and index.
   ISBN 978-0-8014-7509-2
   1. Information organization—History. 2. Information storage and retrieval systems—History. 3. Information society—History. I. Title.
   Z666.5W75 2007
   020.9—dc22
                    2007006290

Cornell University Press strives to use environmentally responsible suppliers and materials to the fullest extent possible in the publishing of its books. Such materials include vegetable-based, low-VOC inks and acid-free papers that are recycled, totally chlorine-free, or partly composed of nonwood fibers. For further information, visit our website at www.cornellpress.cornell.edu.

Paperback printing   10 9 8 7 6 5 4 3 2 1

For my parents

*Our own Middle Age, it has been said, will be an age of
"permanent transition," for which new methods of adjustment
will have to be employed . . . an immense work of bricolage,
balanced among hope, nostalgia and despair.*

Umberto Eco, "Living in the New Middle Ages"

Contents

Introduction   1

1   Networks and Hierarchies   5

2   Family Trees and the Tree of Life   22

3   The Ice Age Information Explosion   39

4   The Age of Alphabets   48

5   Illuminating the Dark Age   78

6   A Steam Engine of the Mind   99

7   The Astral Power Station   122

8   The Encyclopedic Revolution   143

9   The Moose That Roared   152

10 The Industrial Library   165

11 The Web That Wasn't   183

12 Memories of the Future   230

Appendixes

A   John Wilkins's Universal Categories   239

B   Thomas Jefferson's 1783 Catalog of Books   242

C   The Dewey Decimal System   245

D   S. R. Ranganathan's Colon Classification   247

Acknowledgments   251

Notes   253

Index   271

Introduction

Ever since the Web first started to flicker across the world's computer
screens, we have seen a bull market in hyperbole about the digital age.
Visiting San Francisco at the height of the 1990s dot-com boom, Tom
Wolfe noted the particular brand of euphoria then sweeping the city.
Wolfe, who made his journalistic bones chronicling the raptures of
the city's psychedelic pranksters in the 1960s,[1] spotted a similar strain
of quasi-mystical fervor taking hold among the young acolytes of the
digital revolution. "Much of the sublime lift came from something
loftier than overnight IPO billions," he wrote, "something verging on
the spiritual." Enthusiastic dot-commers "were doing more than simply developing computers and creating a new wonder medium, the
Internet. Far more. The Force was with them. They were spinning a
seamless web over all the earth."[2] In the Day-Glo pages of *Wired* and
a host of also-ran *New Economy* magazines, the so-called digerati were
pumping a rhetorical bubble no less inflated than the era's IPO-fu-
eled stock prices. Writer Steven Johnson compared the dawning age
of software to a religious awakening, predicting that "the visual metaphors of interface design will eventually acquire a richness and pro-
fundity that rival those of Hinduism or Christianity."[3] Elsewhere,
supercomputer pioneer Danny Hillis argued that the advent of the

World Wide Web signaled an evolutionary event on par with the emergence of a new species: "We're taking off," he wrote. "We are not evolution's ultimate product. There's something coming after us, and I imagine it is something wonderful. But we may never be able to comprehend it, any more than a caterpillar can imagine turning into a butterfly."[4] More recently, inventor and futurist Ray Kurzweil has gone so far as to suggest that we are undergoing a "technological change so rapid and profound it represents a rupture in the fabric of human history," an event so momentous that it will trigger "the merger of biological and nonbiological intelligence, immortal software-based humans, and ultra-high levels of intelligence that expand outward in the universe at the speed of light."[5] Could the arhats themselves have painted a more dazzling picture of enlightenment?

Mystical beliefs about technology are nothing new. In 1938 H. G. Wells predicted that "the whole human memory can be, and probably in a short time will be, made accessible to every individual," forming a so-called World Brain that would eventually give birth to a "widespread world intelligence conscious of itself."[6] Similar visions of an emerging planetary intelligence surfaced in the mid-twentieth century writings of the Catholic mystic Teilhard de Chardin, who foresaw the rise of an "extraordinary network of radio and television communication which already links us all in a sort of 'etherised' human consciousness" that would ultimately metamorphize into "a single, organized, unbroken membrane over the earth."[7] Teilhard believed that this burgeoning networked consciousness signaled a new stage in God's evolutionary plan, in which human beings would coalesce into a new kind of social organism, complete with a nervous system and brain that would eventually spring to life of its own accord. Teilhard never published his writings—the Catholic Church forbade him from doing so—but his essays nonetheless found an enthusiastic cult following among fellow Jesuits like Marshall McLuhan, who took Teilhard's vision as a starting point for formulating his theory of the global village.

Today, the torch song of technological transcendentalism has passed from the visionary fringe into the cultural mainstream. Scarcely a day goes by without some hopeful dispatch about new Web applications, digital libraries, or techno-capitalists spending billions to wire the developing world. Some apostles of digitization argue that the expanding global network will do more than just improve people's lives; it will change the shape of human knowledge itself. Digital texts will supplant physical ones, books will mingle with blogs, and fusty old library catalogs will give way to the liberating pixie dust of Google searches. As the network sets information free from old physical shackles, people the world over will join in a technological great awakening.

Amid this gusher of cyber-optimism, a few dissidents have questioned the dark side of digitization: our fracturing attention spans, the threats to personal privacy, and the risks of creeping groupthink in a relentlessly networked world. "We may even now be in the first stages of a process of social collectivization that will over time all but vanquish the ideal of the isolated individual,"[8] writes critic Sven Birkerts. In this dystopian view, the rise of digital media marks an era of information overload in which our shared cultural reference points will dissolve into a rising tide of digital cruft.

For all the barrels of ink and billions of pixels spent chronicling the rise of the Internet in recent years, however, surprisingly few writers seem disposed to look in any direction but forward. "Computer theory is currently so successful," writes philosopher-programmer Werner Künzel, "that it has no use for its own history."[9] This relentless fixation on the future may have something to do with the inherent "forwardness" of computers, powered as they are by logics of linear progression and lateral sequencing. The computer creates a teleology of forward progress that, as Birkerts puts it, "works against historical perception."[10]

My aim in writing this book is to resist the tug of mystical techno-futurism and approach the story of the information age by looking squarely backward. This is a story we are only beginning to understand. Like the narrator in Edward Abbott's *Flatland*—a two-dimensional creature who wakes up one day to find himself living in a three-dimensional world—we are just starting to recognize the contours of a broader information ecology that has always surrounded us. Just as human beings had no concept of oral culture until they learned how to write, so the arrival of digital culture has given us a new reference point for understanding the analog age. As McLuhan put it, "one thing about which fish are completely unaware is the water, since they have no *anti-environment* that would allow them to perceive the element they swim in." From the vantage point of the digital age, we can approach the history of the information age in a new light. To do so requires stepping outside of traditional disciplinary constructs, however, in search of a new storyline.

In these pages I traverse a number of topics not usually brought together in one volume: evolutionary biology, cultural anthropology, mythology, monasticism, the history of printing, the scientific method, eighteenth-century taxonomies, Victorian librarianship, and the early history of computers, to name a few. No writer could ever hope to master all of these subjects. I am indebted to the many scholars whose work I relied on in the course of researching this book. Whatever truth this book contains belongs to them; the mistakes are mine alone.

I am keenly aware of the possible objections to a book like this one. Academic historians tend to look skeptically at "meta" histories that go in search of long-term cultural trajectories. As a generalist, I knowingly run the risks of intellectual hubris, caprice, and dilettantism. But I have done my homework, and I expect to be judged by professional standards. This work is, nonetheless, fated to incompleteness. Like an ancient cartographer trying to draw a map of distant lands, I have probably made errors of omission and commission; I may have missed whole continents. But even the most egregious mistakes have their place in the process of discovery. And perhaps I can take a little solace in knowing that even Linnaeus, the father of modern biology, was a devout believer in unicorns.

1

Networks and Hierarchies

*I am a firm believer that without speculation there is no good
and original observation.*
                Charles Darwin, Letter to A. R. Wallace, 1857

When the Spanish conquistadores first encountered the Zuni people
of the North American southwest, they noticed something strange
about their villages. The tribe had divided each of its six "pueblos"
(as the Spanish called them) into a set of identical quadrants, aligned
with the four points of the compass. Each quadrant housed a troop
of clans within the larger tribe: The clans of the Crane, the Grouse,
and the Evergreen lived in the north; the clans of Tobacco, Maize,
and Badgers lived in the south. Each clan enjoyed a set of special
relationships with the natural world. To the people of the north belonged wind, winter, and the color yellow. The people of the west
knew water, spring, and the color blue. The people of the north made
war. The people of the west kept the peace. When the villagers sat
together, they sat apart, like hawks and doves. To the four cardinal
directions, the Zuni added three vertical ones: the sky, the earth, and
a middle realm in between. In the sky, all the colors of the world
swirled together; down below, the earthen realm was black. In the
middle, everything came together; heaven and earth were joined. To
one of these seven directions the Zuni assigned everything in the
cosmos: animals, natural elements, supernatural forces, social responsibilities, families, and individual members of the tribe. This all-

encompassing system equipped the Zunis with a taxonomy of the natural world, a social and political system, a mythology, and a framework for spiritual belief.[1]

The Zuni system represents one people's solution to a problem we all share: how to manage our collective intellectual capital. For more than 100,000 years, human beings have been collecting, organizing, and sharing information, creating systems as varied as the cultures that produced them. Along the way, we have invented a panoply of different tools: taxonomies, temple archives, books, libraries, indexes, encyclopedias, and, in recent years, computer networks.

Today, we live in an age of exploding access to information, awash in what designer Richard Saul Wurman calls a "tsunami of data." Human beings now produce more than five exabytes* worth of recorded information per year: documents, e-mail messages, television shows, radio broadcasts, Web pages, medical records, spreadsheets, presentations, and books like this one. That is more than 50,000 times the number of words stored in the Library of Congress, or more than the total number of words ever spoken by human beings.[2] Seventy-five percent of that information is digital. Most of it will soon disappear. Amid this welter of bits, perhaps some of us worry, like Plato's King Thamus, whether our dependence on the written record will weaken our characters and create forgetfulness in our souls.

As the proliferation of digital media accelerates, we are witnessing profound social, cultural, and political transformations whose long-term outcome we cannot begin to foresee. Organizational charts are flattening, as electronic communication tools enable employees to bypass old chains of command; national borders are growing more porous, as networked data flows across old boundaries; and long-established institutional knowledge systems (like library catalogs) are fast becoming anachronisms in the age of Web search engines. Wherever networked systems take root, it seems, they disrupt the old hierarchical systems that preceded them. Indeed, a faith in the death of

*5,000,000,000,000,000,000 bytes, or 5,000,000,000,000 megabytes.

hierarchy has become a durable nostrum of the digital age. In the popular 1999 tract *The Cluetrain Manifesto*, the authors proposed a credo for the Internet age: "hyperlinks subvert hierarchy."[3] That sentiment captures the widely held belief that the rise of the Internet signals the permanent disruption of old institutional bureaucracies and the birth of a new, enlightened age of individual expression: a renaissance of creativity and personal freedom. In this utopian view, hierarchical systems are restrictive, oppressive tools of control, while networks are open, democratic vehicles of personal liberation. When networks triumph over hierarchies, then, humanity takes a great leap forward.

This comforting narrative is, alas, too tidy by half. Networked information systems are not entirely modern phenomena, nor are hierarchical systems necessarily doomed. There is a deeper story at work here. The fundamental tension between networks and hierarchies has been percolating for eons. Today, we are simply witnessing the latest installment in a long evolutionary drama.

Since the words "network" and "hierarchy" will recur throughout this book, let me spend a moment with the terms. A hierarchy is a system of nested groups. For example, an organization chart is a kind of hierarchy, in which employees are grouped into departments, which in turn are grouped into higher-level organizational units, and so on. Other kinds of hierarchies include government bureaucracies, biological taxonomies, or a system of menus in a software application. Computer scientist Jeff Hawkins suggests that human memory itself can be explained as a system of nested hierarchies running atop a neural network.[4] A network, by contrast, emerges from the bottom up; individuals function as autonomous nodes, negotiating their own relationships, forging ties, coalescing into clusters. There is no "top" in a network; each node is equal and self-directed. Democracy is a kind of network; so is a flock of birds, or the World Wide Web.

Networks and hierarchies are not mutually exclusive; indeed, they usually coexist. We might, for example, work for a company with a formal organization chart; at the same time, we probably also maintain a personal network of colleagues that has no explicit representation in the formal organization: a network within a hierarchy.

Similarly, the Internet—ostensibly a pure network—is actually composed of numerous smaller hierarchical systems. At its technical core the Internet works by breaking large groups of data into small packets, tiny hierarchical units of information stored on a server which are then dispersed across the network and reassembled in a client application, such as a Web browser. At a higher level, much of the content of the Web is generated within organizational hierarchies— like companies, educational and nonprofit institutions, and government agencies—as well as by ostensibly self-directed individuals who nonetheless rely on hierarchical organizations (like computer manufacturers or service providers) to participate in the network. And for all the seeming flatness of the global Internet, most of us make sense of the Web in hierarchical terms: by navigating through menus on a Web site, for example, or selecting from a narrow list of search results. In other words, networks and hierarchies not only coexist, but they are continually giving rise to each other.

Hierarchy

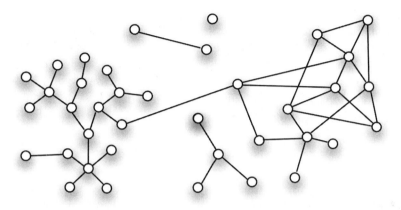

Network

Science writer Howard Bloom has suggested that the tension between networks and hierarchies is not an exclusively human phenomenon, but part of a deeper process embedded in the fabric of the
universe itself, stretching all the way back to the Big Bang.[5] We needn't
look quite so far back, however. Two billion years will do.

CULTURAL EVOLUTION AND OTHER HERESIES

While our reliance on networked information systems may seem like
an acutely modern dilemma, we are not the first generation—nor
even the first species—to wrestle with the problem of information
overload. The information age started not with microchips or movable type, but with the first flowering of complex life. To approach
the history of information systems from a purely human-centered
perspective is to overlook the lessons of billions of years' worth of
evolutionary history. Just as our brains carry around some very old
reptilian equipment, so our collective strategies for managing information bear the traces of patterns that took shape long ago.

John Locke famously argued that "beasts abstract not." But in

recent years, thanks to the breakthrough work of geneticists and evolutionary psychologists, we are beginning to appreciate the surprising complexity of nature's nonhuman information systems. The
animal world is rife with examples of organisms developing collective strategies for accumulating, storing, and distributing information in groups. An assertion like that seems to beg for a definition of
the word "information," so let me offer one:

> Information is the juxtaposition of data to create meaning.

If we accept the familiar construct of information as lying on a
continuum from data to wisdom (data > information > knowledge
> wisdom), then there is no question that other animals create, share,
and organize information. And while animal minds may not harbor the abstractions of human thought, they frequently employ
information-pooling strategies that bear startling resemblances to
our own.

To understand how these systems work requires taking a big step
back into our biological past; but before we set out on the murky
terrain of evolutionary theory, let me sound a note of caution. Many
social scientists (and more than a few biologists) tend to regard evolutionary explanations of human culture with a skepticism bordering
on outright hostility. Ever since the well-chronicled sociobiology wars
of the 1970s and 1980s, scholarly debates have raged about the appli-
cability of evolutionary theory to human culture. The conventional
argument goes something like this: *Homo sapiens* achieved anatomical modernity some 100,000 years ago. Since then our genes have not
evolved in any significant way. Therefore, the term "evolution" simply
does not pertain to the brief span of human culture. Human culture,
they argue, is a complex phenomenon that progresses independently
of biological evolution. Evolution is at best a metaphor—and at worst
a sloppy syllogism—for cultural change: the stuff of eugenics, Social
Darwinism, and worse. The late Stephen Jay Gould, among others,
made eloquent arguments against the notion that human culture
evolves in any biological sense. "Using the same term—evolution—
for both natural and cultural history obfuscates far more than it en-

lightens," he wrote.[6] Human culture, then, cannot be reduced to simple biological processes, and the sheer variety of human culture would seem to prove its independence from biology. In this view, the process of natural selection simply deposited us on the precipice of culture; everything we have achieved since then we have done by—and to—ourselves.

In recent years, however, the srict doctrine of cultural relativism has started to reveal chinks in its conceptual armor. Thanks to break-through work by sociobiologists and evolutionary psychologists, many scientists are now embracing the possibility that natural selec-tion operates at multiple levels of the biological hierarchy—up to the highest levels of human culture. Furthermore, they are beginning to appreciate the complexity of "culture" in other species, and to recog-nize the possibility that certain social behaviors may have evolved in concert with biological evolution. "To say that human behavior and our other attributes cannot be analyzed in evolutionary terms re-quires acceptance of a genuinely bizarre position," argues John Alcock, "namely, that we alone among animal species have somehow man-aged to achieve independence from our evolutionary history."[7] Through the filter of evolutionary psychology, we can begin to ex-plore the possibility that cultural behaviors once thought uniquely human—such as the ability to organize information—may have a deeper evolutionary lineage.

In 1970 biologist Lynn Margulis proposed a revolutionary hy-pothesis about the origin of complex organisms, suggesting that the relationship between networked and hierarchical systems is deeply woven into the fabric of life itself. To make a particularly long story short: About two billion years ago, the first multicellular organisms—eukaryotes—took shape as host bacteria and began to allow other bacteria to take up residence within them, gradually conscripting their formerly independent siblings into a kind of cellular serfdom. These early complex life forms came into existence not as fully formed organisms but rather through a gradual process of evolving social cooperation. Eventually, as teams of bacteria began to reproduce in tandem with their host organisms, they coalesced into nucleated cells capable of reproducing themselves. The first multicellular life forms came into being, then, as self-organizing networks. Gradually, those networks gave rise to an emergent hierarchy: the complex organism. These self-directed biological hierarchies, in turn, began to interact with one another, forming new higher-level networks that, in turn, coalesced into more complex biological hierarchies. From this escalating fugue of hierarchies and networks, life has evolved.

By 500 million BC, complex organisms of a trillion cells or more began to take shape: the first insects, clams, and birds, equipped with highly specialized organs like eyes, nerve cells, and memory coils. As their neural powers grew, these animals became more autonomous. But independence came at a price: The more complex life forms became, the more isolated they became from one another. To compensate for the loss of old physical bonds, they began to develop what Bloom calls "the synapse of the social brain"[8]: imitation. By following each other's behavioral cues, certain animals could pool their sensory data, processing collective experience with a capacity far exceeding the abilities of the lone organism. Imitation provided the glue that bound these increasingly self-directed animals into a higher order of organization: social networks. They became, in effect, superorganisms.

A biological superorganism—like an insect colony, a flock of birds or a school of fish—is both a network and a hierarchy; it emerges from the networked interaction of individual organisms, in turn giving rise to higher-order hierarchies. As individual organisms transmit information to each other, they strengthen the bonds that unite the group. But what, exactly, is being transmitted? Information is, after all, noncorporeal; it is not a physical "thing" (even though it may take expression in the physical environment). Yet there is no question that animals are transmitting some kind of "thing" to each other. So what exactly is it?

In his influential 1975 book *The Selfish Gene*, evolutionary biologist Richard Dawkins dubbed the thing a "meme." Other biologists have variously labeled it a mnemotype, idea, idene, sociogene, or concept.[9] But only "meme" has managed to penetrate the popular vernacular. Whatever term we use, there is no question that other animals regularly record, share, and preserve information that has no physical manifestation. The exchange of memes, moreover, appears to exert a direct influence on the process of natural selection. Biologists have learned a great deal about how memes travel between individual members of a social group, mapping the trajectories of information exchange from individual to individual; less well understood are the higher-level dynamics that characterize the interactions of memes at the group level.

One highly speculative explanation of how nature's "mass minds" operate comes from Bloom, whose unconventional theories and colorful rhetoric have marked him as an agent provocateur in mainstream scientific circles. Bloom postulates that the phenomenon of collective intelligence emerges from the interplay of five essential forces: conformity enforcers, diversity generators, inner judges, resource shifters, and intergroup tournaments. Conformity enforcers (like worker bees or middle managers) ensure that the group as a whole maintains sufficient cohesion to survive adverse conditions; diversity generators (like stray ants or artists) are the "odd ducks" who generate alternative hypotheses for the group to consider, thus ensuring variation; intergroup tournaments (like the waggle dances of bees or scientific debates) enable societies to test alternative hypotheses; inner judges reward productive behavior and punish deleterious actions. Finally, resource shifters (like alpha chimpanzees or corporate executives) make sure successful adaptations receive the support they need to benefit the group as a whole.[10] Bloom's model, while intriguing, is too figurative to pass any empirical test. Nonetheless, respected evolutionary biologists like Margulis and David Sloan Wilson have recognized value in his original, if decidedly left-field, conception of the global brain. We do not have to accept Bloom's theory as hard science, however, to appreciate it as a metaphor. As Alfred North Whitehead put it, "It is more important that a proposition be interesting than that it be true. But of course a true theory is more apt to be interesting than a false one."

Today, we can find ample evidence throughout the natural world of networked superorganisms pooling information, organizing and distributing that information to the right individuals at the right time, and preserving successful group strategies for future generations. Insect societies provide the most often cited example of how seemingly simple creatures can process information with a sophistication seemingly not predicted by their genetic blueprints. In 1946 biologist Karl von Frisch won a Nobel Prize for deciphering the syntax of bees' famous waggle dances, the carefully choreographed tournaments that enable beehives to identify the location of food supplies with astonishing precision. Certain bees scout a particular area for potential food sources and then return to the hive to present choreographed "reports" on what they found. As each bee makes it presentation, the group as a whole registers its level of enthusiasm and compares incoming reports to make a group decision about where to look for food next. No individual bee possesses the intelligence to make such a decision, but as a group, the bees generate a collective "mind" far more clever than the sum of its tiny-brained parts. Elsewhere, studies have shown that, while an individual honeybee can retain a piece of data in its memory bank for up to six days, the hive as a whole can retain that same piece of data for up to three months—double the life span of a single bee.[11]

Some insect colonies display even higher-order behaviors that rely not just on social displays but that actually involve coding their memes onto the physical environment. In 1959 biologist Pierre-Paul Grassé coined the term "stigmergy"[12] (meaning "incite to work") after studying how termites erect their monumental nests. Grassé observed that termites build nests by dint of a brutally simple algorithm: A single termite carries a chewed pellet of dirt in its jaws; whenever it encounters a slightly elevated mound of dirt, it drops the pellet. When a number of termites begin to drop pellets on the same mound, a small clump begins to form; other passing termites, detecting the clump, begin to drop their own pellets, and the mound grows. If one mound starts growing in close proximity to another, the termites will begin scuttling back and forth between the mounds, building diagonally to join them together. From these simple rules, great cathedral-like artifacts emerge. They are living information systems.

Ants, too, exhibit a capacity for stigmergy, communicating to each other through pheromone trails that guide their collective behavior. In one study, researcher Jean-Louis Deneubourg provided an ant colony with two separate tree branches, each a pathway to the same food supply. Individual ants immediately began charging blindly down both paths. Within a few minutes, however, the entire colony had collectively chosen the shorter of the two branches. As the first wave of ants returned from their round-trip journey, they began signaling their remaining compatriots to follow their trail. As the collective pheromone trail grew stronger, the entire colony abandoned the unscented trail and flocked down the fast path to the food supply.

Ants' dual roles as both actors and signals make them a compelling reference model for computer programmers. The new field of "swarm intelligence" has grown up in recent years to explore the application of insect-like solutions to practical problems like computer network design. At Hewlett-Packard, a research team developed a network routing system based explicitly on the tracking behaviors of ant colonies, consisting of a large number of tiny computer programs that wound their way through a distributed network, searching out the least congested routes. Depositing "virtual pheromone" trails at each node, the swarm of programs quickly deduced the fastest path through the network.

Whereas other forms of communication in the natural world typically involve one-to-one transmission between individuals, stigmergy involves at least one step of intermediation: encoding information on an external object. It is a mechanism for indirect collaboration, equipping life forms with what philosopher Ron McClamrock describes as the ability to "enforce on the environment certain kinds of stable properties that will lessen our computational burdens."[13] In other words, stigmergy allows social groups to harness the physical world as a memetic storehouse (something at which our own species has long excelled).

While insect societies provide nature's most elegant examples of information systems that transcend the capacities of individuals, the animal kingdom is rife with other examples of species that share information in groups. In an oft-cited bird study in 1950s England, a small population of English tits stumbled upon the secret of pecking through aluminum milk bottle caps, as a means to get at the milk inside. The new strategy soon took hold among the tit population at large, and an avian meme took flight. An epidemic of bottle pecking spread across the surrounding counties, as successive generations of tits learned the fine art of milk larceny from their peers. In New Zealand, flocks of oystercatcher birds have developed their own idiosyncratic customs for cracking open mussel shells: Some groups hammer the shell until it opens; others pry it open with their beaks. All oystercatchers are born with the capacity for either behavior; the sole determinant of how an individual bird behaves appears to rest entirely on the bird's social affiliation. In other words, social networks—not genetics—may determine how behavioral information gets transmitted.

While insects and birds demonstrate how information systems emerge in species whose intelligence ranks far below our own, we can find examples of complex social networking behaviors in more intelligent animals, notably the primates. Throughout the primate world, social networks provide a fast conduit for innovation and information-sharing that help the group as a whole adapt to its environment.

In Japan a troop of hungry macaques stumbled on an innovative process for separating edible wheat from indigestible sand. On one island an enterprising macaque came up with a handy trick: By throwing the entire mixture of wheat and sand into the sea, the macaque discovered that the wheat would float to the top while the sand sank to the bottom. Success begat imitation; soon after the first macaque stumbled on the wheat-sifting technique, the practice spread through imitative "word of mouth"; within 5 years the entire macaque population of Japan had learned to sift their wheat.[14] Our closest cousins, chimpanzees, also display highly localized traditions that persist across generations. Some chimpanzee troops use rocks to break open nuts; others rely on tree trunks. Some groups have figured out how to use twigs as rudimentary "fishing rods" for digging up ants; others forge long hooked branches into tools for retrieving figs. These local traditions get passed down through generations purely through social transmission, not genetic inheritance. In a similar study, biological anthropologist Carel van Schaik and his colleagues discovered a group of orangutans on the western coast of

Sumatra that had developed highly localized customs for using tools. One group had perfected an intricate procedure for removing seeds from the toughened husks of the *Neesia* tree, by stripping the bark from twigs and using the rudimentary tools to jimmy open the husks.[15] This particular trick seems to have emerged only within one local population; other nearby groups in similar environments had no such innovation, and their *Neesia* seeds went uneaten. The original group had also developed a series of other tool-use innovations, far outstripping the achievements of the surrounding communities. Why did one group of orangutans prove so consistently innovative while their nearby cousins languished? The key to cultural innovation, it seems, has something to do with population density. Van Schaik hypothesizes that "populations in which individuals had more chances to observe others in action would show a greater diversity of learned skills than would populations offering fewer learning opportunities. And indeed, we were able to confirm that sites in which individuals spend more time with others have greater repertoires of learned innovations."[16] The orangutans of Saaq crossed a threshold of social proximity that enabled them to adapt more quickly and successfully to their environment. As we will see later in the book, a similar phenomenon recurs among human social groups, where population density appears to determine the velocity of technological change. Social concentration, it seems, is the engine of innovation.

In addition to imitative learning, primates traffic in another, more subtle, form of information exchange: emotion. We may think of our own emotions in highly personal terms such as joy, sadness, anger, jealousy, and love. Across the primate kingdom, however, emotional expression plays another, broader social role in facilitating the transfer of memes between group members. Recent primate research also suggests that emotional expression may have something to do with our capacity for symbolic expression. "Symbol formation results from a series of stages of affective transformations," writes psychiatrist Stanley Greenspan, suggesting that symbols arose not from the use of human spoken language but from a deeper emotional wellspring grounded in the primate limbic system (the part of the brain that controls emotions). Greenspan has formulated an intriguing theory that suggests an evolutionary progression of symbolic language: from engagement and signaling (like reacting to a mother's facial expressions) to simple call-and-response interactions (like sharing environmental data) to elaborate greeting rituals (like courtship or coalition building) to "co-regulated affective signaling" (like organizing hunting parties with differentiated roles).[17] Greenspan believes that this progression of signaling behavior evolved in concert with a series of genetic mutations among our primate ancestors that would ultimately equip *Homo sapiens* with our uniquely developed capacity for symbolic expression.

If this startling theory of human symbolism holds true, it suggests a radical rethinking of the origin and function of symbols. Our symbols may function not just as embodiments of abstract linguistic ideas but as conveyors of much deeper, preverbal emotional truths that spring from the source of all emotions: families. As we will see in the next chapter, the structure of family relationships has exerted a profound influence on the subsequent shape and structure of human information systems. Relationships between parents and children, siblings and extended family members, form a psychological template that resurfaces over and over again in the way we seem to structure the relationships between thoughts and ideas, providing an implicit structure for the earliest taxonomic systems.

This emotional dimension of symbols may offer a partial explanation for why certain kinds of information systems prove more successful than others. Systems based on artificial ideologies, which lack a reinforcing emotional power, routinely fail to persist. For example, when communist regimes attempted to rewrite their countries' histories in a new ideological light, those efforts eventually faltered in the face of their citizens' own shared memories. "Because families continue to transmit to their children a more basic nonverbal presymbolic emotional 'truth,'" Greenspan argues, "these symbolic fabrications vanish immediately upon the collapse of the dictatorships that enforce them."[18] If our capacity for symbolic abstraction really rests so deeply in our limbic system, that may well explain why our most resilient information systems—like folk tales, urban legends, and religious traditions—seem to flourish by passing through the strong social bonds of personal relationships rather than relying solely on institutional power or ideologies. As we will see later in this book, oral traditions have proved particularly durable over the years, usually outlasting more elaborate written systems that come and go with the rise and fall of their institutional sponsors.

THE "EVOLUTION" OF INFORMATION SYSTEMS

So far, we have seen how the deep biological history of networks and hierarchies has given rise to the escalating complexity of nature's information systems. We have seen how that process has equipped other species with the ability to preserve information beyond the life span of the individual organism through social imitation and pooling, and by encoding memes onto their physical environments. And we have seen how, among primates, deep-seated emotional responses provided the semantic scaffolding for the emergence of symbolic expression—all of which bring us to the brink of human culture. Now we must stop and ask: Can the evolutionary narrative take us any farther? Or does it end 100,000 years ago, when *Homo sapiens* reached their current anatomical state? Are our information systems still "evolving"? This is no small question.

The most coherent scientific theory of how evolutionary forces shape human culture comes from Pulitzer Prize–winning biologist E. O. Wilson, the father of sociobiology. While Wilson's theories remain controversial in some humanist circles, as they have since the sociobiology wars of the 1970s and 1980s, his basic model of the relationship between genes and culture has become widely accepted among many mainstream biologists. Based on his lifelong study of insect colonies and his pioneering theoretical work on the intersection of biology and culture, Wilson has proposed a theory to explain how the exchange of memes (or culturgens) influences the process of genetic evolution. "Culture is created by the communal mind," he writes, "and each mind in turn is the product of the genetically structured human brain. Genes and culture are therefore inseverably linked."[19]

Wilson's theory of gene-culture coevolution hinges on the interaction of two key operators: memes and epigenetic rules, or neural
processes that govern certain aspects of cognition. Epigenetic rules
come in two flavors: Primary epigenetic rules govern our immediate
sense perceptions, such as our universal tendency to perceive the color
spectrum in four basic color groups, or our ability to distinguish the
sound of human voices from other kinds of noise; secondary epigenetic rules operate at a higher level of abstraction, affecting the way
we integrate our sense perceptions, such as the tendency for all human beings to classify objects into opposing pairs like black and white,
life and death, heaven and earth—notions that have no physical component in the human brain, yet seem to recur across human cultures.
Secondary epigenetic rules predispose us to draw certain kinds of
distinctions; culture fills in the blanks. Individuals with a strong disposition to following particular epigenetic rules are more likely to
survive, and therefore pass on their genes, than those with a weaker
disposition to following the rules. For example, individuals who avoid
snakes out of fear are more likely to pass on their genes than individuals who step boldly in front of a rattler. So people with a genetic
makeup that predisposes them to fear snakes enjoy a decided evolutionary advantage. While there is probably no actual gene that tells us
to fear snakes, fear of snakes has nonetheless a clear adaptive advantage that gets passed along from generation to generation. So we can
hypothesize the presence of an epigenetic rule disposing us toward a
fear of snakes.

Epigenetic rules may also explain the prevalence of certain narrative archetypes that recur across human cultures: the creation myth,
the hero's descent, trickster gods, scary monsters, and visions of the
apocalypse.[20] The sheer prevalence of these stories across every known
culture suggests the strong likelihood that human beings share some
kind of inborn disposition toward particular cultural patterns. To return to the snake example: Serpents recur as symbols throughout
human cultures, often taking on mythic forms. "Owing to the power
of fear and fascination given them by the epigenetic rule," Wilson
writes, "[snakes] easily acquire additional mythic meaning; they serve
in different cultures variously as healers, messengers, demons, and

gods."[21] It is no coincidence that snakes have been a leading cause of human mortality throughout our species' history, so it should come as no surprise that the occurrence of serpent imagery tracks closely to the prevalence of poisonous snakes in particular regions. That rule in turn influences the course of the larger cultural system. The social group accrues an adaptive advantage by cultivating a mythology to ensure the persistence of valuable information across generations: namely, that it's a good idea to be afraid of snakes. In other words, Eve's hateful old serpent may boast a very old pedigree indeed: the epigenesis of Genesis?

The similarities in human behavior among otherwise disparate cultures suggest the strong possibility of epigenetic rules at work. But where exactly do these rules exist? They are not hardwired into our DNA; there is no physical mechanism to decode. Rather, they are invisible dispositions that arise from a complex combination of factors, including genetics. But we cannot see epigenetic rules any more than we can see gravity. The only path to discovering these rules lies in a process of reverse engineering, by looking for the presence of universal human behaviors that manifest across cultures.

Anthropologist Donald Brown has devoted his career to compiling what many social scientists now consider the authoritative list of "human universals," a catalog of 200 behaviors that appear to recur in every known human culture. The list stretches from the sublime—beliefs about death, rituals, and symbolism—to the ridiculous—toys, tickling, and jokes. The list also includes no fewer than 12 types of classification: age, behavioral propensities, body parts, colors, fauna, flora, inner states, kin, sex, space, tools, and weather conditions.[22] All of these behaviors are likely influenced by the presence of epigenetic rules.

If Wilson's theory of epigenetic rules is correct, then it may well answer the question of whether information systems literally "evolve." To continue probing that question, the next chapter will look for evidence of epigenetic rules at work in one of our species' most ancient information systems.

2

Family Trees and the Tree of Life

Civilization begins with a rose.
Gertrude Stein, *As Fine as Melanctha*

Walking through the Peruvian rain forest with a guide from the local Aguaruna tribe, anthropologist Brent Berlin listened intently as his companion reeled off the names of all the plants and the animals they encountered. Berlin was impressed not only with the tribesman's encyclopedic knowledge of the forest, but with the elaborate taxonomy he seemed to be using: categorizing plants and animals into species, genus, and family—echoing the familiar Linnaean taxonomy that most modern biologists rely on today. "To find 'simple savages' controlling an extensive body of knowledge akin to the scientific fields of botany and zoology," Berlin later wrote, "is truly remarkable."[1]

Even more remarkable, Berlin has since discovered, is the complexity of so-called folk taxonomies in other tribal cultures around the world. From the outback of Australia to the islands of Papua New Guinea to the depths of the Amazon, indigenous peoples not only create highly developed classification systems, but they do so in strikingly similar ways: with plant or animal "families" divided into nested hierarchies, often using exactly the same categories. For cultures that developed in geographical isolation over tens of thousands of years, what could possibly explain such close parallels? Are taxonomies somehow wired into our genetic makeup?

For many of us the word "taxonomy" probably conjures images of academic drudgery: obscure Latin names, plodding textbooks and pallid grad students discussing the finer points of flora and fauna. Few nonbiologists ever give the subject much thought, and even among many biologists taxonomy has fallen into disrepute as a backwater of the life sciences. But for the greater part of the past 100,000 years, the practice of biological classification ranked as one of humanity's most essential cultural pursuits. "Some people dismiss taxonomies and their revisions as mere exercises in abstract ordering," writes Stephen Jay Gould, "a kind of glorified stamp collecting of no scientific merit and fit only for small minds that need to categorize their results. No view could be more false and more inappropriately arrogant. Taxonomies are reflections of human thought; they express our most fundamental concepts about the objects of our universe."[2]

What exactly is a taxonomy? A taxonomy, in its simplest form, is a system of categories that people use to organize their understanding of a particular body of knowledge. The oldest and most familiar taxonomies involve plants and animals. And while most of us may spend little time thinking about taxonomies, we use them every day. For example, take a common animal like a tabby cat. Most of us would agree that a tabby is a kind of cat, that cats are mammals, and that mammals belong to the larger category of animals. So, the taxonomy of, say, a brown long-haired tabby cat might look something like this:

Animal
Mammal
Cat
Tabby cat
Brown long-haired tabby cat

Now a biologist would consider this particular taxonomy woefully inadequate. The formal Linnaean taxonomy that most of us studied in some long-ago biology class uses a more detailed system that allows for up to nine levels of categorization, each accompanied by a signature Latin name. So, using the example above, the equivalent Linnaean taxonomy would look like this:

Kingdom: *Animalia*
Phylum: *Chordata*
Class: *Mammalia*
Order: *Carnivora*
Family: *Felidae*
Genus: *Felis*
Species: *Catus*

In this system, the long-haired tabby is a subspecies of the species *Felis catus*. While the Linnaean system may be more accurate, for most of us it doesn't mean much. The first group of categories, while it might not pass scientific muster, nonetheless represents the kind of informal "taxonomy" that most of us rely on each day to make sense of the world around us.

For tens of thousands of years, human beings have been doing just this: giving names to things, and sorting those things into categories ("mammals," "birds," and "fish"). The oldest taxonomies stretch far back into our species' past—and perhaps even farther into our pre–*Homo sapiens* lineage (although this possibility inevitably remains a matter of speculation). Indeed, our ability to classify things may be one of our species' great evolutionary differentiators.

Throughout our species' time on earth, we have relied for survival on collecting and disseminating accurate information about the world around us: knowing which animals we can eat, which plants are poisonous, and so forth. For humans living in hunter-gatherer or tribal societies, folk taxonomies are fundamental tools of group survival. It would stand to reason, then, that natural selection played some role in the formation of these systems. Individuals born with an aptitude for taxonomy would likely stand a higher chance of reproductive success. If you could remember which snakes were poisonous, which mushrooms you could eat, which animals you could tame, you stood a better chance of passing on your genes to the next generation. No single human being could possibly catalog the entirety of nature's creation from scratch; it would take too much time and a great deal of trial and error (often of the life-ending variety). Folk taxonomies took generations to build.

While conventional histories of science often credit scientific pioneers like Linnaeus and Aristotle as the first taxonomists, in truth taxonomies have a much longer history. The earliest folk taxonomies almost certainly predate literate civilization by thousands of years. While we may never know precisely how our ancient forbears classified the natural world, we can surmise a great deal about how these systems worked from the study of modern-day tribal societies. Every human culture ever observed has created its own taxonomy of plants and animals. Many of those taxonomies are still alive and well today. "Our predisposition to classify at all is an ancient trait," writes Berlin, "and clearly has an adaptive advantage."[3]

While the details of individual classification systems vary widely, the structure of these taxonomies reveals remarkable similarities. Something in our cognitive makeup seems to drive us to categorize the natural world in hierarchical terms: perhaps the effect of epigenetic rules (see Chapter 1). While we can never know exactly what our ancient ancestors' taxonomic systems may have looked like, we can make informed speculations by contrasting the taxonomies of modern tribal cultures with traditional European systems that almost certainly contain traces of earlier prehistoric systems.

What can the study of comparative taxonomies teach us about preliterate human communities? Anthropologist Cecil Brown conducted the first comprehensive study of how preliterate human social groups organize their knowledge of the animal world. Surveying a broad range of folk classifications across numerous language groups, Brown sought to determine the level of agreement between geographically disparate cultures. The parallels, he discovered, run surprisingly deep. Even the most seemingly divergent cultures seem to employ almost identical strategies for organizing information, following a pattern that Berlin dubbed "ethnobiological rank," or the use of hierarchical categories to describe the characteristics of plants and animals. According to Berlin, every tribal community ever studied appears to share a universal tendency to divide their knowledge of plants and animals into five or six nested categories.[4]

	Name	Description	Examples		
1	Unique Beginner	The highest level of taxonomic inclusion	Plant	Animal	Computer
2	Life Form	The first order of division, always "polytopic" (consisting of at least two members)	Tree	Mammal	Apple Computer
	Name	*Description*	*Examples*		
3	Generic	A "psychologically primary" category, usually identified with a unique name	Oak tree	Dog	Macintosh
4	Specific	A secondary name, usually involving a qualifier added to the generic name	White oak tree	Hound dog	Mac Mini
5	Varietal	The final level of granular description	Swamp white oak tree	Bassett hound	Mac Mini G4 1.42 GHz
	Affiliate	A horizontal or "meta" category that might include members of multiple genera	Deciduous trees	Pets	Personal computers

Not only is a rose a rose, then, but a flower is a flower, a plant is a plant, and so on. All human cultures appear to share the habit of categorizing flora and fauna using a similar structure; they also reach surprising degrees of consensus on the substance of those categories. Among the most commonly observed biological groupings are trees, small plants, bushes, vines, and grass. In the animal world the most common zoological classifications include bird, fish, snake, "wugs" (what we colloquially call "creepy-crawlies": small creatures that always include insects, often spiders, and sometimes worms), and mammals. And the similarities go even deeper. Every culture also seems to agree that things have "real names"—that a rose is more a "rose" than it is a "plant." This psychologically primary category always lands squarely in the middle of the taxonomy, suggesting that not only do all cultures share a disposition toward creating nested taxonomies but that they also seem to recognize one category as being more accurate or true than the others.

Why are taxonomies so universal? Our capacity for classification seems to spring from two basic cognitive capabilities: binary discrimination (the ability to tell one thing from another) and lateralization of the human brain (the ability to string thoughts together). Once we distinguish two objects from each other, we can hold the objects in our minds long enough to recognize a conceptual distinction between them. This is how we distinguish black and white, male and female, good and evil, us and them. These basic categories in turn give rise to higher-level distinctions. For example, we can recognize the difference between a deer and an antelope, yet we can also recognize the ways in which they are alike. This ability to contrast degrees of sameness and difference provides the conceptual foundation for hierarchical thinking. So we can recognize that a deer and an antelope are simultaneously different (belonging to separate species) and alike (belonging to a larger family of species that also includes bison but does not include, say, rabbits). Working our way up through levels of similarity between animals, we might eventually come up with something like "mammals." Our prehistoric ancestors spent a great deal of time doing just this, creating categories to describe the living things around them.

Why do people around the world seem to reach such similar conclusions about the natural world? Surely there is nothing inherent in the plants or animals themselves. As Darwin later proved, Aristotle's notion of idealized forms was classical wishful thinking. We can only assume that our innate disposition toward the animal kingdom reflects a kind of evolutionary consensus. How can we explain the remarkable consistency of these information systems across far-flung cultures? There is no gene, as far as we know, that dictates the structure of taxonomies, yet all human beings seem to share a certain disposition toward categorizing and naming things in structurally similar ways. Such a cultural universal tendency seems to point to the strong likelihood of an epigenetic rule at work. Just as we perceive similar degrees of the color spectrum or a need to tell stories to each other, we seem to have a deep inborn urge to categorize the world around us.

The evolutionary advantage of taxonomic consensus seems self-evident. Perhaps we can imagine our distant ancestors huddled around a fire planning the next day's hunt; surely it would benefit the group as a whole if everyone could agree on a goal of hunting "bison" as opposed to, say, "mammals." Similarly, reproductive advantage would accrue to those people who knew to tread carefully around "snakes," rather than worrying about "reptiles" in general, or making fine-tooth distinctions between green snakes and rattlers. The psychological primacy of the genus seems to make eminent evolutionary sense.

The remarkable similarities between folk taxonomies suggest that categorical thinking cannot be the product of human cultural idiosyncrasy. The parallels simply run too deep; there must be an evolutionary basis. Just as all human beings are born with a disposition toward spoken language, so we are also born with a tendency toward hierarchical categories. Wilson's theory of gene-culture co-evolution seems to offer the most plausible explanation: epigenetic rules that dispose us toward a certain kind of categorical thinking.

PROTOTYPE THEORY

If epigenetic rules do indeed equip us with a disposition toward recognizing things as having "real names" at a certain level in a taxonomic hierarchy, then it stands to reason that such a disposition might continue to reverberate even after human beings moved on from thinking about plants and animals to consider larger bodies of subject matter. The structure of folk taxonomies seems to have shaped the way human beings create all kinds of categorical meaning. In his classic 1958 essay "How Shall a Thing Be Called?" philosopher Roger Brown observed that "the dime in my pocket is not only a dime. It is also money, a metal object, a thing, and, moving to subordinates, it is a 1952 dime, in fact, a particular 1952 dime."[5] Yet somehow most of us would likely call a dime a "dime."

Brown's intuition meshes exactly with Berlin's model of ethnobiological rank, suggesting that our ancient taxonomic tendencies influence our perceptions of other kinds of categories as well. According to Brown, the dime is the thing's "real name," reflecting the same notion of psychological primacy that Berlin identifies with the generic level of categorization. Linnaeus too seems to have recognized the primacy of the genus, placing it at the heart of his own classification system. Berlin's research into folk classification reveals the same result: that the genus occupies a central position as the "real" name of any given organism. The genus represents a kind of focal point in our orientation to the world, from which all the other categories derive.

We could also speculate as to an epigenetic basis for the final level of categorization, the cross-reference; for example, "edible plants" or "dangerous animals." It is surely no great stretch to suppose that our facility for cross-referencing, for creating "meta" categories, stems from this capacity to pull otherwise unrelated things into a category of the mind.

In this universal human tendency to organize information into categories, we can also recognize the familiar contours of networks and hierarchies. A folk taxonomy is a classic hierarchical system, but it depends for stability on the reinforcing presence of a network. Categorical hierarchy provides a framework capable of scaling to encompass the phenomenal world, while the underlying social network cements its role in the culture and ensures its longevity from generation to generation. This archetypal pattern of hierarchical taxonomy reinforced by social networks echoes repeatedly throughout the history of humanity's subsequent information systems.

Recent research into human–computer interaction seems to back up the claim. In 1996 IBM researchers discovered that, when Web users tried to navigate their way around the IBM Web site, they become lost once they traveled beyond five or six levels deep in the menu structure, even though the site comprised a series of menus extending 14 or 15 levels down. Perhaps at some unconscious level, our experience of navigating the Web owes something to our evolutionary disposition toward understanding the world in terms of taxonomies.

While we may never be able to model the epigenetic rules governing taxonomic systems precisely, the presence of such rules would suggest that the structure of our modern classification systems—with their hierarchical categories, binomial naming schemes, and cross-referencing—are not the product of individual human genius (which is not to denigrate the contributions of great taxonomists like Aristotle and Linnaeus), but that these systems emerged over a much longer period stretching deep into our genetic past. If taxonomy is rooted in our evolution as a species, the structure of these systems should also have a corresponding cognitive basis in the human mind. And indeed, the human mind appears to be particularly well suited to think in terms of hierarchical categories. Here we must refer briefly to the work of prototype theorists, who have pioneered a new understanding of how the mind creates categories.

Psychologist Eleanor Rosch pioneered prototype theory, a breakthrough model of human cognition that predicts how the mind assigns things to categories not only based on cultural information but through a process of direct sensory engagement with the phenomenal world. Her theory suggests that people form categories based on "prototypes," or best examples of a particular kind of thing. The theory explains, for example, why people in different cultures tend to recognize similar types of colors or similar kinds of animal species. For example, consider the following pictures of birds (see facing page). If you had to select one of the images below as the best example of a "bird," which one would you choose?

Chances are, you would pick the second image as the best example of a "bird." The crane on the left is taller than most birds; the penguin on the right cannot fly; but the bird in the middle is similar in size and shape to most other kinds of birds, so it falls closest to the best example or prototype.

Prototype theory suggests that we have not only an innate disposition toward categories, but also that we have an ability to iden-

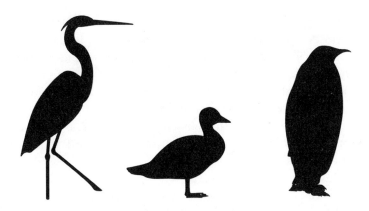

tify levels of gradation within those categories. This capacity for gradation—that is, the ability to recognize that things may be both different and similar at the same time—holds the key to our capacity for hierarchical categorization. One-dimensional categories are inherently dissatisfying to the human brain; we seem to have an innate need to separate things into finer-tuned distinctions. As a result, we form nested categories to describe the relative similarities and differences between things. In all likelihood, folk taxonomies evolved in concert with our cognitive facility for hierarchical categorization.

Rosch's work has, alas, been widely misinterpreted. A simplistic reading of her research would suggest that categories are determined through perception alone—that is, that there are categories inherent in the world. Rosch herself even subscribed to this view in her early work, giving rise to much of the subsequent misinterpretation. But she later revised her theory, coming to the conclusion that prototypes themselves do not determine the semantic categories that people formulate; rather, these are determined through a more complex process of cultural transmission. "Prototypes do not constitute a theory of representation for categories," she wrote. "The facts about prototypes can only constrain, but do not determine, models of representation."[6] In other words, the categories themselves are transmitted through culture, but the human brain is born ready to receive the transmission.

In his landmark book *Women, Fire and Dangerous Things*, linguist George Lakoff wrote a sweeping refutation of the classical (or objectivist) view of categories. The classical view stems from the Aristotelian notion of things having intrinsic characteristics, ideal forms. It is predicated on the possibility of universal truth based on the observation of derived properties. This approach served as the foundation of the modern scientific method and Linnaean taxonomy; it would later run afoul of findings in evolution. Classical categories proceed from disembodied ideals and support the notion that ideas inhabit another plane of thought.

> To question the classical view . . . is thus to question the view of reason as disembodied symbol-manipulation and correspondingly to question the most popular version of the mind-as-computer metaphor. Contemporary prototype theory does just that—through detailed empirical research in anthropology, linguistics, and psychology. . . . [H]uman categorization is essentially a matter of both human experience and imagination—of perception, motor activity, and culture on the one hand, and of metaphor, metonymy, and mental imagery on the other. As a consequence, human reason crucially depends on the same factors. And therefore cannot be characterized merely in terms of the manipulation of abstract symbols.[7]

Our capacity for categorization, in other words, has a biological basis, in terms of both individual cognition and our larger social interactions. Prototype theory also meshes seamlessly with Wilson's theory of gene-culture coevolution. The human brain appears to have evolved in concert with the social transmission of categorical information. As a result, we are all born with a deep-seated need to understand the world in terms of categories and to share that understanding with each other.

BEYOND FLORA AND FAUNA

Our long heritage of taxonomic thinking has influenced more than just the way we label plants and animals. For tens of thousands of years, these archetypal information systems weaved themselves into the fabric of human social life. Folk taxonomies became deeply entwined with the first mythologies, taking on progressive layers of meaning that became embedded in our cultural heritage. In 1903 the sociologist Emile Durkheim, along with his colleague Marcel Mauss, published a pioneering study of the larger social role of folk taxonomies entitled *Primitive Classification*. In one of the first studies of its kind, Durkheim surveyed the taxonomic practices of aboriginal peoples in Australia and North America. His research led him to probe the little-understood relationship between classification systems and human social organization.

Durkheim posited that the structure of classification systems hewed closely to the structure of existing family and kinship networks, expressing a deep unconscious need for members of tribal societies to project their otherwise inscrutable kinship relationships onto the outside world. When people described the natural world, therefore, they did so by invoking the language of family relationships: Plants and animals belonged to "families." The fir tree was the child of the category "tree," the sibling of the pine, and perhaps a distant cousin of the bush, but it was no relation to a chicken. Tribal conceptions of the natural world paint the animal kingdom as one big interlocking web of families. Thus, natural classification systems reflected existing kin relationships; the vastness of the natural world provided a kind of conceptual mirror that allowed tribe members to ponder the larger web of connections among themselves.

In Australia, Durkheim observed how aboriginal tribes classified the natural world using a system that meshed seamlessly with their own tribal organization. Each tribe was divided into "moieties," or social units, each of which in turn was subdivided into so-called marriage classes, and further subdivided into smaller clans. Each of these clans, in turn, claimed an affiliation with some natural element: the trees, the plains, the sky, the stars, the wind, the rain. Each clan also followed certain dietary restrictions according to their marriage class (members of one class ate opossum, kangaroo, dog, and honey, while members of another class ate emu, bandicoot, black duck, and certain snakes). Like the Zuni people (see Chapter 1), the aboriginal tribes used their own family structures as living containers for categorizing information about plants, animals, and the natural elements.[8]

Looking deeper into the symbolic relationships between family organizations and the associated animals and elements, Durkheim discovered the correlation between family subdivisions and the ethnobiological ranking systems. "In fact the moiety is the genus," he wrote. "The marriage class is the species; the name of the genus applies to the species," and so forth. "We are no longer dealing with a simple dichotomy of things," wrote Durkheim, "but with hierarchized concepts." For these remote tribal societies, Durkheim came to the conclusion that the structure of early human classifications reflects macro social structures, projections of human social relationships. The two systems reinforce each other—indeed, in the "primitive" mind they are indistinguishable.

The first categories may have emerged as outward expressions of existing social relationships: an attempt to make visible otherwise invisible relationships like "parent," "sibling," or higher-level abstractions like "family." As Hobart and Schiffman write, "Genealogy provides the ideal classificatory tool, for it narrates a sequence of actions. It thus sustains the tradition while, at the same time, subjecting it to a hierarchical ordering that clarifies the nature of various figures. When gods are considered, genealogy becomes a means of understanding the cosmos . . . when mortals are considered, it becomes an encyclopedic framework for historical and geographical as well as social information."[9]

Durkheim believed that the tendency toward categorical hierarchy simply reflects the natural hierarchy of family structures, thus explaining the prevalent human tendency to describe groups of plants and animals in kinship terms. The family tree, in other words, works as a two-way metaphor: Families are shaped like trees, and trees are shaped like families. "The first logical categories were social categories; the first classes of things were classes of men, into which these things were integrated. It was because men were grouped, and thought of themselves in the form of groups, that in their ideas they grouped other things, and in the beginning the two modes of grouping were merged to the point of being indistinct." So in Durkheim's view, categories derived from existing social structures, forming a conceptual template into which the tribes poured their knowledge about the natural world. "Moieties were the first genera; clans, the first species. . . . It is because human groups fit one into another—the sub-clan into the clan, the clan into the moiety, the moiety into the tribe—that groups of things are ordered in the same way."[10]

If tribal classifications do indeed represent externalized projections of social relationships, it seems fair to surmise that these systems must also entail some level of emotional investment. These systems succeeded because they tapped into the reinforcing power of human emotion by mirroring existing family relationships. If we accept Greenspan's assertion that higher-order information exchange relies on emotional triggers in our limbic system (see Chapter 1), then we could accept Durkheim and Mauss's assertion that "a species of things is not a simple object of knowledge but corresponds above all to a certain sentimental attitude."[11] Berlin, however, questions Durkheim's conclusions about the social origins of taxonomies: "[T]he ethnobiological data suggest strongly that [Durkheim and Mauss] were wrong in their proposal on the social origins of classification. My strong intuition is that it was just the other way around; knowledge of natural kinds and the similarities and differences between and among species provided the model for the social classifications that humans ultimately constructed to provide meaning to social relations."[12] In other words, perhaps people did not create taxonomies to mimic the structure of social relationships; instead, they modeled their social relationships after their observations about the natural world. Regardless of which came first—the human family or the taxonomic one—there is no question that taxonomies and human social structures evolved in concert with each other.

Multilayered, socially pregnant taxonomies would eventually find a complex and beautiful expression in advanced mythological systems like those found in Greece, China, and elsewhere, where systems of astronomy, astrology, geomancy, and divination merged into complex, highly stylized classification systems with deep taxonomic roots. The Chinese folk classification centers on the division of space into four cardinal points, each of which is further divided in two, resulting in eight compass points that, like the Zuni system (see Chapter 1), represent the natural elements: heaven, earth, clouds, fire, thunder, wind, water, and mountains. For example, the south is associated with the father principle, as well as with sky, pure light, force, the head, heaven, jade, metal, ice, red, and horses. In opposition to the fatherly south stands the motherly north, associated with earth, darkness, docility, cattle, the belly, and cloth, among other things. Thus, the basic genealogical principle of mother and father expands into a broad classification system framing the Chinese people's understanding of the world. Each direction is also associated with a season (each of which is further subdivided into six, making for the 24 seasons of the Chinese calendar), an animal (the dragon to the east, red bird to the south, white tiger to the west, and black tortoise to the north), a color, an element, and certain underlying principles.[13]

The classification of natural phenomena into eight categories resembles the strategies employed by other human cultures that developed oceans away: The Australian Aborigines, Zunis, and numerous other human societies have developed analogous systems relying on the correlation of cardinal directions with seasons, animals, elements, and genealogical relationships.

The Chinese astrological calendar also has deep taxonomic roots, connecting each year in a 12-year cycle with a totemic animal: rat, cow, tiger, rabbit, dragon, snake, horse, goat, monkey, rooster, dog, and pig. The animals divide into four groups of three, each associated with a compass direction and with one of four natural elements (fire, water, earth, wind). Thus the entire classification system pulls together an integrated worldview, encompassing time, geography, the animal kingdom, and elemental forces. As Durkheim and Mauss put it, "Here we have, then, a highly typical case in which collective thought has worked in a reflective and learned way on themes which are clearly primitive."[14] The guiding principles of Chinese classification provided the philosophical framework guiding everything from architecture (as in the well-known practice of *feng shui*) to affairs of state, personal relationships, and the Chinese conception of the natural world. Over a period of several thousand years, Chinese civilization became a living manifestation of a vast and all-encompassing classification system. The Chinese system provides perhaps the most compelling example of an ancient classification that survived and adapted itself through long periods of upheaval: wars, empires, and the emergence of a vast institutional bureaucracy.

On the other side of the world, the people of ancient Greece were developing an astrological and divinatory system conceptually not far removed from the Chinese system, predicated on relationships between space, time, and the elements. Here again, the system began with the correlation of natural elements with certain directions, colors, and natural phenomena, all framed in terms of genealogical relationships—in this case, between the gods. For example, Poseidon, the Greek god of the seas, was the brother of Demeter, the goddess of agriculture. Artemis, the moon goddess, was the sister of the sun god Apollo. Ares, the brutal god of war, was brother to Athena, the goddess of wisdom, justice, and the arts. Each god, in turn, represented a set of naturally occurring phenomena. Often, the gods would appear under alternate guises. "Every god has his doubles," writes Durkheim, "who are other forms of himself, though they have other functions; hence, different powers, and the things over which these powers are exercised, are attached to a central or predominant notion, as is the species to the genus or a secondary variety to the principal species."[15] Like other mythological systems, the Greek pantheon employed the familiar construct of family relationships to invoke a web of semantic relationships (see Chapter 4 for a further discussion of Greek mythology).

In human cultures throughout the world, ancient preliterate mythologies reveal this pattern of gods and other supernatural beings as coded entities, organized into families, who represent the phenomenal world. The oldest mythologies, with their divine genealogies, echo the familial structure of folk taxonomies, forming a hierarchical scaffolding to allow preliterate peoples to organize their knowledge about the natural world. As the pantheon of gods and mythic relationships grew over time, specialized gods began to cluster into increasingly narrow categories, until finally the smaller gods became mere echoes or alternate names of their former selves. As these early classification systems grew in complexity, along with the human social structures that created them, they also laid the groundwork for the gradual erosion of superstitious belief. As Durkheim and Mauss put it, "Mythological classifications, when they are complete and systematic, when they embrace the universe, announce the end of mythologies."[16] Even in our highly systematized age, however, we still feel the reverberation of old mythologies, the ancient archetypes of the classifying mind.

3

The Ice Age
Information Explosion

In ancient Peru, Incan messengers used to travel across the Andes carrying a bundle of woven thread known as a *Quipu*, or "talking strings." When a messenger arrived at his destination, he would deliver his news while reeling off knots in the string like a rosary. For the Incas, a people with no written language, the *Quipu* served as their core information technology: It was a newspaper, a calculator, even a repository of laws. A skilled *Quipucamayu* ("keeper of the Quipus") could use the device to tell complex stories by weaving the colored threads together. Each thread represented a different facet of the narrative: a black string marked the passage of time, while other colored strings symbolized different characters or themes in a story: rulers, neighboring tribes, gods.[1] By juxtaposing the multicolored strings of the story along the black-stringed axis of time, the *Quipucamayu* could "write" almost any kind of narrative. Despite a total lack of writing as we would understand it, the Incas managed to keep track of enormous stores of information by manipulating these symbolic objects.

Until recent years, historians tended to give nonliterate cultures short shrift as systems thinkers. In the popular Cave Man stereotype, prehistoric people were cultural simpletons, too preoccupied with

Drawing of a *Quipu*, from *Meyers Konversations-Lexikon* (1888).

survival to pursue the loftier avenues of civilization. While main-stream academic views have shifted to accommodate a growing appreciation for preliterate societies, our mainstream culture still harbors a vague prejudice against people who don't know how to write. As a result, we often fail to appreciate the richness and complexity of nonliterate cultures and what they can teach us about the way our minds work. As it turns out, preliterate societies not only exhibit surprisingly complex cultural behaviors, but in many cases make innovative use of symbolic information technologies to record, store, and distribute their shared knowledge.

While symbolism may seem like an intrinsically human capacity, the practice of using external symbolic artifacts emerged only in our relatively recent past. *Homo sapiens* reached anatomical modernity at least 100,000 years ago, yet it took us more than 60,000 years to begin producing the kinds of symbols that most of us recognize as the manifestations of human culture. For most of human beings' time on earth, we have behaved in ways barely distinguishable from our Neanderthal cousins: foraging in loose-knit groups; fashioning rudimentary tools like sticks, rocks, and spears, occasionally burying our dead. Then, about 30,000 to 40,000 years ago, our ancestors suddenly started displaying a whole tapestry of symbolic behaviors: decorating bone knives, stringing bead necklaces, making paintings. "In a blink of geological time," as science writer John McCrone puts it, "one line of hominids suddenly became symbolically minded and self-aware."[2] That we should have survived for so long without producing symbolic artifacts is hardly surprising. After all, every other species on earth has managed to survive without producing a single bead necklace, cave painting, or pop music CD. The question that still vexes many researchers is this: Why did we cross the threshold to symbolic expression so quickly? Human mythologies are rife with explanations for the emergence of symbolic thought: Eve biting the apple, the appearance of a primordial Buddha, or the arrival of mystical space aliens, to name a few.

There is also a more mundane explanation, one grounded squarely in the archaeological record. The arrival of symbolic expression appears to have coincided almost exactly with a period of rapid climate change, starting about 45,000 years ago, when the last great ice age sent glaciers out across much of the earth's surface. As temperatures plunged, our ancestors started competing over dwindling food supplies. Competition for resources brought people into closer social proximity, and that proximity appears to have triggered the emergence of symbolic expression. Call it a primordial tipping point.

In the popular stereotype of "primitive" or preliterate societies, we might think of our ancestors as big game hunters from time immemorial, but in fact we come from a long line of scavengers. For our first 60,000-odd years, *Homo sapiens* were scrappy opportunists who foraged for plants, chased foxes and beavers, and lunged after rabbits and pigeons. As global cooling sent temperatures plummeting, however, those once-easy pickings ran scarce, and our ancestors had no choice but to set their sights on, literally, bigger game.

Now, any able-bodied biped can thwack a pigeon, but stalking a woolly mammoth, or an 8-foot-tall prehistoric cow, takes teamwork. Faced with the choice between starvation and banding together to hunt larger prey, humans started working together. Whereas once they had moved in loose-knit bands with little or no social structure, now they started collaborating in larger groups, hunting big animals, huddling in caves for warmth, and forging the kinds of social bonds nec-

essary to support an expanding body politic. Social relationships grew
more complex, demanding new forms of mediation. And somewhere
along the way, people started making symbols.

For ice age humans, symbols appear to have emerged only after
we came in from the cold and started working together. The first un-
ambiguously symbolic objects were beads and pendants, usually
made of stone, shells, or ivory. These objects would have been worth-
less as tools; their only plausible function had to involve some form
of symbolic expression. While we can never know exactly what these
objects meant to people, archaeologists comfortably speculate that
beads may have served as emblems of social identity, marking affiliation with a particular band or tribe, denoting gender, or marking
major rites of passage like coming of age or marriage. The use of
these totems seems to suggest the value in having a means to identify
oneself and one's status in a larger social group. In small groups,
people can easily recognize each other as individuals. The larger a
group becomes, the harder it gets for everyone to know each other. In
lieu of face-to-face recognition, people started relying on external
signifiers as a way to communicate information about themselves:
social rank, marriage status, and so forth. As ice age humans began to
shift their way of life from loose-knit bands to larger tribal communities, they began to build what Kuhn et al. call "ornament technology,"[3] using a lattice of symbols with shared meaning to signal status
and form the basis for new kinds of relationships. The use of beads
and other totems facilitated what Gamble calls a "release from proximity," a rudimentary kind of social contract built around a shared
understanding of what certain symbols meant. With an agreed set of
symbols in place, human groups could begin forging wider networks
of trust. And from those networks, new kinds of hierarchies emerged.

During the Upper Paleolithic period, starting about 35,000 years
ago, people seem to have devoted enormous time and energy to making beads of astonishing sophistication, with painstaking attention to
detail. In one European ice age community, bead making seems to
have turned into a mass obsession, with over 14,000 beads appearing
at one 28,000-year-old burial site. "These beads were very important
to these people," says White. "They spent thousands of hours of their

life making ivory beads even though they were living within 150 kilometers of a huge glacial ice sheet."

Beads seem to have functioned not only as communication objects within particular groups, but also as units of cultural exchange between otherwise disparate groups. At the caves of Altamira in Spain, archaeologists have discovered an enormous variety of symbolic objects—ostrich-shell beads, ivory figurines, seashells, pieces of amber—suggesting that the site may have served as a trading post for ice age Europeans: a hub on the regional trading network and a nexus for a kind of proto-commercial exchange. The sheer variety of styles suggests that different social groups gathered there to exchange these artifacts (and probably other goods as well) as a means of solidifying social relationships or forming alliances. These early trade networks served much the same purpose as the Internet today: as a vehicle not just for commercial exchange but also for forging social bonds between far-flung communities.

The emerging technology of symbolic communication would wreak lasting changes on the structure of social organization. Symbolic communication provided a networked communications platform that allowed more complex social—and eventually political—hierarchies to emerge. In other words, the relationship between symbolism and political power stretches back at least 30,000 years.

Given that human beings survived so long without symbols, however, why has symbolic culture proved such a durable adaptation? As we have seen in the previous chapters, symbols are more than just semantic emblems; they rely on emotional responses lodged deep in our limbic systems. Understanding this emotional aspect of symbolic expression sheds light on why some systems of symbolic expression persist while others fail. Effective symbols trigger deep-seated emotional responses. In all likelihood, there are epigenetic rules governing our responses to certain kinds of symbols. By triggering limbic system responses, simple totems like beads and pendants allowed people to transfer emotional bonds from people to objects; in turn, the objects could function as charged particles of emotional meaning, enabling people to forge increasingly far-flung

Drawing of a bead necklace from the
neolithic site of Pigna (Italy), by Paolo
Orsi, *Bullettino di Paleontologia Italiana*
48 (1929).

ties with each other. In ice age communities, beads and pendants
were imbued with emotional meaning that could invoke responses
between strangers grounded in the deeper emotional bonds of kinship: Power, loyalty, or even something like love?

Today, we still rely on certain kinds of symbols in much the same
way as our ice age forbears. The use of symbols as tokens of social
trust is evident across the World Wide Web, where people routinely
rely on disembodied symbols to evoke emotional responses and forge
bonds of trust with each other: for example, the use of icons in
instant messaging applications to represent emotional states (smiley
faces, angry faces, sad faces, etc.); or trust ratings on eBay, where complete strangers routinely transact business with each other purely on
the basis of iconic representations of social capital. Similar trust
mechanisms play a crucial role in facilitating the success of user reviews at *Amazon.com*, and any other number of Web sites where
people routinely exchange information and seal bonds of trust with
complete strangers. These interactions are not so far removed from
the symbolic exchanges of trust and coding of social rank that ice age
people achieved using beads, shells, and necklaces.

Symbolic expression, then, originated not just as an aesthetic or a spiritual pursuit but also as a pragmatic adaptation to changing environmental conditions. "Art is a cultural equivalent of mutation," says New York University archaeologist Randall White. "We know that bipedalism was caused by a genetic mutation that allowed some creatures to be able to stand upright, and that proved advantageous. What about the individual or social group that creates drawings of animals? What is the adaptive value of that? Well, for one thing, it creates the ability to communicate with each other through images," says White. From this perspective we can view ice age art as more than just a first foray into spiritual or aesthetic expression, but also as a practical adaptation to changing environmental conditions. "We've tended to think of the imagery from this period as 'art' in the soft sense that people were into evocative images, and animals really meant a lot to them, etc.—and maybe they did. But you also have people who are capable, using artwork, of showing someone else how an animal behaves, or where best to plant a spear, or any number of practical applications."[4]

We often think of "art" as a rarefied form of human achievement, a capacity that emerges only during periods of relative prosperity. Maslow's famous hierarchy of needs places cultural expression at the very top of the pyramid, expressing the common assumption that humans come to worry about aesthetic expression only after we secure our supposedly "basic" needs like food, shelter, and physical security. But the archaeological record suggests that symbolic expression was no esoteric exercise; it was a matter of survival. Symbolic expression seems to have played a critical role in cementing social relationships. As Durkheim writes, "in all its aspects and at every moment of history, social life is only possible thanks to a vast symbolism."

White has studied the evolution of art among ice age cultures and has concluded that art played an essential role in enabling *Homo sapiens* to survive during this period. "People don't think about art as a necessity," says White. "But it seems to have arisen as an attempt to cope with some very difficult circumstances. Art corresponds to periods of stress much more than it corresponds to periods of well-being and leisure. There is no question that art is not being produced as a result of people having more spare time; it is being produced when all hell is breaking loose and people don't have enough to eat."[5]

The most spectacular examples of ice age art are the famous cave paintings of Cro-Magnon Europe. At the caves of Lascaux, Altamira, and a host of smaller sites, the charcoal-and-pigment paintings and etched figures of bison, mammoth, and even rhinoceroses have captivated the public imagination for years. While the purpose of these paintings inevitably remains a subject of speculation,[6] most scholars agree that the paintings served at least in part as a practical method for building social consensus. In all likelihood, cave paintings served more than just a ritualistic or an aesthetic purpose; they may also have functioned as informational tools, the preliterate equivalent of a how-to manual or encyclopedia. Cave paintings allowed social groups to coalesce around fixed images, shared reference points that gave them a way to align their thoughts around a common object . Just as stigmergy provides a mechanism for indirect collaboration between individual members of a social group, so cave paintings may have served as a means for people to introduce social constraints on each other's behavior.

While historians typically assign writing a special status as the harbinger of "civilization," the building blocks of complex information systems were in place long before the first scribe set stylus to clay. "Each society creates culture and is created by it," writes Wilson. "Through constant grooming, decorating, exchange of gifts, sharing of food and fermented beverages, music, and storytelling, the symbolic communal life of the mind takes form, unifying the group into a dreamworld that masters the external reality into which the group has been thrust."[7] Human beings have invested long millennia in forging social bonds through the stigmergy of symbols, invoking our shared yearning to make our dreamworlds real.

The ice age information explosion brought humanity to the brink of literacy. For tens of thousands of years, the infrastructure of tribal information systems—folk taxonomies, mythological systems, and preliterate symbolism—created the conditions for the emergence of literate culture. For most of our species' time on earth, we relied on oral traditions—storytelling, folk taxonomies, and gesture—to preserve and transmit information between generations. The advent of symbols would change the shape of human social organization, bringing people together in larger social groups and, eventually, leading them across the threshold to an even more revolutionary adaptation: writing.

4

The Age of Alphabets

Nigerians used to believe that the first writers were monkeys. Ancient Chinese people credited a sacred turtle.[1] The Mayans and Assyrians attributed the sons of their respective creator gods. Certain Arab traditions maintain the first writer to have been no less a person than Mohammed. Stories explaining the origins of writing vary as widely as the cultures that produce them, but every human society that has crossed the threshold to literacy has assigned writing a status worthy of myth.

A more prosaic account for the origins of writing might take us to the city of Uruk, in the ancient kingdom of Sumer. By about 5000 BC, a growing population was coalescing into the first human settlement to resemble a city: "a mind-defeating jumble of temples, dwellings, storerooms, and alleyways,"[2] as historian Thomas Cahill describes it. The people of Uruk, having mastered a few basic agricultural techniques, had started to settle in a growing population center with a flourishing trade and increasingly specialized classes of workers: farmers, merchants, builders, and a ruling class of elite citizens. It was the world's first boomtown.

The sheer concentration of people created a cauldron of technological innovations. During this period, ancient Sumerians invented the wheel, sailing ships, molded bricks, metals, and architectural breakthroughs like vaults and domes. They were the first people to divide the day into hours.[3] Amid such a prolific period of innovation, the typical Sumerian might have scarcely noticed the curious little etchings that merchants were starting to make in clay tablets while they tried to keep track of their accounts.[4] The booming commercial trade in Uruk created an unprecedented volume of transactions: As merchants struggled to keep up with an expanding commercial economy, they needed to develop better systems for keeping track of their accounts. The first forms of writing emerged "not for magical and liturgical purposes," writes V. Gordon Childe, "but for practical business and administration."[5]

Samuel Johnson once remarked that "no man but a fool ever wrote except for money." Indeed, if it weren't for money, we might have no writing at all. Much as we like to think of writing as the fruit of high culture, all literature originates from the basest of all commercial transactions: sales receipts.

Writing appears to have emerged with little fanfare, arising as a practical innovation to take advantage of two prior technologies: drawing and counting. The earliest tabulating devices were notched bones dated to 35,000 to 20,000 BC—the earliest known representations of numbers. By the ninth century BC, clay tokens had emerged as units of basic currency—appearing almost simultaneously in Mesopotamia, Iran, Sudan, Palestine, and Syria. The first written notations were called *bullae* (tokens). Shaped like disks, cones, spheres, tetrahedrons, ovoids, cylinders, triangles, or animal heads, each token represented some form of commercial transaction: records of purchases, debts, or contractual obligations. The oldest specimens yet discovered date back as far as 3500 BC. By 3000 BC the earliest examples of what we would recognize as "writing" emerged, when merchants began transcribing the contents of *bullae* onto clay tablets.

As written tablets took hold as a commercial technology, a new class of professional scribes emerged. These early knowledge workers facilitated trade by serving as trusted third parties who could record transactions between two or more parties. A typical written receipt might read something like this: "Offer Gentleman B the enclosed message from Gentleman A."[6] After kneading wet clay into a cylinder or tablet, the scribe would record the details of the transaction by scraping marks into the surface using a wedge-shaped stylus. Both parties would put their marks on the tablet. The scribe would place his own seal, and the contract would be baked into the permanent record. Because clay dried quickly, the scribes had to work fast; this was no medium for poetry. Once the tablet was baked, the scribe would then deposit it on a shelf or put it in a basket, with labels affixed to the outside to facilitate future search and retrieval.

Linguist Walter J. Ong has charted a pattern of social transformation that appears to recur across human cultures that have made the transition to literacy. Writing invariably emerges at first to support commerce. This phase marks a period of "craft literacy," during which "writing is a trade practiced by craftsmen, whom others hire to write a letter or document as they might hire a stone-mason to build a house, or a shipwright to build a boat."[7]

The clay-based information economy would dominate the ancient Near East for the next 2,500 years, as networks of trade spread to neighboring regions that in turn created their own local scripts. The yeomen Mediterranean scribes, equipped with their styli and lumps of clay, provided a bedrock layer of trust that supported a growing network of commercial activity. Just as beads and bone totems had enabled ice age people to expand their social circles, so writing served a similar purpose, enabling otherwise unknown parties to forge reliable social bonds cemented by new forms of documents like contracts, laws, and religious rites. The new technology thus facilitated another degree of social abstraction, enabling people to coalesce into farther-flung social networks. From these networks, new kinds of hierarchies would soon emerge.

THE KNOWLEDGE BUREAU

As literary craftsmen began to accumulate power over the conduct of day-to-day transactions, a new kind of collective entity began to form around them. Just as ancient bacteria had joined into complex organisms, so the ancient scribes slowly came together into larger social organisms: institutions.

While writing had originated as a tool for helping individuals buy and sell, its use gradually expanded to encompass larger-scale governmental and religious functions. The economic power of writing afforded scribes a social status second only to the king, increasingly concentrating power in the hands of a literate bureaucratic elite. The escalating complexity of these relationships, coupled with the need for third parties capable of providing both authority and trust, gave rise to multiperson knowledge bureaus predicated on the power of the written word. As human settlements grew, the stewardship of writing slowly passed from the hands of individual craftspeople to fall under the purview of new organizational entities: institutions. The first government bureaucracies, religious temples, and educational institutions began to take shape.

As writing gave rise to increasingly complex institutions, writing itself became more complex. At the Ebla site in Syria, archaeologists found a literary treasure trove of 2,000 tablets dating as far back as 2300 BC. Most contain records of routine transactions involving textiles, olive oil, cereals, and other staple products. The Ebla site also contains another set of tablets, set apart from the rest in a neat pile atop the other manuscripts. These tablets contain different kinds of lists that serve no apparent transactional purpose: lists of birds and fish, geographical locations, the names of professions. One tablet consists solely of a list of the other tablets (though not in any discernible order). Another such "meta" document appears at the ancient Hittite site of Hattusas, near Ankara, where archaeologists discovered what appears to be the first-known bibliographic record: a list of other documents that includes title pages and rudimentary colophons containing brief descriptions of each tablet. For example:

> Eighth tablet of the Dupaduparsa Festival, words of Silalluhi and Kuwatalla, the temple priestess. Written by the hand of Lu, son of Nugissar, in the presence of Anuwanza, the overseer.[8]

In addition to information about the author and subject of the document, each colophon included a number, indicating that the tablets were stacked in a predictable sequence. The colophon also allowed for a brief set of keywords to provide readers with a glimpse of the document's contents, a kind of primitive abstract to help prospective readers limn the contents of a tablet before investing the time to read it. The Hittites had mastered all the basic functions of a library catalog, capturing information about authors and subjects in a digestible form and adding call numbers to help users retrieve the document they wanted. Melvil Dewey[9] would have been proud.

List making has always constituted an important form of writing. Long before anyone started producing the familiar narrative documents that we associate with "writing" today, the first true writers were list makers. Indeed, we may have an epigenetic proclivity for creating lists rooted in the lateral sequencing of the human brain, as evidenced in the tiered oral lists of folk taxonomies. The first written lists emerged as a growing tide of transactions produced more and more documents, forcing people to develop new mechanisms for organizing the growing sprawl of data: tokens, then lists, then lists of lists, then bibliographical systems for organizing entire collections. By 3000 BC the scope of written knowledge had grown to the point where Sumerian temple libraries contained commercial records, grammars, mathematics texts, books on medicine and astrology, and religious scriptures. Also fueling the Sumerian writing boom was the emerging institution of the temple. Ancient temples functioned as more than just purveyors of ritual; they were also the first national banks, lending out money at interest to individuals and small businesses. The Sumerian Savings and Loan managed an enormous volume of transactions, each recorded on a separate clay record, which in turn found its way into periodic "roll-up" reports issued on a weekly, monthly, and annual basis. Indeed, while we might think of information technology as a newish field, in fact Information Technologist may rank among the world's oldest professions.

Invoices and accounting records paved the way for records of taxes and tributes, property records, deeds, and property transactions, with graphic symbols confirming their legality. These early records, written on clay tablets or papyrus or engraved in bronze or copper, formed the foundation of government archives that would eventually grow to include laws, decrees, property records, contracts, treaties, and chronicles of events involving the state itself: the outcome of battles, the succession of monarchs, and other chronologies. Slowly, these chronological records took on the trappings of literature. "Since records of military conquests and biographies of kings often included as much fiction as fact, they added an element of literature to an otherwise staid collection."[10] Over time the great stream of oral tradition found its way into print.

As the scope of recorded information expanded, scribes began dividing into professional specialties with increasingly narrow domains of knowledge: the *dubsar kengira* specialized in the classics; the *dubsar nishid* plied mathematics; the *dubsar ashaga* labored at geometry. In the temples, scribes began to write down old spells and legends. As academic specialties began to coalesce, temples began to establish formal writing education programs to ensure the continuity of skills from generation to generation. As growing numbers of scribes mastered the literary arts, they began to produce more varied texts on, for example, astronomy, prophesies, and scientific observations.[11] The prolific Sumerian scribes created such a bulwark of recorded knowledge that by the time Sumerian civilization fell into decline it had created a written legacy that would reverberate for millennia.

Eventually a new Semitic power rose in Babylon, displacing the Sumerians. Although the Babylonians spoke their own language, they preserved the written record of Sumerian religious texts, whose ancient pedigrees lent them an air of authority not unlike the veneration that more recent cultures have ascribed to the Bible, Koran, or Torah. As the Babylonians displaced the Sumerians, they placed a great emphasis on preserving the old civilization's textual legacy, in much the same way that European nations went to great pains to preserve the ancient legacies of Greek and Latin literature. Like learned Europeans during the Middle Ages, the Babylonians established a bilingual standard: with a spoken vernacular for the common people and an exalted written text—Sumerian—for preserving ancient holy truths.[12] Why did the Babylonians invest so much effort in maintaining old texts in the language of an older empire? Historian A. C. Moorehouse speculates that for the Babylonians "there was a deep bond between producing documents and maintaining political legitimacy." Recognizing the essential relationship between the written word and political power helped cement the authority of the state over the older, preliterate, symbolically minded tribal cultures.

The relationship between written language and political legitimacy stretches deep into antiquity. Just as the earliest literate cultures had invented fables to explain the spellbinding power of the written word, later civilizations would invoke mythologies to assert the bond between writing and the political authority of the state. Ancient Romans attributed the prosperity of their empire in part to the purchase of three divine books by the ancient King Tarquin. According to the story, Tarquin bought the volumes from the prophetess Sibyl only after spurning her original offer of nine books, six of which she proceeded to burn out of spite. Realizing his mistake, Tarquin quickly came to his senses and snapped up the remaining volumes. Those books would later occupy a place of honor in the Roman forum, providing a tangible bridge from the mythic world to the present, until they were finally destroyed along with the empire during the great sieges. The Assyrians assigned a similar mythological significance to the power of writing in their tale of Zu, a lesser god who steals a divine tablet from the ruling god Enlil and brings it to Assyria. The tablet is said to reveal the fate of the gods, thus granting the Assyrian kingdom a measure of power over the gods themselves.

Throughout the ancient world, writing played a crucial role in the expansion of empires. In the seventh century BC, King Ashurbanipal took control of Mesopotamia, establishing the great Assyrian empire. As one of his first acts, he commanded his scribe Shadunu to collect every available written artifact in the kingdom. "No one shall withhold tablets from you," the king decreed, "and if you see any tablets and ritual texts about which I have not written to you, and they are suitable for my palace, select them, collect them and send them to me." Executing the king's decree, Shadunu traveled the countryside impounding every written tablet he could find. He confiscated every single document from every temple and private home in the kingdom. Eventually, he returned with a vast collection of poems, proverbs, hymns, fables, omens, horoscopes, incantations, prayers, and more than 500 drug recipes.[13] From this act of imperial confiscation the world's first library emerged. In addition to a vast array of factual records, King Ashurbanipal's collection included a literary component: the now-famous legend of Gilgamesh, 12 tablets of the old Babylonian account of the great flood, and numerous translations of older Sumerian stories. Of the 25,000 tablets later excavated at the vast Royal Library at Nineveh, more than two-thirds were created in response to orders from the king. Just as Ptolemy would later build his library at Alexandria by confiscating books from incoming ships, Ashurbanipal built his library through coercion. And lest there be any doubt about who owned the books, the king ordered that every book in the kingdom carry this royal inscription:

> Palace of Ashurbanipal, king of the world . . . who has possessed himself of a clear eye and the choice art of tablet-writing, such as none among the kings, my predecessors, had acquired. The wisdom of Nabu, the ruled line, all that there is, have I inscribed upon tablets, checking and revising it, and that I might see and read them, have I placed them within my palace.[14]

Some manuscripts he further commended to posterity, "for the sake of distant days." The books also included a warning that anyone who stole or vandalized a book would be subject to a curse "terrible and merciless as long as he lives." The king instituted rules requiring a high degree of bibliographic control: Every text would be copied in a consistent format, bearing the name of the scribe and the name of the king. The library also bore several hallmarks that would become characteristic of subsequent early libraries: forming part of a temple dedicated to the worship of a deity, following stated acquisitions guidelines, and employing a dedicated staff conversant in multiple languages. Of the organization of the library we know almost nothing. But we do know that it proved instrumental in supporting the expansion of the Assyrian empire. Armed with a vast arsenal of recorded information about governance, military strategy, weapon making, agriculture, mathematics, and other topics, the empire stood poised to dominate the region.

The earliest libraries were first and foremost vessels of political power, consolidating the accumulated intellectual capital of the early nation-states and providing a durable link with the past by invoking religious authority and asserting a relationship to the gods. The gods, by extension, protected the library, and the genealogical relationships of the gods, echoing old folk taxonomies, found a new manifestation in the nested hierarchies of state institutions.

The first libraries existed primarily to support these growing imperial hierarchies. In China, the earliest known library dates to 1400 BC. In Egypt, Rameses II established a sacred library at Thebes in 1225 BC. The first Indian manuscript collections date as far back as 1000 BC. Each of these great imperial civilizations seems to have progressed along a markedly similar (though far from identical) path: Agricultural settlements developed a commercial facility for writing, enabling them to make the transition from tribal societies to nation-states. As some of those nation-states grew into empires, they began producing more varied forms of literature that were eventually gathered into libraries.

The fates of those libraries would prove no less turbulent than the empires that built them. Indeed, the advent of literacy and book making has invariably been accompanied by violence and political turmoil. When the Emperor Shi Huangdi consolidated power over the Chinese Empire in 213 BC, he promptly ordered an imperial biblioclasm, commanding the destruction of every book in the kingdom. Soldiers demolished the old royal library, a priceless trove of early Confucian and Taoist texts known as the Heavenly Archives (whose most famous curator was Lao Tzu). After clearing the brush of the prior regime's intellectual legacy, the emperor created a new library, complete with a new classification system to reflect the new imperial order. That system eventually coalesced into the great ancient Chinese library classification system known as the Seven Epitomes. The scheme divided the library's holdings into six top-level categories: Military, Science, Technology, Medicine, Poetry, and Philosophy. The epistemological hierarchy also manifested itself in the political structure of the new empire. As a ministerial administration took shape to support the new imperial priorities, the hierarchy of the library became the hierarchy of the state. But this new classification, like the one it supplanted, would last no longer than the empire that supported it. When the Wei Dynasty later took power, the new imperial librarian Cheng Moe established yet another new classification scheme to replace the old one, reflecting a new set of imperial priorities, boiling everything down to four categories: Classics, Philosophy, History, and Literature.

Centuries later, when the Spanish conquistador Cortés arrived in sixteenth-century Mexico, he discovered a civilization that had mastered the art of book making a full thousand years earlier. The Aztec libraries contained an enormous collection of manuscripts about history, myth, biographies, herbalism, mathematics, and all kinds of local lore. When the conquistadors arrived, Bishop Diego de Landa ordered them to burn every one of the bark-clothed books, because they "contained nothing but superstitions and falsehoods of the Devil."[15] While it may be tempting to bemoan the wanton destruction of an indigenous culture at the hands of a European imperialist power, the Spanish were not the first invading force to raze an Aztec library. Just a century before the Spanish arrived, a conquering Aztec ruler named Itzcóatl burned the previous royal library to the ground, clearing the intellectual brush for a new Aztec history written in his own mold.

The violent history of libraries is a mirror of empire building: hierarchical systems emerging from violent political upheavals, only to collapse, disintegrate, and give rise to new emergent systems. Ever since the first temple libraries emerged in Sumeria around 3000 BC, libraries have flourished and fallen with the empires that supported them. From ancient Sumer to India to China to the Aztec kingdom, the same pattern manifested again and again: first came literacy, then the nation-state, the empire, and ultimately the intellectual apotheosis of the empire, the library. When empires fall, they usually take their libraries with them.

The greatest library of the ancient world, of course, was the legendary Library at Alexandria. Today, Alexandria enjoys an almost mythic status as the archetypal temple of ancient wisdom. Why does Alexandria, alone among all the great libraries of antiquity, occupy such a special place in the popular imagination? Alexandria was more than just a large collection of books; it was the apotheosis of a whole new way of thinking that departed radically from the old imperial information systems of the preclassical era. To understand why Alexandria still matters, we need to understand a thing or two about the Greeks.

FROM MYTHOLOGY TO ONTOLOGY

Sometime after 2000 BC, troops of mounted warriors swooped down from the Caucasus Mountains, through the Balkans, and into the valleys of the Greek peninsula. They terrorized the indigenous population of farmers, ultimately subduing them and establishing a series of new kingdoms throughout the region. During the so-called Mycenaean Age (approximately 1600 to 1200 BC), a succession of small monarchies emerged that looked a lot like other regional kingdoms throughout the Near East. Like the Sumerians and Babylonians before them, the Minoans and Mycenaeans established a caste system predicated in part on the legitimating power of the written word. A ruling class of kings, attended by literate scribes and priests, established royal institutions, hoarded wealth, and wielded power over the illiterate populace of farmers and soldiers. Once again, it seemed, literacy was emerging along a familiar trajectory, with the technology of the written word serving to prop up ruling institutional hierarchies. But this time things would turn out differently.

The first Greek civilization came crashing to an end around 1200 BC, through a series of political disruptions that would be immortalized in Homer's *Odyssey*. The first Greek kingdoms collapsed, and the region descended into an ancient equivalent of the Dark Ages. The arts of literacy deteriorated and then vanished. State institutions disintegrated, and Greek culture vanished into a historical black hole, leaving almost no written trace for more than two centuries. As the first Greek kingdoms collapsed, people reverted to earlier tribal ways, reembracing their old oral traditions. The disintegration of institutional hierarchies created a fallow ground for ancient social networks to reemerge.

In this renewed oral culture, ancient myths took on new vitality. As we saw in Chapter 2, these mythologies were more than just popular stories; they reflected a deep-seated disposition to understand the world in terms of family relationships, shaped by the same epigenetic rules that govern the structure of folk taxonomies. The tales of Greek mythology originated from earlier traditions in Sumer, Babylon, Ugarit, and Bogazköy, which in turn derived from even older tribal myths. These overlapping streams of narrative myth extended like a vast cultural watershed across the ancient Near East. In the structure of these ancient stories, we can find the echoes of old taxonomic hierarchies. Hesiod's *Theogony*, the canonical version of the Greek myths, portrays a family tree of the gods that runs about five to six levels deep, just like a folk taxonomy, with each god representing a particular element of the natural world. Zeus is the god of thunder, Poseidon the sea, Hades the underworld, and so on. The relationships among the gods describe allegories and metonymies encoded in a structure of "family" relationships.

The diagram below shows a partial glimpse of how the family relationships among the gods unfold. Chaos, the primordial abyss, gives birth to Gaia, the Earth, who in turn gives birth to Cronos, the Harvest, who begets the family of gods most familiar to humans: Hestia, Zeus, Hera, Hades, and Poseidon. Zeus and Hera, the archetypal king and queen, give birth to Athena, the goddess of civilization; Ares, the god of war; and Hephaestus, the god of technology. Ares gives birth to Phobos, the god of fear, and Harmonia, the goddess of harmony. The whole system functions as a kind of vast cultural encyclopedia, cross-referenced using the familiar structure of family genealogy. The stories of Zeus and the gods also narrate metaphorical relationships among natural phenomena. For example, Okeanos and Tethys give birth to rivers and streams; Hyperion and Thela to the sun, moon, and dawn; and so forth. The familiar myth of the Muses—the divine beings said to inspire poets and artists—represents more than just a superstitious belief in the possibility of divine inspiration. "The Muses' genealogy is transparent allegory," writes classicist Robert Lamberton. "Offspring of power and memory, they embody the prestige and authority of the highest of the gods.

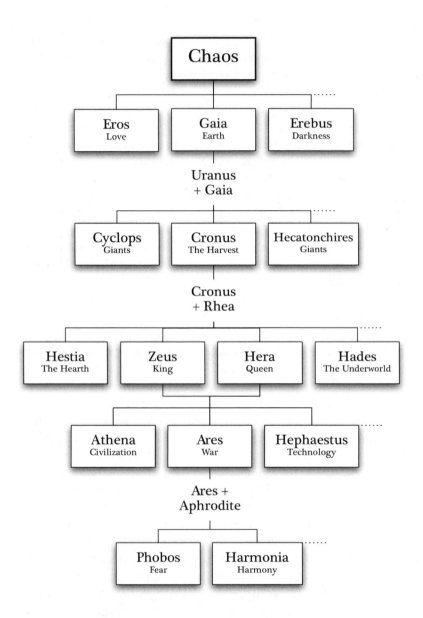

A partial genealogy of the Greek gods, adapted from Hesiod's *Theogony*.

Memory, in this context, is not the capacity eroded by Alzheimer's or obliterated by Korsakov's syndrome but rather a fine-tuned programming in a vast range of cultural skills and information."[16] The *Theogony* thus serves as a taxonomic prototype for the structure of Greek thought.

While it would be outrageously simplistic to suggest that the rich tapestry of Greek mythology boils down to one big taxonomy, nonetheless the basic structure of these divine genealogies seems to echo the implicit structures of ancient folk taxonomies. Note that the most popular gods—the Olympians—appear roughly in the middle of the hierarchy, in a position corresponding to the genus, the "psychologically primary" category in folk taxonomies (see Chapter 2).

The structure of the gods' families holds glimpses of older oral traditions that predated the first era of Greek kings, traditions that spread through the pure network of oral traditions, unfettered by priestly bureaucracies. "From the earliest glimpses we have into Greek tradition, the poets and visual artists, not the priests, were the bearers of the traditions about the divine," writes Lamberton. "The contrast with the priest-ridden cultures of the East has often been drawn but cannot be too much emphasized. The Greeks had no Moses, and their first theologians were entertainers—Homer and Hesiod."[17] In the years following the disappearance of the old state hierarchies during the Greek Dark Ages, poets strengthened their command of the old stories and, by extension, the transmission of cultural tradition.

By the time Greek civilization reemerged from its writing-less silence in the ninth century BC, the Greeks were living in a new world. Poetry had taken the place of scriptures and royal decrees. Soon it would provide the foundation for a whole new kind of literate culture. Whereas the earlier Greek civilization had used a form of writing derived from the imperial Babylonian script, this time the Greeks borrowed a new script from their trading partners, the Phoenicians. The Phoenicians used a phonetic writing system, with letters signifying sounds rather than ideas. The Greeks adapted this alphabet to their native oral language, in the process hitting on a radically simplified style of writing. Their new alphabet contained just 24 symbols. It was easy to learn. In the earlier Greek civilization, literacy had required long years of training and imperial support; it was only for the elites. Now, almost anyone could learn to read and write. This time the Greeks would not succumb to the old imperial "tyranny of the book."[18]

The Greeks took up the new form of alphabetic writing with enthusiasm. While the old empires had used writing largely for affairs of state—government archives, administrative records, hagiographies of their rulers—the newly literate Greeks put writing to more populist ends. Emerging from a period of reengagement with their older oral heritage, mythologies, and folk traditions, the Greeks started writing down their old stories. By the time of the great civic festivals of Athens in the sixth century BC, readers were clamoring for standardized versions of their old myths. This period saw a great shift in the nature of storytelling, from an era when poems enjoyed a fluid structure in the ever-shifting versions of oral storytellers to a more rigid and deterministic form, as poems became "frozen and shackled to the interests of political power," as Lamberton puts it. While the stories of the Greek myths contained embedded hierarchies of family relationships between the gods, those hierarchical narrative structures also strengthened the bonds of social networks. "Institutions demand—indeed, impose—stability and are able to harness the power of even such unlikely sources as poetry."[19] While the notion of poems as political tools may strike us as implausible today, the poems of ancient Greece—like the Odyssey, or Hesiod's mythology—went straight to the heart of questions of political legitimacy. The emerging Greek political institutions had a clear vested interest in nailing down standard versions of these texts as safeguards of their own power. These old tales, preserved through the Greek Dark Ages through the aegis of social networks, became important tools in establishing new political hierarchies.

As the old myths became ensconced in writing and embedded in a growing bureaucratic structure, the Greeks began to approach their old stories in a new light. At first most of these stories had fallen into the category of what psychologist Merlin Donald calls "mythic" or integrative thought, in which cultural knowledge is synthesized in the form of densely layered mythologies. Mythic thought, while it may be expressed in writing, harkens back to the oral traditions of tribal cultures. The Greeks, however, took their understanding a step farther. They were, as far as we know, the first culture to make the leap from mythic to "theoretic" thought: that is, the ability to reflect on the process of thought itself. Writing gave Greeks the chance to approach their old myths with a new reflexive stance, cultivating a degree of objectivity that enabled them to compare, assess, and excavate new layers of meaning from the texts. By writing down their old stories, they made the inner logics of these systems visible. Once the text became externalized, it could be subjected to analytical thought, reworked, and even improved on. This process of textualization corresponds to what Merlin Donald calls the "demythologization" of culture. "The first step in any new area of theory development is always antimythic," he writes. "Things and events must be stripped of their previous mythic significances before they can be subjected to what we call 'objective' theoretic analysis. In fact, the meaning of 'objectivity' is precisely this: a process of demythologization." For example, astronomy constitutes the demythologization of astrology, chemistry the demythologization of alchemy, anatomy constitutes the demystification of the human body, and so on. "Before nature could be classified and placed into a theoretical framework, it too had to be demythologized," writes Donald. "Nothing illustrates the transition from mythic to theoretic culture better than this agonizing process of demythologization, which is still going on, thousands of years after it began. The switch from a predominantly narrative mode of thought to a predominantly analytic or theoretic mode apparently requires a wrenching cultural transformation."[20]

This second coming of alphabetic thought left some Greek thinkers with a conflicted relationship to the emerging information technology of the written word. In *Phaedrus*, Plato recounts the story of the Egyptian god Theuth, the discoverer of writing, the "speech of the gods." When he presents his discovery to the Egyptian god-king Thamus, presumably expecting accolades for his breakthrough, the king instead gives him a sharp rebuke. "This discovery of yours will create forgetfulness in men's souls," says the king, "because they will not use their memories; they will trust to the external written characters and not remember of themselves." The king goes on to decry the art of writing as "an aid not to memory, but to reminiscence," warning that readers will become "hearers of many things and will have learned nothing . . . having the show of wisdom without the reality."[21]

This story has often been misinterpreted as Plato's condemnation of writing. In fact, Plato was a great lover of books. He maintained one of the largest private libraries in Athens. The tale is actually a veiled attack on the Sophists, who devoted themselves to the enthusiastic production of knowledge without, in Plato's view, a proper reverence for reading. The Sophists' disposition toward profligate penmanship prompted Aristophanes to deride the ancient Greek capital as "Athens full of scribes."

Plato's story also contains the central paradox of writing: Plato surely knew the story could not possibly have survived without being written down. The story seems to recognize the threat posed by literate culture to earlier oral traditions. Yet the interpolation of oral and literate cultures was the essential factor in the Greek contribution to human knowledge.

Poised at the cusp of the transition from oral to literate traditions, the tales of Greek mythology provide a perfect boundary object for analyzing the effects of this profound cultural shift. They give us a revealing glimpse into the mythic world of the oral traditions that preceded the reemergence of Greek literacy, showing how mythologies rooted in ancient wisdom traditions provided the cultural framework for the great Greek experiment with decoding the process of "knowing" itself. "From the first, Greek thinkers were employing external memory devices to their fullest effect, in a way that was totally new," writes Donald.

> In modern culture, narrative thought is dominant in the literary arts, while analytic thought predominates in science, law, and government. The narrative, or mythic, dimension of modern culture has been expressed in print, but it is well to keep in mind that in its inception, mythic thought did not depend upon print or visual symbolism; it was an extension, in its basic form, of the oral narrative.[22]

Analytic thought gives rise to "formal arguments, systematic tax-onomies, induction, deduction, verification, differentiation, quanti-fication, idealization, and formal methods of measurement"—systematized ways of understanding the world that are all absent from the world of mythic thought.[23] "[T]he natural tendency of spo-ken thought . . . is toward fairly loose narration of events, metaphoric fantasy, and storytelling. Fine-grained analysis of the thought pro-cess itself is difficult, because the memory trace of an oral narration is so ephemeral."[24] The new art of "thinking about thinking" opened the door to introspection—formalized ideas and conjectures, unfin-ished thoughts, and dialogue. The process of demythologization not only affects the forms of human thought but also influences macro structures of social organization. Whereas oral traditions lend them-selves naturally to fluid, self-organizing social networks, written ana-lytic thought creates a different imperative, fostering the kind of linear thinking that seems to beget organizational hierarchies. Donald speculates that "the governing cognitive structures of the most recent human cultures must be very different from those of simple mythic cultures. They exist mostly outside of the individual mind, in external symbolic memory representations, which are de-pendent upon visuographic invention, and they culminate in gov-erning theories."[25] In other words, the shift from mythological to analytic culture played out in the evolving structure of the state itself.

The journey from mythic to analytic thought was hardly a smooth one. Socrates was put to death for lack of reverence toward the gods, and Aristotle later faced the same accusation. But slowly, inexorably, the old mythologies began to make way for a more sys-tematic way of understanding. The process of demythologization that started in ancient Greece continues to this day. While we may live in a highly analytic, systematized culture, oral myths continue to exert a strong pull. Orality has hardly disappeared; indeed, with the rise of electronic media, it may be reemerging. Ong has suggested that we are witnessing the birth of a "new orality" in the form of electronic communications. Just as the Greeks of the classical Dark Age saw new forms of thought emerge when oral and literate cultures began to interpolate each other, we may be witnessing a similar period of cultural renegotiation today, a process whose outcome we probably cannot yet predict.

If the Greek journey from mythic to analytic thought tells us anything, however, it may point to the sheer durability of mythological thinking. Today, most of us still know more about Greek mythology than we do about classical logic. Elementary school students can still tell you stories about Zeus, Hera, and Apollo (while very few of them could tell you anything about Aristophanes). The sheer longevity of these stories, even in our technologically advanced society that ought to be well along the path to demythologization by now, suggests that the enduring resonance of myths may stem from a deeper affinity in the human psyche. Perhaps the ancient epigenetic rules governing folk taxonomy (see Chapter 2) equip us with a subtle longing to understand the world in terms of gods and their families.

FROM ARISTOTLE TO ALEXANDRIA

As Greek civilization spread throughout the ancient Near East, so too did its books. Long before Alexander established his great eponymous library in Egypt, the Greeks had established great halls of learning at Antioch and Pergamum, a library said to contain more than 200,000 scrolls. Athens was the bibliographical center of the Greek world, playing host to a bustling book trade that fueled the rise of personal libraries among a growing class of literate citizens. As public literacy flourished during the age of Sophocles, Aristophanes, Thucydides, Euripides, Aeschylus, and the other great secular writers of ancient Greece, private citizens began to amass growing book collections. By the fourth century BC, a typical Athenian library might contain works by Homer and Hesiod, tragedies, histories, works of poetry and philosophy, and even cookbooks. The largest and most famous of Athens's personal libraries belonged to Aristotle, who not only amassed great numbers of books, but also developed a keen fascination with the question of how to organize his collection. As the scholar Strabo wrote, Aristotle "was the first to have put together a collection of books and to have taught the kings in Egypt how to arrange a library."[26]

Aristotle's interest in organizing books grew out of his passion for mapping the structure of human thought. He devoted enormous energy to questions surrounding the organization of knowledge, postulating theories of logic and taxonomic models that would reverberate for millennia. Aristotle's work on categorization would provide the foundation for a contribution to the heritage of Western thought too vast to be addressed in remotely adequate detail here. Suffice it to say that students of philosophy and the social sciences have spent thousands of years pondering Aristotle's categories.

Aristotle took a special interest in the organization of knowledge about the natural world, devoting a great deal of his work to the search for logical order in the world of visible phenomena. He grounded his work in an exhaustive program of scientific observation, gathering vast amounts of first-hand data about plants and animals, which he then labored to situate in a larger categorical framework. While Aristotle's writings about plants have been lost altogether, his works on the animal kingdom constitute a seminal contribution to biology. He proposed a comprehensive taxonomy of animal life that distinguished mammals from nonmammals, vertebrates from invertebrates, even recognizing that whales and dolphins differed from fish (although he failed to recognize them as mammals). He also introduced the convention of binomial naming: that is, describing a species by its genus (e.g., "felis") and species ("catus"). Reflecting the dominant view of his day, Aristotle mistakenly believed that animal species did not change over time, but rather that they represented instances of fixed, immutable ideal forms stretching back into time immemorial (Darwinian evolution would have been a thoroughly alien concept to the ancient Greeks).

Vertebrates	*Invertebrates*
Quadrupeds (or mammals)	Cephalopods
Birds	Crustaceans
Reptiles	Insects
Fish	Shelled animals
Whales	Zoophytes (or "plant-animals")

Although Aristotle is often credited as the first great taxonomist, his system almost certainly relied on earlier folk taxonomies that had persisted for thousands of years in earlier oral traditions (see Chapter 2). Although his naturalist writings would have a lasting impact on the subsequent course of biology, he receives perhaps a little too much credit as the world's first taxonomist. Aristotle did not invent the concept of genera and species; he simply adapted and codified the ancient oral traditions of folk taxonomies. His great contribution was to make the old implicit structures explicit, and therefore available for inspection and improvement. In so doing, he extracted an analytic system of thought from the remnants of oral traditions shrouded in myth. If we understand Aristotle's categories not just as the insights of a great thinker, but also as the fruition of ancient folk taxonomies long in the making, then perhaps we can also speculate as to why his system (flawed though it was) persisted for thousands of years. By invoking the structure of folk taxonomies, Aristotle's categories may have resonated with epigenetic rules lodged deep in the prehistoric mind. While Aristotle's landmark writing on the natural world owed a great deal to the heritage of folk taxonomies, it also signaled the beginning of the end of the old folkways and the inauguration of a new, systematic approach to scholarship.

Aristotle did a great deal more than simply categorize plants and animals, of course. Building on his research into the natural world, he went on to postulate a metaphysical world view that drew the crucial distinction between matter and form, or what he called "primary" and "secondary" substances. Primary substances referred to the individual instances of particular phenomena; secondary substances referred to their ideal forms, the disembodied templates of human thought.

> Substance, in the truest and primary and most definite sense of the word, is that which is neither predicable of a subject nor present in a subject; for instance, the individual man or horse. But in a secondary sense those things are called substances within which, as *species*, the primary substances are included; also those which, as *genera*, include the species. For instance, the individual man is included in the species "man," and the genus to which the species belongs is "animal"; these, therefore that is to

say, the species "man" and the genus "animal"—are termed secondary substances.[27]

By recognizing the distinction between form and matter, Aristotle believed the human mind could aspire to penetrate higher realms of Truth. In his *Categories*, Aristotle enumerated a comprehensive set of classes and subclasses that he believed could reveal the structure of nature's creation. He believed that any phenomenon in the world could be described in terms of a particular set of characteristics: substance, quantity, quality, relation, place, time, position, state, action, and passion. He further believed that the relationships between phenomena could be explained in terms of a web of semantic relationships: causality, equivalence, identity, similarity, family, inside of, bigger than, and earlier than. By weaving the universe of forms together with these relational threads, Aristotle conceived of human knowledge as a vast interconnected web that extended even beyond the observable world, into incorporeal realms. His famous Great Chain of Being classified all life into a grand cosmic hierarchy, from the lowest realm of minerals to the highest realm of the gods. Unlike the traditional folk taxonomies that concerned themselves with the observable world of plants and animals, Aristotle's taxonomy stretched into the otherworldly domains of gods, angels, and demons:

Aristotle's Great Chain of Being:

Gods
Angels
Demons
Man
Animals
Plants
Minerals

Aristotle's categories would cast a long shadow over the subsequent development of the Western intellectual tradition, influencing the trajectory of European thought, especially during the Middle

Ages, when scholars rediscovered Aristotle and elevated his writings to the level of canonical truth second only to the Bible and the church fathers. Aristotle's taxonomic conventions would persist for more than 2,000 years, until Linnaeus embraced and improved on the Aristotelian system to create the familiar modern Linnaean taxonomy still in use today (see Chapter 9). Aristotle's work on categorizing the phenomenal world reflects his deeply systematic worldview, his conviction that the world could be described in terms of ideal forms. His quest for logical order led to his conviction that the world was ultimately knowable. That conviction not only drove Aristotle's personal ambitions, but also served—along with his personal library—as the intellectual foundation for the greatest library of the ancient world.

THE UNIVERSAL LIBRARY

By some accounts the Great Library at Alexandria literally began with Aristotle's own personal collection (other accounts insist that the library only took its conceptual inspiration from Aristotle and that his book collection was buried in Athens after his death, later to be dug up and sold to book collectors). Whether or not the library contained Aristotle's actual books, there is no question that it embodied his ideals. The Great Library at Alexandria was the first library with a truly comprehensive ambition to gather all the world's knowledge under one roof. Established around 300 BC, the library marked an achievement of vast intellectual proportions, ultimately growing to house more than 700,000 items. Unlike the royal libraries that preceded it, the Alexandria library was open to the public.

The structure of the library followed Aristotle's division of knowledge into observational and deductive sciences. The library was also built specifically with Aristotle's peripatetic ideal* of scholarship in mind, with wide colonnades and open spaces to encourage scholars to stroll around and converse about topics of scholarly interest. We can imagine scholars strolling the grounds, papyrus rolls in hand,

---

*Aristotle is said to have taught his students while, literally, walking around.

debating the politics of the day or perhaps a fine philosophical point. In keeping with the great teacher's insistence on open inquiry, the library encouraged "walking around"—both physically and metaphorically. To Socrates, Plato, and Aristotle, intellectual freedom was a paramount civic value (they would surely have bristled at the scholarly territorialism and narrowcast specialization of the modern academy), and the architecture of the library reflected that point of view.

Today, Alexandria occupies a special place in the popular imagination as a symbol of the lost era of classical scholarship and as the site of one of history's great biblioclasms, the place where the great tide of classical learning rose, crested, and finally crashed into oblivion. But the real story of Alexandria turns out to be considerably less tidy than the myth. Its birth was less idealistic, its life less peaceful, and its death less cataclysmic than the popular fable suggests.

When Ptolemy I established the royal library, Alexandria was a new city, populated by military people, traders, and assorted hangers-on. As an intellectual center, it could scarcely hold a candle to Athens. But the city's first ruler, Ptolemy, fancied himself a scholar, having composed a detailed history of Alexander's conquests and studied geometry with no less a mathematician than Euclid. Determined to attract scholars to his young city, Ptolemy offered enormous incentives for learned men to come to his new metropolis at the mouth of the Nile. He invited poets, writers, and scientists to live in the city and work at its famous museum, offering them room and board in the royal palace and a generous tax-free salary, as well as the guarantee of lifetime employment. As a final inducement, he built the world's first great library (actually called a museum), whose ambitions were nothing short of universal. By the time of Ptolemy's death, the collection had grown to 200,000 books. By the time Julius Caesar arrived in 47 BC, the library had swelled to 700,000 volumes. The library's signal achievement was the sheer magnitude of its collection, orders of magnitude larger than any library before it and larger than any library that would follow for more than a thousand years.

The library's stated acquisition policy was simple: Acquire everything. The Alexandrian rulers built the great library not just as an act of imperial generosity but also through fiat, confiscation, and occasionally subterfuge. According to one story, Ptolemy III sent to Athens for a collection of tragedies by Aeschylus, Sophocles, and Euripides, giving them a substantial cash deposit along with a promise to copy the manuscripts and send the originals back to Athens. Upon receiving the prized volumes, the king promptly reneged on his promise, keeping the originals and sending back copies instead. As the library acquired new volumes, it stored them in a vast warehouse where they awaited cataloging (library acquisition backlogs are nothing new).

Like other great libraries of history, the Alexandria library mirrored the struggles of the empire that begat it. Its rise and fall rested entirely on the stability of its patron empires, and like all institutional knowledge systems, it ultimately proved no more durable than its imperial patrons. The Greek heyday of self-organized scholarship was over, and the new imperial age after Alexander would give birth to a great institutional consolidation of knowledge. The emperors' intentions were not, in other words, purely Arcadian. They recognized the political value of intellectual capital. Ptolemy I's advisor Demetrius saw the importance of a library not only in promoting the flourishing of scholarship but also ensuring the newly relocated empire a competitive advantage over neighboring rivals in terms of science, technology, and statecraft. Toward that end, the library implemented history's most aggressive collection development program: confiscating books from private citizens and insisting that all ships harboring at the docks yield whatever books they carried as the price of entry to the port. And while the scholars at the library enjoyed near-total academic freedom, with a wide mandate to roam where their minds would take them, in truth they were a little less free than we might like to imagine. While scholars were under no obligation to pursue any particular discipline, they were nonetheless beholden to the patronage of the emperors. As the Alexandrian institution grew, it began to suffer from the curse of many a state educational organ: intellectual conservatism. The residents of the so-called museum were putatively free to pursue their intellectual interests, but royal patronage exerted a subtle and ultimately stultifying influence. None of the Alexandrian scholars, so far as we know, felt quite so free as to question the imperial system of government. Alexandria became a haven for scholarly sycophants or, as Timon of Philius put it, a "chicken coop of the muses." As library historian Leslie W. Dunlap writes, "The Museum typified the derivative culture of Alexandria: significant original creations were rare indeed, but here the laurels of Greek civilization were kept green for seven centuries."[28] Indeed, given hundreds of years' worth of munificent imperial support, perhaps the most remarkable thing about the library is how little original scholarship it actually ever produced.

Alexandria's first librarian was a scholar named Zenodotus, who had won fame for his efforts at standardizing the old Homeric texts. A pioneering figure in library science, Zenodotus introduced the first library classification scheme, a rudimentary subject scheme that assigned texts to different rooms based on their subject matter. At first the library had no catalog; the collection was its own catalog. Curators attached a small tag to the end of each scroll, describing the work's title, author, and subject. Although this elementary bibliographic data constituted the first systematic abstraction of metadata, those data remained physically affixed to the material book. During the library's initial period, this approach worked well enough, as long as the collection remained small enough that readers could peruse its contents simply by walking around the room. One of the early librarians, Aristophanes of Byzantium, is said to have read the entire collection himself.

While the library served as, in effect, its own catalog during the early years, eventually the collection reached a size of such magnitude that readers needed a better way to navigate it. The poet and librarian Callimachus was the first to undertake the job of creating a separate catalog of the collection, a comprehensive bibliography known as the *Pinakes*, or "Tables of Persons Eminent in Every Branch of Learning Together with a List of Their Writings." Although he succeeded in cataloging only one-fifth of the entire collection, his catalog was an impressive undertaking, filling no less than 120 scrolls and earning Callimachus a place in history as not only Alexandria's greatest poet but also the world's first great bibliographer. Alas, the *Pinakes* failed to survive the library's destruction, but thanks to descriptions by contemporary writers, we know something of its structure. It consisted of a set of tables, broken down in a top-level distinction between poetry and prose, further divided into subcategories. Interestingly, the *Pinakes* was not a classification of works but of authors (apparently, the Alexandrian librarians saw no problem with literary typecasting). From what we know of its structure, the classification broke down as follows:

Poetry	Prose
Dramatic poets	Philosophers
Tragedy	Orators
Comedy	Historians
Epic poets	Writers on medicine
Lyric poets	Miscellaneous

Within each table, authors' names appeared in alphabetical order, accompanied by a brief biographical description. The catalog was the library itself, with each room representing a broad subject area: verse, prose, literature, science, and so forth. As the Alexandrian collection mushroomed to over 500,000 volumes, the task of maintaining the catalog by hand outstripped the ability of the librarians to keep pace. Over time the library began to institute a two-tiered system that gave preference to major authors, ensuring their historical longevity at the expense of lesser scribes.

The story of Alexandria's demise has long been the subject of competing myths. One story lays the blame for its death at the feet of Julius Caesar, who is said to have burned the library as a defensive ploy against a storming Alexandrian mob. Another story sets the blame 700 years later, at the feet of the Muslim conqueror Amr, who is said to have followed the advice of a caliph who advised him: "Touching the books you mention [at Alexandria], if what is written in them agrees with the Book of God, they are not required; if it disagrees, they are not desired. Destroy them therefore."[29] Other scholars believe the library persisted in some form until about 270 AD, when the emperor Aurelian laid waste to the city while fighting a rabid insurgency. Whatever the circumstances of its demise, we know the library's end came as a result of armed conflict; its fate was inexorably tied to the fate of its empire.

Today, the library stands as an idealized symbol of scholarship and learning. But the tale of its rise and fall also tells an instructive story about the inherent instability of institutional systems. And its burning, while surely a great historical tragedy, marks only one in a long progression of historical biblioclasms.

AFTER ALEXANDRIA

While Alexandria occupies a special place in the popular imagination as the iconic library of the ancient world, libraries flourished throughout the Greek and Roman worlds. As Rome began appropriating Greek culture starting in the fourth century BC, Roman citizens populated their private libraries from the great book markets in Athens, Rhodes, and Alexandria. Wealthy citizens collected decorative books to ornament their homes, while less affluent Romans could buy small unadorned books for a few coins. Prominent Roman citizens like Cicero built vast personal libraries. The fashion for book collecting reached such a height that the poet Ausonius satirized the folly of citizens who increasingly purchased books for ornamental purposes:

> That thou with Books thy Library hast fill'd
> Think'st though thy self learn'd and in Grammar skill'd
> Then stor'd with Strings, Lutes, Fiddle-stricks now bought;
> Tomrrow thou Musitian may'st be thought.[30]

Shortly before his death in 44 BC, Julius Caesar decreed that a great public library should be built. A statesman named Pollio picked up the imperial charter after Caesar's assassination and started building the first great Roman public library with the support of no lesser public intellectuals than Catullus, Horace, and Virgil. Located near the Roman forum, the library consisted of two distinct collections: one block for Latin works and another for Greek. This precedent of dividing the library into two parallel collections would persist in subsequent Roman libraries, as generations of Romans built new public libraries modeled on Pollio's original. Centuries later, early Christian libraries would follow this model of bibliographical bicameralism, splitting their books into collections for Christian and pagan works.

By the fourth century AD, Rome had no fewer than 28 public libraries. While none of these libraries came anywhere close to approximating the vast Greek collections at Alexandria and Pergamum, they played a visible role in everyday Roman life. The typical Roman library stood in close proximity to a temple or palace, usually conjoined by rows of columns. Walking inside, the citizen would traverse a front entryway with busts of famous poets and authors, arranged into their separate chambers for Latin and Greek. The larger libraries featured bookcases with numbers corresponding to entries in a master catalog listing. As in Alexandria, each scroll bore a tag identifying its author and title. The bookcases opened out onto reading rooms, where library users could peruse a chosen manuscript; some libraries permitted private borrowing.

Roman libraries also served as intellectual salons, housing literary, social, and political groups. While only a fraction of Rome's residents would likely have availed themselves of these services, the public mission of the library nonetheless signaled a continuation of the Greek commitment to public scholarship. In many Roman communities, libraries were attached to the public baths. The library system was administered by a *procurator*, with each individual library headed by a librarian with a staff of assistants and copyists who made up the preponderance of the library staff. Librarians enjoyed high esteem during this period. Martial describes Sextus, the librarian of the Palatine, as having "intelligence approaching that of a god."[31]

By the fourth century AD, Roman libraries had spread throughout the empire, from Africa to Britain. Roman scribes distributed their copied manuscripts throughout the conquered territories; these far-flung collections would later prove instrumental in preserving the heritage of classical literature. By the latter days of the Roman empire, however, public love of learning began to degrade into an all-out embrace of Greek Epicurianism. Libraries languished as citizens increasingly devoted their energies to sensory pleasures. Coupled with the pacific influence of Christianity, a love of the good life overwhelmed the old farmer-soldier ethic of the early Republic, and the old ideals—including the long tradition of civic bibliophilia—began to diminish. By 378 AD, Ammianus reported an empire whose citizens had relinquished their former love of knowledge in favor of pleasures of the flesh:

> [I]n place of the philosophers the singer is called in, and in place of the orator the teacher of stagecraft, and while the libraries are shut up forever like tombs, water-organs are manufactured and lyres as large as carriages, and flutes and huge instruments for gesticulating actors.[32]

In our age of pop music, TV dramas, and Broadway musicals, perhaps some of us can identify with Ammianus's lament. Just as the old hierarchies of the Roman Empire started falling into decay, so too did its libraries. By the fifth century, Rome's great public libraries had all but disappeared, either destroyed at the hands of the Vandals or carted away to the new capital in Constantinople. By the sixth century they were gone. The old hierarchies of the Roman empire—and its imperial libraries—gave way to a period of intellectual chaos, creating a fallow ground from which new forms of knowledge would soon emerge.

5

Illuminating the Dark Age

A scholar is just a library's way of making another library.
Daniel C. Dennett, *Consciousness Explained*

An Irish legend holds that one night in the middle of the sixth century, Saint Columba borrowed a manuscript from his guest Saint Finnian, staying up all night inside the church to copy the rare text. According to the legend, Columba's fingers shone like candles, lighting up the whole church.[1]

With the collapse of the Roman Empire in the fifth century, Europe lost more than just its imperial government; it also lost thousands of texts—Plato, Aristotle, Cicero, Virgil—the intellectual foundation of the *Pax Romana*. As the Goths and Vandals swarmed into the city, they burned the libraries and government archives, annihilating the empire's collective intellectual capital. During the so-called Dark Ages that followed, the scorched earth of the old empire gave way to the reemergence of smaller, close-knit societies not far removed from the tribal chiefdoms of old. While the institutional template of the old imperial bureaucracies persisted in the form of the growing Roman church, daily life for most Europeans reverted to a more tribal mode of existence. The old hierarchies of the state collapsed, and Europe entered a period in which literacy waned, while older oral traditions and kinship networks reasserted themselves. To invoke the evolutionary metaphor, the Dark Ages were a period of mutation and drift. Across Europe this seemingly regressive period provided fertile ground for a series of new technologies that would soon begin to take shape. Most of this innovation would happen in a few isolated corners of Christendom, within the cloistered walls of early monasteries.

In the century before the fall of Rome, the unwieldy 12-foot-long papyrus scrolls of Alexandria had started to cede room on the shelves to a new form of document: the codex book, so named because it originated from attempts to "codify" the Roman law in a format that supported easier information retrieval. The new format boasted a more navigable interface, featuring leafed pages bound between durable hard covers. Not only was the new format more resilient than the carefully wound scrolls that preceded it, it facilitated a new way of engaging with the text. Scrolls, by their physical nature, demanded linear reading from start to finish. They required a commitment on the part of the reader and resisted attempts to extract individual nuggets of information. But with a codex book, readers could now flip between pages easily to pinpoint any passage in a text. As Hobart and Schiffman write, "The codex had the potential to transform the manuscript from a cumbersome mnemonic aid to a readily accessible information storehouse."[2]

The new technology of the book ushered in a whole new way of reading: random access. A document no longer had to be read from top to bottom; its pages could be flipped, allowing the reader to move around at will. By letting users move freely from page to page, the new book allowed readers to form their own networks of association within a particular text. Scrolls, on the other hand, encouraged linear reading. The book also had one more considerable advantage over the old scrolls: portability. While collections of papyrus scrolls and codex books coexisted in late Roman libraries, the destruction of the empire saw most of the great old library collections burned, plundered, or scattered. The codex book format proved hardier and more portable than the old scrolls; as a result, many scrolls failed to survive the fall of the Roman empire, and a great deal of the literature that lived on did so between the covers of bound books.

By the fifth century AD, Rome had conquered much of continental Europe and most of the neighboring island of Britannia, dispersing copies of books that would eventually make their way into monastic libraries throughout the former provinces. For all of Rome's far-flung conquests, one island had always lain just beyond its reach: Ireland (or, as it was called, Hibernia). Throughout the era of Roman conquest, the Irish had lived in tribal communities not far removed from the preliterate cultures of Mesopotamia, Australia, or North America. Knowing nothing of reading, let alone Aristotle, people lived in small social groups with warring feudal kings and a shamanistic religious tradition, Druidism. Lacking any form of written language, they relied on oral traditions, mythology, and a web of symbols to preserve their understanding of the world. The old Druidic system was conceptually not far removed from the multilayered ancient folk systems of China, Greece, or aboriginal Australia.

The Irish Celts were a famously bellicose people, who warred with each other and occasionally raided neighboring England, where in the early fifth century a group of Irish pirates brought back a recalcitrant young slave named Saccath. After working naked in the fields tending goats for several years, the slave managed to escape his captors and find his way to Gaul, where he spent the next 12 years at the monastery of Saint Germain, learning to read and studying the Gospels. Eventually, he decided to leave the monastery, vowing to return to Ireland to spread the word of God among his former captors. In the course of fulfilling that aspiration, the onetime slave—known to us now as Saint Patrick—would forever alter the course of Western European thought.

While Saint Patrick was not the first Christian missionary to reach Ireland, he was certainly the most successful. Within a mere 30 years he managed to convert the entire Irish population to the new faith. While Patrick's success undoubtedly had a great deal to do with his personal charisma, he also had technology on his side. Patrick introduced the Irish to the written word. He returned to Hibernia armed with a copy of the Latin Gospel. That lone volume would become the catalyst for Ireland's encounter with literacy. Patrick initiated the long process of transplanting the literate culture of classical antiquity into the shamanistic oral culture of Ireland. The result was an extraordinarily successful cultural adaptation. The drift of classical literacy to the remote island culture resulted in a beautiful new art form with lasting cultural consequences: the illuminated manuscript.

While the Irish were hardly the first tribal culture to come in contact with the literary arts, their experience differed in one important respect from previous historical encounters with literacy. Before the emergence of the bound book, literate cultures had always introduced the technology of writing to nonliterate people in a linear format: in stone, clay tablets, or papyrus scrolls. The Irish were the first people to learn to read from books. Ever since, Irish literacy has been inextricably bound (so to speak) with the form of the book.

The sudden introduction of this new, random-access form of writing to a previously illiterate tribal society sparked a collision of cultures that would yield dazzling literary byproducts. In short order the Irish managed to embrace both writing and books, while imbuing them with their own unique cultural sensibilities. In the coming centuries, Ireland would become a kind of literary research and development laboratory, populated by talented scribes with a knack for innovation, working together in an environment largely insulated from the continental ravages of the Dark Ages. For the next 500 years the Irish scribes not only preserved the classical texts of the old Roman world, they also recorded their own indigenous Celtic mythologies and folklore, infusing bound books with their cultural heritage of storytelling and symbolism. Unencumbered by the institutionalized hierarchies of Rome and knowing nothing of government bureaucracies, religious institutions, or schools, the tribal people of Ireland took to literacy with zeal. Newly literate Irish monks began to navigate the great corpus of classical and scriptural knowledge. At first the early Irish manuscripts were artistically primitive affairs, scratched out on poor-quality vellum (made from cows' stomachs) and stuffed with cramped and inconsistent handwriting. But the scribes learned quickly and soon showed a remarkable aptitude for the literary arts, mastering the finer points of majuscule and minuscule scripts, making notes in the marginalia, and decorating their texts with clever, sometimes provocative, illustrations. Within a century they were producing manuscripts of astonishing beauty. These new kinds of books would become the gold standard of European illuminated manuscripts. Within two centuries, Irish scribes were producing breathtaking specimens like the *Book of Kells* and later the *Lindisfarne Gospel*. The illuminated manuscript became Dark Age Ireland's national art form.

For the scribes, copying manuscripts was an act of private devotion and contemplation rather than a rote task. While the popular historical stereotype paints the monastic scribe as a dour clerical type, making laborious transcriptions—like the famous Xerox TV commercial caricature—the early Irish scribes were in truth anything but human copy machines:

> [The scribes] did not see themselves as drones. Rather, they engaged the text they were working on, tried to comprehend it after their fashion, and, if possible, add to it, even improve on it. In this dazzling new culture, a book was not an isolated document on a dusty shelf; book truly spoke to book, and writer to scribe, and scribe to reader, from one generation to the next. These books were, as we would say in today's jargon, open, interfacing, and intertextual—glorious literary smorgasbords in which the scribe often tried to include a bit of everything, from every era, language, and style known to him.[3]

The scribes found ample opportunities for exploration in making sense of these imported coded texts. Their capacity for inventiveness and experimentation stemmed in no small part from their near-total isolation from the Roman Church, which elsewhere on the continent was beginning to establish a governing structure with restrictive rules for its burgeoning monastic orders and churchmen. But in Dark Ages Ireland the scribes enjoyed a great deal of artistic leeway.

The Irish scribes not only preserved countless important texts but in the centuries that followed also propagated those texts back to a continental Europe that had descended into near-barbarism. Most of the great Roman libraries failed to withstand the ravages of the Dark Ages. And while a few monasteries managed to preserve important collections of church texts and works by classical authors, no one else came close to approaching the artistic innovations of the Irish scribes. Without the Irish contribution, Europe might well have lacked the intellectual fortitude to withstand the expansion of Islam in the early Middle Ages. Eventually, the Irish style would work its way back to the continent, and conversely, continental scribes would influence the Irish to adopt a more conventional style. Irish monks began to adopt the uncial script style of the continent, while the Irish techniques of lavish illustration and marginalia seeped into the continental manuscripts. The cultural mutations of the Irish manuscripts became part of Europe's cultural DNA.

The early Celtic Church that began in Ireland soon spread across the Irish Sea to Scotland and then to England (and eventually, as far as Iceland and Italy). In contrast to the great institutional hierarchy of the Roman Church that would eventually displace it, the early Celtic Church was mostly a grassroots operation, self-organized, gender-harmonious (monks could marry), and geared primarily around individual contemplation rather than institutional dogmatism. While the Roman Church would eventually flex its political, economic, and military muscle to bring the wayward Irish scribes (and their British colleagues) back into the administrative fold, during the critical period following the collapse of Rome, Ireland harbored a period of remarkable literary innovation that would have lasting consequences for European culture. The legacy of the early Celtic Church—with its antihierarchical, individualist emphasis—would reverberate for centuries.

In the archetype of the Irish scribe—the original literary intertwingler—can we recognize a distant ancestor of today's blogger? Working outside of any traditional institutional hierarchy, engaging whatever topics interest him, interpolating words and images using a newly introduced communications technology, the scribe and the blogger seem like kindred literary souls. While we should be careful of stretching the parallel too far, the introduction of new technology in both cases seems to have given rise to a new ethos of self-directed writing, holding the promise of entirely new forms of expression.

The medieval manuscript not only opened up the possibility of random access to the contents of a document but also gave rise to new forms like marginalia, inline illustrations, and layered type styles that allowed readers to engage medieval manuscripts in a manner not far removed from what we now think of as hypertext. The scribes recognized the importance of visual cues, fusing words and images to create juxtapositions of meaning beyond the mere concatenation of words on a page. The Irish style of manuscript, with its lower minuscule-style typeface (as opposed to the uncial style prevalent on the European continent), became the artistic signature of the early Celtic Church. Irish scribes brought the style to England, where it flourished in the great monastery at Lindisfarne and became the foundation for the early English scriptoria that produced such works as the *Lindisfarne Gospel.*

One signature of the *Lindisfarne Gospel* is its Canon Tables, symbolic arches containing cross-references between sections of the Gospel. Designed to resemble a church, the Canon Tables were both metaphorical (a symbol of God's word housed in the church) and practical reference tools enabling the reader to move between related sections in the text, a kind of illuminated hypertext.

While historians of the book celebrate the artistic achievements of great manuscripts like the *Lindisfarne Gospel* and the *Book of Kells,* the vast majority of books produced in the early scriptoria were simpler affairs, intended for practical purposes. Scriptoria often produced durable copies of the Gospels to equip Christian missionaries on their journeys across the continent, where they used the texts to convert the pagans they encountered by wielding the power of God's "spell" ("Gospel"). The popular image of illuminated manuscripts suggests that they were the property of cloistered monks counting their proverbial angels on the heads of pins, but many early manuscripts went out into the world. Their physical heft and rich symbolism proved to be powerful physical totems against the disembodied oral traditions that held sway over the illiterate souls the missionaries intended to save. Often, when missionaries first encountered a pagan tribe, they would approach their prospective converts bearing a cross in one hand and a book in the other. To the illiterate tribes the book carried far more power as a symbolic object than as a container of words, representing what Christopher de Hamel calls "tangible proof of their message"[4] and a potent counterargument to ethereal oral traditions.

Canon Table, from a Bible made for the monks of Saint Albans Abbey in 1170.
Cambridge: Corpus Christi College, MS. 48, fol. 201v. Reproduced by permission
of The Master and Fellows of Corpus Christi College, Cambridge, England.

For the next thousand years, the monastic art of book making would play a central role in the spread of Christianity.

While the books functioned primarily as containers of written words, they also relied heavily on visual symbolism; it was through the power of images that the missionaries could captivate their illiterate audiences and then spellbind them with the ability to decipher the strange codes accompanying the images on the page. The Venerable Bede describes the importance of skillful imagery in the early spread of the Gospel, noting that the effect of pictures was "to the intent that all . . . even if ignorant of letters, might be able to contemplate . . . the ever-gracious countenance of Christ and his saints."[5]

As the craft of the manuscript progressed, the art of illumination became integral to the form. As a priest visiting Ireland in 1185 put it, "Look more keenly at [the illuminated manuscript] and you will penetrate to the very shrine of art. You will make out intricacies, so delicate and subtle, so exact and compact, so full of knots and links, with colours so fresh and vivid . . . the more often I see the book, the more carefully I study it, the more I am lost in ever-fresh amazement, and I see more wonders in the book."[6] These books, full as they were of "knots and links," represented a weaving of written meaning and imagery that would flourish in the age before Gutenberg. Before automated printing ushered in an era of relentlessly textual books, the information architecture of the Dark Ages revolved around the union of word and image.

In the ancient archetype of the monastic scribe, perhaps we can recognize a distant ancestor of today's multimedia artisans. Like the self-directed artists of the scriptorium, today's generation of online writers and artists take an unexplored new medium—the Web—into their own hands, fusing words and images, interpolating old texts, and creating whole new forms of expression that, like the illuminated manuscripts of a millennium past, are brimming with vivid colors, knots, and links.

HOUSES OF MUMBLERS

At about the same time that Saint Patrick was escaping his masters in Hibernia, a Roman nobleman named Cassiodorus was engineering an escape of his own. During the siege of Rome, he had witnessed the destruction of the last great Roman libraries, the Palatine and Ulpian. Although he stayed in Rome during the early years of rebuilding, he felt uneasy about the gathering political might of the church, ultimately deciding to forsake the ravaged city in search of a contemplative life. He abandoned the city and traveled to southern Italy, where his family maintained a country estate at Calabria. There he decided to establish his own little monastery.

The little monastery would eventually tower over the European intellectual landscape, playing a crucial role in preserving the Roman literary heritage and pioneering techniques of book production and library cataloging that would reverberate for more than a thousand years. While other European monasteries already had libraries of their own, Cassiodorus envisioned his scriptorium as more than just a literary archive. He saw it as an active center of scholarship and book production guided by an ethos of spiritual contemplation. He called it the Vivarium, "a place for living things."

Cassiodorus envisioned the scriptorium not as a musty archive but as an active center of learning, as a place where each monk "may fill his mind with the Scriptures while copying the sayings of the Lord." He also envisioned the scriptorium as a kind of missionary center, turning out copies of holy texts to be distributed across the growing expanse of Christendom. "What [the monk] writes in his cell will be scattered far and wide over distant Provinces,"[7] he wrote. The Vivarium soon became the most prolific center of book production the world had ever seen, churning out copies of works that eventually became canonical texts throughout Europe. Employing a small cadre of literate monks, Cassiodorus initiated a program of copying and translation that would become a template for a scholarly enterprise that flourished in European monasteries well into the Middle Ages.

In contrast to the inventive and sometimes freewheeling Irish scribes, Cassiodorus was a strict literary constructionist, holding his monks to a high standard of exactitude and consistency as they turned out uniform copies of the Gospels and other scriptural works as well as classical Greek and Roman writings. In their quest for efficiency the monks pioneered new techniques of book production, introducing efficient new binding techniques and engineering a system for mechanical lighting that enabled them to work on their copying projects well into the night.

Cassiodorus did more than institute an efficient literary assembly line; he also postulated a philosophical framework that attempted to impose a higher order on the whole enterprise. Having fled the authoritative strictures of the church and its hierarchical doctrines, Cassiodorus felt at liberty to propose his own system for classifying the growing body of works now in his charge. In his landmark work, *Institutiones divinarum et saecularium litterarum* ("Foundations of Divine and Secular Literature"), he laid out a sweeping system of thought that proposed a unified organizational scheme for both scriptural and secular texts. Here he proposed a new hierarchy of knowledge, starting with the titular dichotomy between divine and secular works. Within each top-level category, he proposed a mirrored ordering scheme. Believing that the pagan wisdom of the ancients contained seeds of God's truth, he arranged his books in a bipartite system, juxtaposing the sacred wisdom of the scriptures against the practical knowledge of the ancients. Within the divine realm, the Bible occupied the top spot in the hierarchy, followed by the church fathers, then later and lesser commentaries. On the secular side, Homer occupied the lead position in the literary pecking order, followed by subsequent Greek and Roman poets, orators, dramatists, and historians. The system constituted, as Matthew Battles puts it, "a diptych of mirrored orderings of the divine and the worldly."[8]

Just as the ancient Romans had split their collections between Roman and Greek authors, Cassiodorus instituted a bifurcation between Christian and pagan writings that would reverberate for centuries in libraries and scriptoria throughout Western Europe. The system would become the foundation of medieval library catalogs for the next thousand years, serving as the de facto classifying scheme for most monastic libraries. Eventually, even the Vatican adopted Cassiodorus's scheme.

In addition to establishing a basic subject-level hierarchy, Cassiodorus introduced important innovations at the level of textual analysis. He established the practice of annotating texts in the marginalia and posited numerous lower-level classification schemes, like the one he devised for categorizing the psalms, which he divided into categories by the holy number of 12:

1.   the carnal life of the Lord;
2.   the nature of His deity;
3.   the multiplied peoples who tried to destroy Him;
4.   that the Jews should cease their evil ways;
5.   Christ crying out to the Father in the passion, and being resurrected from the dead;
6.   penitential Psalms;
7.   the prayers of Christ, chiefly in His human nature;
8.   parables, tropes, and allegories, telling the story of the life of Christ;
9.   psalms beginning with the exclamation Alleluia;
10.   "gradual" psalms, fifteen in sequence;
11.   the praises of the Trinity; and
12.   seven Psalms of exultation at the very end.[9]

At its peak, Cassiodorus's library numbered perhaps 700 books, a far cry from the 700,000 scrolls at Alexandria. But what they lacked in volume they made up for in attention to craft. Given the limited resources of monastic scriptoria and lacking the great aggregating power of the old empire, the focus of libraries shifted away from the brute accumulation of knowledge toward perfecting the craft of reproduction and textual exegesis. The scriptoria were dedicated primarily to the preservation—not the production—of knowledge.

The creation of a codex book required the cooperation of several skilled workers: a skinner, a parchment maker, a beekeeper (for wax tablets), perhaps a painter, a book binder, and of course the ink-stained scribe. Often monasteries would employ illiterate scribes to make copies of texts; they were considered more accurate copyists because they lacked the ability to inject their own ideas into the text.

The monks' relationship to books was deeply shaped by the oral culture that surrounded them. A page was not a flat slab of data but a

Drawing of a monastery book cabinet, from a fourteenth-century edition of the *Roman de Troie* by Benoît de Saint-Maure. Paris, Bibliothèque Nationale, ms. fr. 782, fol. 2v.

living template for the spoken word and the refracted image. Understanding the medieval mind requires an imaginative leap. "For the monastic reader," writes critic Ivan Illich, "reading is a much less phantasmagoric and much more carnal activity: the reader understands the lines by moving to their beat, remembers them by recapturing their rhythm, and thinks of them in terms of putting them into his mouth and chewing."[10] Indeed, monasteries were sometimes known as houses of mumblers. As Ong puts it, "Manuscript cultures remained largely oral-aural even in retrieval of material preserved in texts. . . . [R]eaders commonly vocalized, read slowly aloud or *sotto voce*, even when reading alone, and this also helped fix matter in the memory."[11]

As the old hierarchies of the Roman empire disintegrated into a period of chaos, new knowledge networks emerged at the hands of self-directed agents like Cassiodorus and the Irish scribes. Rejecting traditional political hierarchies (as personified in the Roman Church), the monastic scribes prized individual intellect as the most reliable vessel of God's truth, pursuing new pathways and forging new ways of knowing from which new ontological hierarchies would eventually emerge.

FLOWERS FROM THE WALLED GARDEN

Throughout the Dark Ages, the monastic scribes protected countless classical texts and scriptural commentaries, preserving the flame of literacy while most of the continent reverted to the old feudal system. During this period, monastic libraries maintained their own small idiosyncratic collections of books. The monk responsible for tending the books was known as the *armarius*. In many monasteries this monk held a position of high esteem, second only to the abbott. The typical monastic library owned at least one Bible, and most maintained editions of works by major theologians like Augustine and perhaps Jerome. They also collected a flotsam of lesser commentaries, classical poems, lives of the saints, local laws, and assorted popular lore. Books were difficult to come by, and so most of these collections remained small, typically numbering only a handful of volumes, rarely more than a hundred. Given the high costs associated with producing illuminated manuscripts, monasteries valued their books as prized assets. Monks kept detailed records of their holdings with written lists that looked more like an inventory of land holdings than a library catalog. Some of these inventories seem to list books in order of perceived value to the monastery, while others list them in chronological order, and others used organization schemes that remain entirely inscrutable. For example, the library in Würzburg, Germany, maintained a list of 34 books, arranged in a seemingly idiosyncratic order starting with *The Acts of the Apostles*, followed by Gregory the Great's *Cura Pastoralis* and *Dialogues*, a commentary by Jerome, Bede's ecclesiastical history, and theological works by Augustine and Ambrose. The list appears to follow a determined logic, but the structure of the catalog remains anyone's guess.

The forty-eighth chapter of the Rule of Saint Benedict prescribes that each monk should read exactly one book per year, decreeing that "at the forty-day period [of Lent] they each receive a single book from the library, and each shall read the entire book from front to back;

Portrait of a scriptorium monk at work, from William Blades, *Pentateuch of Printing with a Chapter on Judges* (1891).

these books shall be given back at the beginning of the [next] Lenten season."[12] Monasteries guarded their collections closely; books were far too valuable for individual monks to own (with the notable exception of the Dominicans, who allowed their friars to keep small personal libraries).

While the monastic scribes did their best to preserve the heritage of written thought inside the monasteries, outside the cloister most people had reverted to the old ways of oral folk traditions and symbolism. For most of the thousand years before Gutenberg, reading was an almost entirely lost art.

In the eighth century, Europe witnessed a brief renewal of literacy when King Charlemagne instituted a revival of book learning in his imperial court, echoing the literary ambitions of the old empires. Although the so-called Carolingian Renaissance would ultimately falter, it sparked a resurgence of interest in books and reading that marked a high point of literate culture in the era before Gutenberg.

Like Ashurbanipal and Ptolemy I before him, Charlemagne recognized the political potency of a great imperial library. Unlike any other European king of the era, he also seems to have harbored a deep personal passion for reading. Throughout his reign he devoted enormous resources to building a library fit for an emperor. When Charlemagne needed to find a suitably learned man to build his great library, he looked across the channel to England, whose scribes had by 782 established the English monasteries as Europe's literary powerhouse. He invited a renowned scholar from York named Alcuin to his court, charging him with assembling the greatest library in Christendom. After arriving at Charlemagne's court, Alcuin soon sent word back to his old school in York:

> I say this that you may agree to send some of our boys to get everything we need from there and bring the flowers of Britain back to France that as well as the walled garden[13] in York there may be off-shoots of paradise bearing fruit in Tours.[14]

Alcuin collected works by Statius, Lucian, Terence, Juvenal, Tibullus, Horace, Claudian, Martial, Servius, and Cicero, among many others. The English monk set about establishing not only a great imperial library but also a central repository for distributing template manuscripts to be copied and disseminated widely across the growing empire. To that end Alcuin introduced a new simplified style of script, now known as Carolingian minuscule, that enabled monks to copy works more quickly to speed up the distribution of texts across the far-flung empire. The letters you are now reading on this page are the direct typographic descendants of Carolingian minuscule.

As the Carolingian libraries grew, monastic librarians began recognizing a need to keep better track of their assets. A few monks began listing their books chronologically. Eventually, some of them began creating higher-level categorical schemes, usually derived from Cassiodorus's system. At the Abbey of Saint Riquier, monks separated the books into discrete collections: one section for the Bible and theological works, one section for school books and grammars, and a third section for liturgical texts. "As humanism sought to recapture the sublimities of ancient Latin, on the one hand, and to authenticate Scriptures—and the power of the church—on the other," writes Battles, "its libraries recapitulated the symmetries of classical antiquity."[15]

Within each category the books would be arranged in a rough chronology (alphabetical order would not emerge again until the twelfth century). As monks copied each other's texts, they became increasingly interested in the questions of librarianship: Which texts should they acquire, and how should they be organized? For guidance in developing their collections, monastic librarians would consult popular bibliographical works like Jerome's *De viris illustribus* and Cassiodorus's *Institutiones*—seminal guides to book collecting that would provide monastic librarians with a template for growing their collections. As these standardized bibliographies began to circulate among medieval libraries, they provided the foundation for an emerging scholarly network. Libraries began coordinating their collections, arranging them with similar structures, and learning to rely on each other for access to hard-to-find works.

In 1170 the first known "scrutinium" or catalog emerged—a reckoning of the monastery's collection of books. "With this invention," write Illich and Sanders, "the book became dislocated from the sacristy." The Sorbonne established the first Union Catalog. The 1495 catalog of the Carthusian cloister Salvatorberg in Erfurt stands as the largest known catalog of the late Middle Ages. It contains a list of authors arranged chronologically (rather than alphabetically), with each entry accompanied by a brief biographical sketch of the author, along with cross-references to other works by the same authors. These catalogs, all printed as codex books, provide a glimpse into the emerging semantic structure of medieval libraries.

In Rome, Pope Sixtus IV initiated the great expansion of the Vatican Library, establishing the role of *scriptores* or, roughly, curators of the collection (a position that has persisted at the library ever since). The Vatican Library catalog of 1475 offers a revealing glimpse into the evolving organization of knowledge in the world's most powerful institution. The library adopted Cassiodorus's convention of splitting its books into sacred and secular collections. "Up one side of the great library ran a series of tables with books chained to them; on the opposite side ran a series of secular works that roughly paralleled the arrangement of the sacred texts. The library must have looked something like this:

Sacred	Secular
The Bible	Aristotle
Fathers of the church	Astrologers and mathematicians
Doctors of the church	Poets
Saints	Orators

The next room contained works in Greek, broken down along similar lines. The Vatican catalog's semantic balancing act would fail to hold up over time, but it marked an important impulse toward reasserting an institutional hierarchy as a means of preserving intellectual order.

The efforts of the monastic scriptoria would reverberate for centuries to come. The organizational schemes of these libraries proved remarkably durable. Indeed, the heritage of the modern library catalog traces its lineage directly back to the catalogs of Cassiodorus.

THE ARABIAN LEGACY

While the European monasteries played an important role in preserving classical texts, their collections remained paltry compared to the great libraries that were taking shape a world away in the lands of Islam. "Bagdad in its glory abounded with libraries," writes library historian James Westfall Thompson. Before the city fell to the

Mongols in 1258, there were no fewer than 36 libraries in the great city, supplied by more than 100 book dealers tending stalls in the great bazaars. The last vizier, Ibn al-Alkami, personally owned 10,000 books. The historian Omar al-Waqidi is said to have possessed 120 camel loads of books, while a scholar named al-Baiquai needed 36 hampers and two trunks to transport his collection. Legend has it the library at Tripoli held three million books, including 50,000 Korans (although historians believe those numbers were probably exaggerated). In Cairo the caliph al-Aziz established a school library with 100,000 volumes (some say 600,000) of bound books, including 2,400 Korans illuminated in gold and silver. The collection also included books on law, grammar, rhetoric, history, biography, astronomy, and chemistry. The library stored its collections in large presses behind a series of locked doors, each with a list of the books contained inside nailed into the front. In 1004 AD the caliph al-Hakim opened a so-called House of Wisdom in Cairo, said to contain 1.6 million books.[16] In contrast to the closely held literary treasures of the European monasteries, the caliph threw his library doors open to the public.

> The books were brought from the libraries ... and the public was admitted. Whoever wanted was at liberty to copy any book he wished to copy, or whoever required to read a certain book found in the library could do so. Scholars studied the Koran, astronomy, grammar, lexicography and medicine ... books in all sciences and literatures of exquisite calligraphy such as no other king had ever been able to bring together. Al-Hakim permitted admittance to everyone, without distinction of rank, who wished to read or consult any of the books.[17]

While Europe languished in the Dark Ages, Islamic libraries flourished, preserving a huge swath of the heritage of classical thought. Greek, Hindu, and Persian books found their way by the thousands into the great libraries of Islam. The rise of Islamic libraries seems at first like an improbable outcome. Mohammed did not read or write, and the indigenous Arab tribes had no written heritage. Traditionally, they were storytellers, preserving their legends, poetry, and genealogies through oral transmission. Thanks to a confluence of historical circumstances, these nomadic storytelling people became the curators of the ancient world's philosophical legacy.

Ancient books followed a circuitous path to the Arab world. When the emperor Justinian closed the great school of Athens, seven of its most prominent teachers went into exile, eventually finding refuge in Persia. They brought their books with them. Before long Persia became a repository for Greek philosophy, poetry, and science. Hundreds of translators (mostly Hellenized Syrians) arrived to translate the great works of classical antiquity from Greek to Persian. When the Arabs later conquered Persia, they assumed control of this great body of texts, which they proceeded to translate into Arabic. After centuries of isolation and illiteracy, the Arabs (like the Irish) experienced an abrupt, dramatic encounter with the literary heritage of the ancients. And like the Irish, that encounter would reshape their culture. For more than 500 years the Arabs went on to foster a period of scholarship that would fuel their rise to regional dominance and technological progress that made early medieval Europe seem, by comparison, like a cultural backwoods. As Gibbon put it, "The age of Arabian learning continued about five hundred years . . . and was coeval with the darkest and most slothful period of European annals."[18]

In Baghdad, Cairo, and Cordova, learned Jews played an important role in the expansion of Muslim philosophy, producing generations of diligent scholars who contributed to the expansion of learning in the Arabic world. The works of Hippocrates, Galen, and Ptolemy were preserved entirely from Hebrew sources. The Muslims generally treated their Jewish population well, following the Prophet's instruction to act indulgently toward their Jewish brothers.

Eventually, the Arabian intellectual heritage began to seep back to the European continent, primarily via the conduits of southern Italy and Spain (where Muslim culture flourished for almost 700 years). While copies of many ancient works ultimately wound their way from the Islamic libraries into the European scriptoria, many more were lost. The Mongol invasions left many of the great Muslim libraries in embers. After the Moors were expelled from Spain in 1492, the emperor Charles V ordered the burning of all books written in Arabic.

Those texts that survived long enough to resurface in Europe, however, would help seed a new respect for science and a revival of ancient wisdom that would ultimately pave the way for the great philosophical awakening of the European Renaissance.

6

A Steam Engine of the Mind

In Victor Hugo's *Notre Dame de Paris*, a scholar sits in his study carrel inside the great cathedral, contemplating a strange new artifact that has just landed on his desk: a printed book. Surrounding the new book are piles of old illuminated manuscripts. The scholar walks to a nearby window and gazes out on the silhouette of the great cathedral. "*Ceci tuera cela*," he says: This will be the end of that.

Just as the advent of alphabetic writing caused massive social disruption across the ancient world, so the new technology of the printing press would transform the social and political worlds of medieval Europe. The Gutenberg revolution would destabilize the old feudal and religious hierarchies of the Middle Ages, enabling a growing class of literate Europeans to reach out to each other in new ways, forging new social bonds that would eventually culminate in the cultural transformations of the Renaissance. While today many of us tend to regard the advent of printing as an unqualified good, its immediate effects were hardly benign. For many Europeans the arrival of this disruptive new technology signaled a bloody road ahead.

By the time Johannes Gutenberg introduced his famous press in 1458, the revolution that would bear his name was already well under way. While the advent of mass printing would accelerate the transformation of Europe's information infrastructure, the seeds of change had already been planted inside medieval monastery walls. To understand the deeper trajectory of the Gutenberg revolution, we need to begin by stepping back a few centuries to the late Middle Ages, when the first glimpses of popular literature were starting to make their way out of the cloisters.

WHY THE ELEPHANT HAD NO KNEES

In early medieval England one of the most popular books circulating among the middle and lower classes was a little volume known as the *Physiologus* or *Bestiary*. Consisting of simple verse descriptions of animals, usually accompanied by colored illustrations, the *Bestiary* tried to explain basic points of Christian doctrine in allegorical terms, by presenting them in the guise of a book about animals. By the late twelfth century, it had become the most popular nonbiblical manuscript of its time—indeed, the first such work to reach a wide lay audience. By the early fourteenth century, almost every monastery and church parish owned a copy; schoolchildren learned it by rote in their classrooms. Ever since the first folk taxonomies emerged, human beings have been naming and categorizing animals. So perhaps it should come as no surprise that the *Bestiary* should prove such a runaway best-seller in pre-Gutenberg Europe.

The work had originated in the early Greek Christian community, persisting through the ages as successive generations of monks copied the manuscript and passed it around from monastery to monastery throughout early Christendom. Its origins stretch far back into classical antiquity. The textual material evolved from a seminal Greek work known as the *Physiologus* (meaning, "The Naturalist"), whose bibliographical lineage stretches through a number of other books dating back to the reign of King Solomon. Parts of the book can be traced back to Pliny and Aristotle, some even further back to stories of Indian, Egyptian, and Jewish origin. In other words, the *Bestiary* contained a healthy dose of folk wisdom from ancient oral tradition. By echoing the themes of popular folk taxonomies and portraying animals as symbols of other divine truths, the *Bestiary* may have

Adam naming the animals, from the *Aberdeen Bestiary*, Folio 5r. Copyright by University of Aberdeen, Aberdeen, England.

struck a deep unconscious chord with its illiterate audience, who may have felt the stirrings of an ancient wisdom tradition at work.

The book was full of allegorical stories, using the figures of animals to tell a larger story about Christian theology to people who lived, for the most part, in an oral culture. We have seen how folk taxonomies give rise to synaesthetic knowledge systems that persist with remarkable fidelity in oral cultures. In the oral culture of the late Dark Ages and early medieval era, the *Bestiary* tapped into this vein of folk wisdom while at the same time serving as a kind of boundary object between oral and literate cultures, introducing illiterate audiences to tales that were undoubtedly meant to be heard aloud yet were nonetheless obviously encased between the covers of a codex book.

The *Bestiary* almost always begins with the image of Adam naming the animals, making a biblical claim for humanity's divine right to name—and, by extension, categorize—the beasts of the earth. "To name is to control," as Whit Andrews puts it, "and to establish primacy and the right of exploitation."[1] In this image, Adam not only names the beasts but also appears to assign a rudimentary taxonomy, allotting each beast to a particular box in his scheme. Each animal's name includes a divine etymology, with families of animals arranged by both family and relative proximity to humankind, with animals "not in man's charge" (the great cats and other wild quadripeds), followed by animals "for use by men" (like horses, cows, and sheep), and finally "beasts" (like dogs, cats, and boar). This image also echoes the folk classifications of preliterate societies in which affiliate classes provide a category for grouping animals by their relationship to human beings as well as by their relationships to each other.

The author (sometimes also known as "Physiologus") attempts to draw instructive moral lessons from the behaviors and qualities attributed to various real and mythical animals. Each chapter conforms to a simple pattern: First, an animal is described in physiological detail; then its properties are shown to illustrate a particular theological point, often buttressed with biblical passages. Elephants were said to have no knees; when they slept, they had to lean against a tree, and the tree in turn symbolized "tree of life," or the pillar of faith. Lions were said to give birth to stillborn cubs, which came to life only on the third day after their birth, symbolizing the Resurrection. And so on. The *Physiologus* made no pretense at scientific accuracy; these were allegorical tales, meant to illustrate symbolic rather than literal truths.

The *Physiologus* traveled through successive generations of copyists from ancient Greece to libraries as far away as Ethiopia, Armenia, Syria, and Rome. It was in its last translation to Latin that the text took on a relatively stable form that would shape the template for a thousand-year run in successive copyists' hands across the monasteries of Europe, eventually finding its way into Italian, French, German, Spanish, and English. During this period of northward migration, the work passed through the hands of generations of monastic scribes, evolving along the way to incorporate local nuggets of animal lore and superstition. With each successive copying, both text and image would change slightly as scribes made alterations from the original. One copy served as the basis for the next, and hundreds of small alterations eventually accumulated into significant changes. By the eleventh century, the work contained descriptions of almost double the number of beasts found in the original *Physiologus*, evolving over time through a long process of mutation. Eventually, these iterations turned the work into a whole new book, no longer called the *Physiologus* but instead the *Bestiarum* ("Animal Book"). By the time the genre reached its English heyday, it began to expand toward a proto-scientific form, including entries that found their way into the work with no apparent religious significance. Isidore of Seville's famous *Etymologies*, for example, contained descriptive materials similar to those found in the *Physiologus* but without the Christian allegories. In these larger works, doctrine and religious interpretation had to share the stage with a more secular and straightforward view of the natural world. Thus, the *Bestiary* began paving the way for the more formal classification systems that would come later at the hands of naturalists like Linnaeus and Buffon (see Chapter 9).

Popular demand for copies of the *Bestiary* fueled the development of inventive new reproduction techniques in the monastic scriptoria, methods that in turn allowed the work to reach even wider

audiences. English bestiaries of the thirteenth century bore remarkable similarities to one another. The text and illustrations mirrored
each other so closely, in fact, that book historians have surmised that
they must have been produced from common master copies. The
practice of using such "model books" for the production of popular
manuscripts flourished in European scriptoria of this period. In the
well-known K manuscript, illustrations reveal small puncture marks
tracing the periphery of each figure, along with one hole in the middle
of the page—some pricked so forcefully that they penetrate through
to the following pages. Samuel A. Ives and Hellmut Lehmann-Haupt
have tried to trace some of these techniques through a careful examination of the physical evidence:

> The central hole in the miniatures probably served to keep the leaves in
> exactly the same position during the puncturing process. After they were
> pricked, the loose sheets were laid onto the pages of the new copies of the
> Bestiary that were being produced at the workshop. Powder was dusted
> through them, the dots [were] joined, forming a fine outline drawing
> perhaps in light pen or thin brush stroke. This was then painted in by
> illuminator, using the originals as color guides.[2]

This process of replication, known as the "punch-transfer" technique, marked an important breakthrough in the technology of book
production. Now, scriptoria could produce copies of the same work
with much greater speed and accuracy. Although the technique was a
far cry from the automated processes of Gutenberg, it marked a major leap forward in medieval information technology. Most of the
surviving bestiaries from this period have a hurried, inelegant quality
to them—further evidence of mass production. While a few finely
wrought specimens survive, the majority bear the mark of hurried
production, with spare illustrations and sometimes sloppy handwriting. Most of the surviving bestiary manuscripts of this period feature
only a single illustration per passage, while earlier versions contained
many more.

In the age just before Gutenberg, the technologies that facilitated
the distribution of bestiaries placed the book in a central role in both
technological and cultural change. Bestiaries became an important

forerunner of later popular books, in both form and content. The images they contained became a cornerstone of popular Christian iconography for centuries to come, cropping up regularly in the church architecture of the day as sculptural adornments in even the simplest of parishes, where illiterate parishioners would listen to sermons and Gospels and then find those lessons reinforced in the visible symbols of the church architecture. Bestiaries also figured prominently in the medieval school curriculum, taking a place as one of the standard instructional texts along with Cato, Aesop, and Prosperus. This entrenchment in the popular nonliterate psyche explains the hold these images would later have on successive English generations. The images so imprinted themselves on the popular consciousness that they eventually appeared in tapestries, paintings, mosaics, and even fabric cloth. English authors from Spenser to Shakespeare to C. S. Lewis regularly drew on animal imagery that can be traced directly back to the *Bestiary*.

Long after the *Physiologus* faded from the popular fancy, the images and themes it contained persisted, insinuating themselves into the symbolism of later ages. The *Bestiary*'s legacy extends beyond our lingering fascination with imaginary animals, however. Its success helped fuel a popular demand for books that would plant the seeds of the Gutenberg revolution.

TOWARD LITERACY

As Europe entered the Middle Ages, the production techniques perfected in the monasteries fueled a rising popular interest in books. Once again, information technology was driving cultural change. While literacy was slowly beginning to spread among the monastic and aristocratic classes during the late medieval period, the vast majority of the population remained illiterate. Folk wisdom still predominated, and oral traditions continued to flourish. But the success of the *Bestiary* suggested a new public role for books and writing as more than just instruments of monastic scholarship, but as vessels of popular wisdom.

Across Europe, literacy was reemerging along the contours of a familiar historical pattern. Just as writing in the ancient Near East had emerged at first in the mode of "craft literacy," supporting commercial transactions, so the reemergence of writing in Europe may have had at least as much to do with Mammon as with God. As historian Brian Stock writes, medieval Europe's reencounter with literacy "would seem to have repeated with minor variations a process that unfolded in the eastern Mediterranean centuries before." Just as in Mesopotamia, "the rebirth of medieval literacy coincided with the remonetization of markets and exchange."[3]

Charlemagne had contributed to the secularization of writing by forbidding priests from conducting business transactions, such as drawing up contracts between illiterate parishioners. With priests barred from creating documents, a new class of secular scribes began to emerge. Coupled with a revival of Roman law in Italy that began to spread across the continent, the newly privatized class of scribblers found a growing market in writing up quotidian documents, including various bonds, pacts, and legal agreements. The privatization of secular writing also yielded an economic incentive for the scribes to market their services. Whereas in the Dark Ages Europeans had largely done business on a word and a handshake, by the fourteenth and fifteenth centuries they increasingly could avail themselves of willing scribes who, for a fee, would write down the details of their business arrangements.

Throughout the Dark Ages most people conducted transactions requiring close personal bonds of trust, like the highly ritualized pledges of fealty between vassals and lords (often sealed with a kiss on the lips). Now these old forms of intimate, person-to-person social contracts started giving way to more detached forms of written agreement. Although the vast majority of the population remained illiterate, the technology of writing exerted a growing influence over people's lives. "When written models for conducting human affairs make their appearance, a new sort of relationship is set up between the guidelines and realities of behavior," writes Stock. Such documents introduce consensual rule sets that constrain social actions. "Moreover, one need not be literate oneself in order to be affected by such rules. A written code can be set up and interpreted on behalf of unlettered members of society, the text acting as a medium for social integration or alienation."[4] In other words, literate civilization is not necessarily predicated on mass literacy.

As written laws and contracts began to proliferate throughout Western Europe in the eleventh and twelfth centuries, the function of writing started to change. Documents were no longer just vessels of information—like the word of God, the poems of Virgil, or tales of fanciful beasts. A new class of documents emerged that functioned less as narrative texts and more as facts unto themselves. "Men began to think of facts not as recorded by texts but as embodied in texts, a transition of major importance in the rise of systems of information retrieval and classification."[5] In a society where most people still could not read, the document served less as a text and more as an externalized "social fact"[6]: its mere existence often mattered more than the particular words it contained. Even today, in an age when most people can read, we still treat many documents this way. For example, how many of us ever read the words in a warranty, a stock prospectus, or a software license agreement? Such legalistic documents typically serve the same function as medieval contracts insofar as they matter more as symbolic seals of trust than as conveyors of textual meaning.

The rise of social documents in the early Middle Ages fueled an expansion of commerce and trade, laying the groundwork for a series of larger social, political, and economic transformations to come. Just as symbolic objects like beads and bone knives had transformed and expanded existing social structures facilitating a "release from proximity," the new technology of secular documents allowed people to forge bonds of trust among people otherwise lacking any social connection. Like tribal beads and jewelry, medieval documents functioned primarily as totemic objects, used to cement social relationships that could extend beyond any one individual's immediate trusted social network. Now two relative strangers could forge a reliable bond in the form of a document, even though in all likelihood neither party could read it. Merchants from distant towns could make pacts with each other; treaties, laws, and institutional charters began to emerge. Whereas writing had once been the exclusive province of holy men, now it passed into the hands of the laity. Merchants had contracts drawn up, government officials documented their laws, and increasingly people learned to govern their own affairs under the aegis of the written word. Even though most people still could not read, documents provided the conduit for medieval Europe to move toward larger and more complex social and political forms.

The technology of writing had been locked for centuries in the monasteries. To medieval Europeans it was an instrument of divine power, a secret accessible only to holy men. As secular literacy started to spread beyond the monastery walls, written words still carried a residual talismanic authority that lent documents an extraordinary symbolic power. The once-mysterious art became part of the fabric of everyday social life.

Late medieval writing was, then, a form of stigmergy (see Chapter 1). Just as ants and termites transform the external environment to introduce coded constraints on each other's behaviors, so medieval documents served a similar purpose as totemic objects designed to regulate behaviors; their function had less to do with textual meaning than with social coercion. "Relationships between the individual and the family, the group, or the wider community are all influenced by the degree to which society acknowledges written principles of operation," writes Stock. A shared recognition of the power of documents can mediate and shape human relationships, whether or not every individual actually knows how to read. This kind of macro literacy "also affects the way people conceptualize such relations, and these patterns of thought inevitably feed back into the network of real interdependencies."[7]

As Europeans found themselves living in an increasingly document-centric world, they started to experience the first rumblings of social and political transformations that would reverberate for centuries. While the changes that swept Europe during this period arose from a complex web of causes and conditions, the new technologies of writing played an important role, helping speed the demise of the old feudal system and fostering a period of turmoil that would reach an apex during the Gutenberg revolution. Ultimately, the impact of new technologies helped spur the growth of new forms of governmental and institutional hierarchies that would take full expression in the Renaissance. Eventually, the technology of secular documentation would even give rise to an entirely new form of government: the "document nation,"[8] a state founded purely on the written word (whose greatest exemplar would eventually be the United States). We are getting ahead of the story now, but suffice it to say that even before Gutenberg invented his press, a medieval information explosion was well under way, and it would prove literally revolutionary.

As secular writing emerged among the mercantile classes, literacy spread. Books were getting cheaper to produce, and more people could read them. The monastic scriptoria, which had once enjoyed a virtual monopoly on book production, were beginning to compete with an emerging institution of secular literacy: the university. During this period leading up to Gutenberg, books began to find an audience among the bourgeoisie, and Europe began to feel the first rumblings of an emerging secular literature.

The growth of universities, coupled with cheaper production materials, meant that monasteries lost their monopoly on the production of books. Now a new class of scholars, teachers, and students began to produce manuscripts of their own, often working with lay craftsmen who began to form a healthy and growing book trade, populated by booksellers, professional copyists, and "stationers."[9] The growing number of secular tradespeople involved in book production led to a flowering of more and more books. Universities began to accumulate books in growing libraries of their own. And as the universities turned out graduates, a new reading public emerged, fueling a market for books whose subjects extended beyond the time-honored genres of scriptural texts and works of classical antiquity. New types of popular texts, written in local vernacular, began to surface: Travel journals, poems, romances, the lives of the saints, and the popular *Book of Hours* started to grace the homes of many medieval households.

During a period stretching roughly from the thirteenth to the fifteenth century, a preliminary information explosion began to take shape, fueled by the introduction of a breakthrough information technology: paper. While the old materials of parchment and vellum had persisted for centuries, the invention of pulp-based paper made it suddenly possible for scribes to produce cheaper editions of popular works, which a growing merchant class could afford to purchase for themselves. The cost of raw materials declined (although the cost of labor did not), and as a result books started to proliferate among a wider audience.

By the end of the fourteenth century, an emerging literate public was consuming books in growing numbers. By the early fifteenth century, books were already being mass produced throughout Europe, through monastic scriptoria and other private-sector workshops capable of turning out hundreds of books at a time. Fueling the spread of writing were innovations like woodblock printing and the punch transfer technique perfected in distributing books to the missionary corps. Demand for books was growing, and the growing corps of secular scribes were finding it difficult to keep up. Conditions were ripe for a technological breakthrough.

A RUMOR IN MAINZ

In 1458 the king of France dispatched one of his spies to the German town of Mainz, where rumor had it that a troop of printers had created an ingenious new device, capable of reproducing manuscripts mechanically. No scribe needed.

The historical impact of Gutenberg's printing press requires no corroboration here. Suffice it to say that without the advent of movable type, we would live in an unimaginably different world. Today, we instinctively view the arrival of the printing press as an unqualified boon: the engine of democracy, modern scholarship, and individual expression. For all its positive byproducts, however, the history of the printing press turns out to be far less rosy than we might imagine.

Gutenberg's machine arrived in Europe not as a benign force for personal enlightenment but as a profoundly disruptive technology that triggered a series of painful and often bloody conflicts. The arrival of the Gutenberg press may have ultimately heralded an unprec-

edented boom in reading and writing, but it also serves as a cautionary tale. Just 10 years before the French king dispatched his spies,
Gutenberg had invented his movable-type system, signaling a staggering technological leap forward from the block printing technology already in use. Recognizing the potential value of his invention,
Gutenberg had sworn his printers to the medieval equivalent of a
nondisclosure agreement, making them promise to breathe not a
word of it outside the print shop. It was a futile promise. Word of the
invention soon found its way out of Mainz and into neighboring
municipalities. By the time the rumor reached the king of France,
word had already started to spread throughout continental Europe.
By 1475 printing presses had popped up as far away as Paris, Lyons,
and Seville.[10]

In the first decades of printing the press found its most eager
supporters among the clergy, who recognized the obvious labor-
saving value proposition and rejoiced in the prospect of expanding
the reach of God's word through the promising new technology.
Scholars, clergy, and other literate people greeted the new technology
effusively. "What an ascent toward God! What ecstatic devotion must
we feel on reading the many books which printing has given us!"[11]
Many of the first printers were themselves monks, eager to use the
new device to spread the word of God far and wide among their fellow monasteries. Little did they realize that this useful contraption
would soon play a role in their own institutions' ultimate downfall.

In the fifteenth century the Roman Church exerted a near-
monopoly on the New Testament, carefully controlling access to the
Bible and other holy texts. Even within the church, only a subset of
elevated priests possessed the skill to read Latin and thus interpret
the Word of God. Churches and monasteries often kept their copies
of the Bible chained to a desk or pulpit, or locked in a cabinet. These
prized holy books were not just vessels of the Word of God; they also
carried a totemic power as symbols of church authority.

At first the Roman Church enthusiastically endorsed the new
printing process, recognizing the potential economy of scale in distributing holy texts to far-flung churches and monasteries. Early
printers would often set up shop at the behest of nearby cathedrals or

Chained Bible in Cumnor Church, England. From William Andrews, *Curiosities of the Church* (1891).

monasteries, who subsidized their set-up costs so that they could provide ready access to copies of the scriptures and other liturgical texts. The early printing business also flourished in part thanks to a bull market in printed indulgences,[12] which now became an increasingly profitable business thanks to the printing press's economy of scale.

The booming printing business soon proved too lucrative a business for the clergy to support by themselves; as the volume of printed documents grew, printing required an increasingly specialized workforce. Private presses were springing up all over Europe, especially in the growing university towns. In larger towns there was an enormous untapped market of wealthy individuals eager to acquire texts previously accessible only to churches and governments able to employ armies of scribes. These wealthy patrons, men like Jean de Rohan (himself a man of letters), functioned much like venture capitalists today. They invested in the presses both for their own enrichment and out of a genuine interest in the propagation of knowledge. In large towns with an academic population, popular volumes included secular works by Aristotle, Aquinas, William of Ockham, and Boethius, as well as traditional religious texts like the works of Saint Augustine and other church fathers.[13]

Depending on local literary appetites, publishers would tailor their offerings to the tastes of particular market segments. Scholastic books were typically printed in black gothic letters. For the common lay reader, vernacular narratives were printed in bastarda gothic. And for an emerging class of readers that today would be called "humanists," classical texts were printed in the new "littera antique" style, the ancestor of today's familiar roman typefaces (like the letters on this page).[14]

Soon the emergence of printed books led to a standardization of typefaces that began to extinguish the idiosyncratic local styles that had flourished in the age of illuminated manuscripts. An alphabet soup of local typefaces gave way to the new roman style. Many scholars came to believe that roman type evoked the clean, economical style of the classical texts they so admired; they regarded gothic texts as overly ornamental, a throwback to old monkish ways. The adoption of roman typeface was more than just a stylistic decision; it also signaled a rejection of medieval scholasticism in favor of the secular wisdom of the Ancients.

The standardization of typefaces would prove the catalytic event in the subsequent movement of information across cultures. Roman type became the equivalent of ASCII type today: a universally recognized standard that speeds the flow of information across a distant network of readers and writers. Within a century of Gutenberg's invention, roman script had taken hold across Europe (although printers in Germany continued to produce works using gothic typefaces, a preference that never completely subsided). Standard typefaces soon led to another form of standardization in the form of the printed book itself. New conventions took hold around the use of "meta" information like title pages, colophons, and framed title pages. These conventions emerged over time and slowly coalesced into standard practices for European printers. The introduction of a convention for bibliographic metadata reverberates to this day; indeed, the title page of this book (and of almost every commercially published book) is the direct heritage of a 500-year-old convention forged in the first few years after Gutenberg.

The rapid growth of the popular book market split the book trade into two broad segments: (1) large folio works intended for institutional collections like libraries, schools, and churches; and (2) smaller *quarto* or *octavo* works for the public at large. This broad market segmentation persisted well into the nineteenth century, contributing to a growing schism between "canonical" and popular knowledge.

By the sixteenth century, mass-produced books were starting to reach a growing population of customers who themselves could barely read. This interim period between the emergence of printing and widespread popular literacy marks the heyday of the illustrated book. Books were increasingly within reach of a public eager to consume books that didn't necessarily demand reading. Popular volumes often included simple line drawings accompanying the text, illustrating stories from the Bible, pictures of saints, or the terrifying visages of demons trying to wrest men's souls.[15] These sturdy xylographic[16] illustrations were simple and clean, intended to serve as informational graphics rather than decorative illustrations. "Book illustration answered a practical rather than an artistic need," write Lucien Paul Victor Febvre and Henri-Jean Martin, "to make graphic and visible what people of the time constantly heard evoked."[17] Like the widely distributed bestiaries, these popular books appealed to readers and non-readers alike. The popular books of this era mark a brief period in which word and image still enjoyed equal prominence on the printed page.

The golden age of illustrated texts in the sixteenth century would not last. Growing popular literacy, coupled with inexorable logic of the marketplace, forced efficiencies in both the production and the consumption of books. "What the steam engine does with matter," writes Newman, "the printing press is to do with the mind; it is to act mechanically, and the population is to be passively, almost unconsciously enlightened, by the mere multiplication and dissemination of volumes."[18] Whereas monastic scribes had produced books almost exclusively for religious purposes—to equip missionaries with books for their travels or to preserve the word of God for their fellow brethren—the printing press transformed book publishing into a for-profit industry. Fifteenth-century publishers, like their descendants today, would publish books only if they felt reasonably assured of turning a profit. The old craft production values of the monastic scriptoria could never survive in the new world of for-profit publishing.

At first publishers turned out great numbers of Bibles and other devotional texts. In the thriving Jewish communities of Italy and Spain, Hebrew printers started publishing traditional Hebrew texts that were welcomed enthusiastically in their communities, where the new technology of printing afforded the possibility of reproducing the dense layered commentaries of Torah scholars.

Eventually, a public appetite for reading fueled the growth of an increasingly secular book trade: calendars, almanacs, and works by classical authors started to appear on bookstore shelves alongside popular religious texts like the *Book of Hours* or the lives of the saints. With a saturated market for traditional religious books, publishers started looking for new profit centers. "Under the mounting flood of new books written for an ever increasing public," write Febvre and Martin, "the heritage of the Middle Ages lost its hold."[19] By 1500 Gutenberg and his professional descendants had already published an estimated 8 million books; by the end of the sixteenth century the number stood close to 200 million.[20]

Publishers were turning out a staggering number of volumes in local vernacular languages, starting with translations of classical authors like Virgil, Ovid, Caesar, Suetonius, and Josephus. Popular contemporary authors started to emerge in Italy, France, and Spain. Writers like Machiavelli, Erasmus, and Rabelais started to find a wide readership, while a new crop of scientific writers like Copernicus started to gain a following in scholarly circles. Books about geography, natural science, and medicine started to circulate. History books were enormously popular. "Gutenberg's invention produced what we today understand as scholarship," writes Landow. "No longer primarily occupied by the task of preserving information in the form of fragile manuscripts that degraded with frequent use, scholars, working with books, developed new conceptions of scholarship, originality, and authorial property."[21] Whereas once the whole business of manuscript production had involved an intimate, largely anonymous collaboration among countless scribes, the press would introduce a new fixity, both to the text and to the concept of the author.

One popular travel book captured the reading public's fancy: Christopher Columbus's description of his voyage to America (published simultaneously in Barcelona, Paris, Rome, and Basel). By sixteenth-century standards it was a runaway best-seller. Yet lest we start to overestimate the impact of the printing press on the daily life of the average European, we should bear in mind that it still took the better part of a hundred years for news of Columbus's "discovery" of the New World to reach most people in Europe beyond a small circle of literate middle- and upper-class readers. For the most part, news still traveled by word of mouth. But that was starting to change.

This was the third great turning of the information explosion. In tribal societies, human cultures had been bound together by unitary knowledge systems in which everyone participated; in the age of city-states and empires, a literate scholarly class had emerged as caretakers of institutional knowledge, while the masses relied on oral traditions, imagery, and socially transmitted knowledge. Oral and literate cultures twirled in separate orbits. This third axial period of information technology would bring those orbits closer together, with occasionally cataclysmic results.

Just as primordial bacteria had walled themselves off from each other to form a new kind of self-directed organism, the new printed book signaled a consolidation of form. Oral traditions existed in a fluid medium, where authorship and provenance were fuzzily delineated. As the printing press took hold, those traditions would find their way into print and become more fixed in the process—forming nucleated texts with, as it were, thicker cell walls.

Handmade manuscripts had been fluid affairs too, produced by teams of craftspeople working in close collaboration to produce labor-intensive intellectual artifacts. Scholarship took place within tightly confined institutional constraints. Now, the old bonds of collaboration and careful engagement had been sacrificed for the virtues of speed, lateralization, and efficiency, and soon scholars would find new ways of communicating with others across institutional barriers.

The new fixity of texts not only led to emerging forms of scholarship but also had both a galvanizing effect on hierarchical institutions—which drew great strength and power from the new invention—and a disruptive effect, as a newfound ease of communication allowed new kinds of public social networks to emerge. Brian Stock has written of how the spread of documents and literacy led to the formation of "textual communities" that coalesced around particular documents, especially religious and political movements that challenged the established organizational hierarchies. Without the printing press, Martin Luther could never have published his 95 theses, or Thomas Jefferson circulated the Declaration of Independence.

The text became a shared object, a replicable unit of information that could move freely through the social body of the literate populace. Textual communities flourished in an era of newly fixed documents, in which meaning was no longer interpreted through a scholastic elite possessed of secret knowledge but freely disseminated to anyone who could read. Movable type granted the text an authority that had previously belonged solely to the church or the monarchy. The coming centuries would witness a series of bloody struggles by which competing social groups tried to claim that authority for themselves.

LEFT-BRAINED LUTHERANISM

In fifteenth-century Germany, as printers started turning out mass quantities of Bibles and works by classical authors, they also started producing pamphlets, handbills, posters, and broadsheets (the forbears of the modern newspaper). Europe was entering a new era of mass communication, fueled by a disruptive information technology whose effects no one could possibly have foreseen. On October 31, 1517, Martin Luther catalyzed the revolution of mass literacy when he nailed his 95 theses on the door of the Augustinian chapel in Wittenberg.

Without the printing press, there likely would have been no Protestant movement. The ease of printing and speed of communication allowed the written word to circulate freely outside the traditional institutional control valves of the church. Before the advent of the printing press, Rome could quash heretics at will; now the "heretics" had a powerful technology at their disposal. Hurriedly printed posters like Luther's soon became the core communications vehicle for the reformist movements fomenting across Europe. Whenever reformists wanted to organize a public meeting, they would draw up a poster, have it printed, and tack it up all over town. The networked communications platform of the posted broadsheet would forever destabilize the old hierarchy of the Roman Church.

"Lutheranism was from the first the child of the printed book," writes historian Elizabeth Eisenstein, "and through this vehicle Luther was able to make exact, standardized and ineradicable impressions on the minds of Europe."[22] Luther hailed printing as "God's highest and extremest act of grace, whereby the business of the Gospel is driven forward."[23] If Christianity is the religion of the book, Protestantism is the denomination of the press.

Protestantism represented more than just a doctrinal departure; it signaled a psychic rift between two very different ways of understanding the world. As Leonard Shlain puts it, "Luther repudiated the colorful ritual of mass, rich with icons. The nexus of the Reformation was the rekindling of the age-old conflict between written words and images."[24] The technology of movable type privileges the written word over the image, elevates left brain over right. Lutheranism represented a cognitive schism as much as a religious one. And while the social and political causes of the Reformation are too complex to catalog in full here, the printing press played a central role in triggering a series of bloody convulsions that would sweep the European continent.

In our modern literate culture, we tend to view the printing press as a force of liberation and an unqualified historical good, the technological wellspring of modern culture. At the time, however, the abrupt introduction of the new technology wreaked a series of calamitous social disruptions. The popular heroic image of Luther nailing his theses to the wall tends to divert our attention from the brutal truth of the Reformation. The Roman Church made every effort to suppress the new polemic literature. The church issued a Papal Bull against Luther's work (which Luther promptly set aflame in protest). When Luther's work started attracting a following in Paris, the church issued another bull forbidding printers from publishing not only Luther but any work not bearing the Church-sanctioned imprimatur of the University of Paris. In the wake of the papal ban, a black market soon sprang up as foreign printers recognized the opportunity to supply Parisian readers hungry for forbidden works. In an effort to stanch the flow of radical and potentially destabilizing books, the king of France issued an edict banning the import of all foreign books. Printers freely ignored the law. Meanwhile, sales of thoughtful writers like Erasmus began to decline in favor of the strident populism of Luther and his ilk. "As Luther's message caught on," writes Shlain, "the illiterate masses nonetheless revolted against the image-centric Church artifacts: smashing statues, slashing paintings, overturning altars. They built new Protestant churches with plain white walls, no images or stained glass—not even a crucifix. These were strictly left-brained affairs dedicated to interpreting the Word—not the Image—of God."[25]

In Germany, Luther inaugurated a stream of religious polemics that took on increasingly poisonous tones. Popular pamphlets with titles like "Pope Donkey" and "Cow Monk" painted vicious satires of the Roman clergy, inciting the lay population to acts of horrific brutality. During the battles of the Reformation, Europe descended into a period of atrocities in which opposing bands of Protestants and Catholics literally gutted each other in the streets. In Holland, when Dutch Calvinists invoked Protestant doctrine as their basis for overthrowing the Spanish Catholic government, the struggle boiled over into a frenzy of brutality. According to writer John Lothrop Motley:

On more than one occasion, men were seen assisting to hang with their own hands and in cold blood their own brothers, who had been taken prisoners in the enemy's ranks. When the captives were too many to be hanged, they were tied back to back, two and two, and thus hurled into the sea. . . . On one occasion, a surgeon at Veer cut the heart from a Spanish prisoner, nailed it on a vessel's prow, and invited the towns-men to come and fasten their teeth in it, which many did with savage satisfaction.[26]

Wherever the Protestant message spread, powered by the new technology of printing, violent upheavals ensued. The century after Gutenberg witnessed a series of violent upheavals that raged across the continent. Peasants embraced the newly translated vernacular Bibles with a revolutionary fervor. Across Germany tens of thousands of peasants refused to pay taxes. Peasant wars broke out, leaving over 100,000 dead. Of course, much of the violence was orchestrated by Catholics as well, inspired by their own understanding of a theology that is, at least in some sense, a "product" of the book. "Despite having recently read the New Testament for the first time," writes Shlain, "many people on both sides behaved in a manner antithetical to the spirit of the Gospels."[27]

Wherever the printing press took hold, conflict seemed to follow. Shlain argues that the introduction of printed books seems to have triggered a kind of mass social pathology that may have stemmed from the jarring introduction of a linear, left-brained communications mode of thought into what had previously been a predominantly oral and visual right-brained culture. Leonard Shlain believes this cognitive disruption explains why printing and literacy seem to have spread in almost perfect lockstep with the rise of witch-burning. As printers brought the left-brained modality of the written word into contact with the old right-brained values of folk traditions and feminine-centered wisdom (as exemplified in the flourishing cult of Mary), masculine values came into open and violent conflict with feminine values. Countless women paid a tragic price. "It was in Germany," as Shlain points out, "the birthplace of the printing press and home to the fastest rise in literacy rates, that the witch craze assumed its most monstrous proportions."[28] In one town 133 witches were executed in one day. In the two villages surrounding Trier, the witch hunters were so successful that only one woman was left alive. Between 1623 and 1631 the bishop of Würzburg (home of the great monastic library) executed 41 girls ages 7 to 11.

The sudden shift from an oral, visually symbolic culture to an increasingly left-brained world of linear written texts may have triggered a deep shift in the European psyche that led, for a time, to a kind of mass psychosis. Paradoxically, when the book first emerged in the latter days of the Roman empire, it had represented a new, more open kind of technology—a kind of analog hypertext—that freed readers from the unidirectional constraints of ancient scrolls. The days of the Irish scribe perusing classical texts were long past, however. Now books were turning into commodities, and the insistent logic of automated production gave them an increasingly linear character. Page numbers appeared, while illustrations dwindled. Unlike the handmade, carefully illustrated manuscripts of the monasteries, the printed book seemed to insist on forward progress.

As the printing press took root amid a series of larger social, political, and religious transformations, newly literate Europe started acting out. "The eerie conjunction of the printing press, steeply rising literacy rates, religious wars and the witch craze seems significant."[29] The sudden rise of alphabetic literacy seems to have accompanied a deep conflict in the collective social brain: a war between left- and right-brained values, in which left-brained values, for a time, emerged victorious after a violent struggle.

The explosion of printing had wreaked havoc with the old institutional hierarchies. Europe was headed into a period of bloody upheaval. Those disruptions echoed in the more pacific world of scholarship as well. No longer could books be easily classified into the simple old Vatican systems of secular and sacred knowledge. There were simply too many books; moreover, an explosion of facts and printed knowledge was taxing the underlying ontologies of knowledge that had guided Western European understanding of the phenomenal world. Disciplinary boundaries were blurring, and the sheer volume of knowledge demanded a more methodical system for organizing humanity's burgeoning intellectual output. The old monastic scriptoria would soon die out; but as the era of printing dawned, the old scholastic ways would enjoy one final flourish.

7

The Astral Power Station

Yea, from the table of my memory
I'll wipe away all trivial fond records,
All saws of books, all forms, all pressures past
That youth and observation copied there
And thy commandment all alone shall live
Within the book and volume of my brain.

Shakespeare, *Hamlet*

In 1532 an Italian fellow named Viglius wrote to his friend Erasmus about his upcoming trip to Venice. He was looking forward to seeing a new invention that had been causing a stir among the town's cognoscenti: a so-called Theater of Memory. Viglius was not entirely sure what the thing was, but he had heard that it was "a work of wonderful skill, into which whoever is admitted as spectator will be able to discourse on any subject no less fluently than Cicero."

Returning from Venice a few weeks later, Viglius wrote again to tell his friend what he had seen. "The work is of wood," he wrote, "marked with many images, and full of little boxes." The theater turned out to be a contraption the size of a small room, housing a complicated apparatus with tiyo gears that opened and closed windows to reveal words and images printed inside. By manipulating the windows a visitor could retrieve nuggets of information on any number of topics: the seven virtues and vices, the teachings of Solomon, the orientation of celestial bodies, and all manner of other medieval factoids. It was a kind of sixteenth-century Rube Goldberg hypertext machine. Step inside, click open a window or two, and presto: the wisdom of the ancients revealed. Viglius reported that the theater's inventor, Giulio Camillo, "calls this theatre of his by many names, saying now that it is a built or constructed mind and soul, and now that it is a windowed one."

For the newly literate Venetian audience, Camillo's contraption must have seemed nothing short of a technological marvel. It was also a perfect metaphor for a dawning era of post-Renaissance information technology. The spread of popular literacy and the erosion of monastic power had created a fertile environment for a new breed of maverick scholars to emerge. Freed of the intellectual confines of the monastic system, a few pioneering thinkers began to experiment with new ways of structuring access to human knowledge: from encyclopedic contraptions like Camillo's to mystical memory wheels, universal classification schemes and artificial languages. Many of these ambitious efforts would meet unfortunate ends, with their progenitors ending up in bankruptcy, burned at the stake, or the butt of famous literary jokes. But ultimately, the Renaissance information technologists paved the way for the emergence of the scientific method and a new secular approach to information systems that still reverberates today.

No one knows exactly what Camillo's theater looked like—no drawings have survived—but Camillo once described the design as follows:

> The Theatre rests basically upon seven pillars, the seven pillars of Solomon's House of Wisdom. Solomon in the ninth chapter of Proverbs says that wisdom has built herself a house and has founded it on seven pillars. By these columns, signifying most stable eternity, we are to understand the seven Sephiroth of the super-celestial world, which are the seven measures of the fabric of the celestial and inferior worlds, in which are contained the Ideas of all things in the celestial and in the inferior worlds.[1]

The machine worked by allowing users to tunnel their way through a series of nested conceptual hierarchies, proceeding from the gross physical plane of the theater to the metaphorical House of Wisdom, then on through successive layers of abstraction, finally ascending to the realm of divine truths to pierce the innermost secrets of the arts. This grand scheme was not Camillo's own. It actually rep-

resented a cheap facsimile of an ancient scholastic practice that had
flourished in Europe's medieval monasteries for centuries: the art of
memory. Camillo, himself a former monk, had left the cloisters several years earlier to seek his fortune in the town squares of Europe.
Determined to make something of himself, he hit on the idea of taking a few tricks he had learned in the monastery and turning them
into a public attraction. He even came up with a catchy tagline: turning "scholars into spectators."

The original monastic art of memory was a far cry from Camillo's
version. In medieval monasteries, generations of monks had perfected
a demanding mental regimen that enabled them to memorize long
tracts of scripture and other information through years of difficult
training. The technique traced its roots to the Greek poet Simonides
of Ceos, who in the fifth century BC described a method for improving one's memory by visualizing a series of *loci* (places) in a particular order, then associating a meaningful image with each place, as an
aid to reminiscence. Aristotle later picked up on Simonides's work,
incorporating the technique into his discussion of memory in his *De
memoria et reminiscentia* ("On memory and recollection"), in which
he described the act of memorization as a visual practice that invoked the "inner eye" of memory to summon *phantasmata* (images)
stored in the "sensitive soul" and making them available to the "intellectual soul" of the logical mind. Aristotle's description of the technique eventually found its way to Rome, where Cicero, Quintilian,
and other rhetoricians embraced the art of memory as an aid to practicing the great Roman art of oratory, using the technique to command vast arrays of facts, quotations, ideas, and topics that they could
pull together extemporaneously while delivering orations.[2]

The classical art of memory faded with the decline of Rome, and
Aristotle's seminal work on the subject fell into obscurity until the
thirteenth century, when European scholars rediscovered *De memoria et reminscentia*. Thomas Aquinas, in particular, wrote a series of
commentaries on Aristotle's work that helped popularize the technique among medieval scholastics, celebrating the technique as a remedy for the inherent frailties of the human mind. Aquinas pointed
out that while the mind was well equipped to recollect the gross de-

tails of physical experience, it was ill suited for remembering "subtle and spiritual things" (a limitation stemming from man's fallen condition). The art of memory, as he saw it, offered monks a powerful tool for harnessing their physical and spatial memory as a means for internalizing God's word. "It is the image making part of the soul which makes the work of the higher processes of thought possible," Aquinas explained. "Hence 'the soul never thinks without a mental picture.'"[3] Aquinas described the art as relying on two essential facilities: association (the ability to relate one concept to another) and order (the ability to arrange spatial memories into nested categories)—in other words, networks and hierarchies.

In its medieval incarnation, the art became a spiritual regimen, requiring years of contemplation and devotion in the quiet of a monastery. Cloistered monks, with no shortage of time on their hands, passed their days memorizing scriptures, religious commentaries, and assorted classical works. At first, monastic practitioners seem to have viewed the art as a kind of practical information technology. One monk, John Willis, postulated that memory "so far as it is strictly taken for the common receptacle of Memorandums, is merely passive . . . in the same manner as Paper preserveth words written therein." He goes on to caution, however, that just as "it is the office of a Scribe, not of Paper, to write and read things written; so to dispose Idea's in Memory, and aptly to use them, is work of Understanding, not of Memory."[4] Memorization, in other words, is no substitute for true learning.

The monastic version of the technique worked something like this: A monk would apprentice himself to a master of the Art, who would teach him to visualize a series of metaphorical images. These might include buildings, palaces, cities, wax tablets, chains, or writing. For example, a monk might learn to memorize a room in a house, containing a series of symbolic objects tied to a particular theme. The theology room might house (surprise) a theologian, his head tattooed with the words *cognitio, amor, fruitio*; his limbs with the words *essentia divina, actus, forma, relatio, articula, precepta, sacramenta*; and so on.[5] The trainee would commit the contents of each room to memory, slowly mastering the painstaking journey from room to room.

Despite the volume of published writing on such a highly visual technique, illustrated depictions are surprisingly rare. The art was largely handed down through direct oral transmission, without external visual aids. One of the few tangible glimpses survives in a Florentine convent, where a fresco depicts Thomas Aquinas seated on a throne amid flying figures representing the seven virtues; to each side sit the saints and patriarchs; beneath his feet lie vanquished heretics; farther down, seven female figures represent the seven liberal arts; then another seven represent the theological disciplines.[6] The fresco provides one of the few physical manifestations of a technique that otherwise resided—and expired—only within its practitioners' minds.

The practice took years to master, but those who succeeded reported astonishing mnemonic feats. One practitioner, Peter of Ravenna, claimed to have memorized more than 100,000 rooms, enabling him to recall from memory the entire canon law, including every related commentary, the full text of 200 complete speeches by Cicero, 300 philosophical sayings, 20,000 legal points, and more.[7] Another enthusiast, Johannes Romberch, in 1533 published a widely read grammar that laid out an elaborate system for memorizing the entirety of theology, metaphysics, law, astronomy, geometry, arithmetic, music, logic, rhetoric, and grammar.

From the late fifteenth century onward, numerous scholastic writers penned treatises on the technique, including Giovanni de Carrara's *De omnibus ingeniis augendae memoriae* (1481), Peter of Ravenna's *Phoenix, sive artificiosa memorabilia,* Guigliemo Gratoroli's *De memoria* (1553), Cosimo Rosselli's *Thesaurus artificiosae memoriae* (1579), and William Fulwood's *The Castle of Memorie* (1562). As European scholastics embraced the art in growing numbers, the practice became increasingly esoteric, eventually devolving into what historian Frances A. Yates calls "a kind of cross-word puzzle to beguile the long hours in the cloister." Often, the monks found themselves turning these memory puzzles into intricate and time-consuming diversions that "can have had no practical utility; letters and images are turning into childish games."[8] Memorization became a kind of monastic fad, often at the expense of learning.

So Camillo's theater represented the culmination of an apostasy long in the making, the conflation of memorization with learning. With the decline of monasticism, however, it also represented an important effort to translate the previously secretive technique for a broader lay audience. And while the simplistic literalism of Camillo's boxes and windows may have represented a debased version of the original art, it also marked a philosophical turning point at the beginning of the Renaissance. It represented, as Yates puts it, "a new Renaissance plan of the psyche, a change which has happened within memory, whence outward changes derived their impetus." By giving the once-ethereal art a concrete form, Camillo transformed the old monastic art into a vehicle for secular aspiration. In so doing, he also anticipated the broader philosophical trajectory of the Renaissance. For the medieval monastics the art of memory was an antidote to the weakness of the human mind; by contrast, "Renaissance Hermetic man believes that he has divine powers; he can form a magic memory through which he grasps the world, reflecting the divine macrocosm in the microcosm of his divine *mens*."[9]

Camillo, it should be noted, never actually completed his theater. He died before he could finish raising the funds to complete his ambitious vision. Soon after Camillo died, the first generation of European humanists began to decry the old scholastic ways. Writers like Erasmus (Viglius's friend) criticized the old medieval art, enjoining scholars to embrace a new rationalism that relied on more "natural" or linear forms of memory. Other influential European thinkers like Philipp Melanchthon, Cornelius Agrippa, and Michel de Montaigne all pilloried the monastic art of memory. Thomas Fuller bemoaned the "Memory-mountebanks" who had corrupted the classical art of memory by locking it in the cloister and keeping it from being used for practical purposes.[10] "For the Erasmian type of humanist the art of memory was dying out," writes Yates, "killed by the printed book, unfashionable because of its mediaeval associations, a cumbrous art which modern educators are dropping."[11] For the early modern humanists, the art of memory "belonged to the ages of barbarism; its methods in decay were an example of those cobwebs in monkish minds which new brooms must sweep away."[12]

BRUNO'S HERESY

As Europe entered into a new period of secular reason and scientific inquiry, the old art of memory would slowly fall into disrepute. At the end of the sixteenth century, however, it would see one more burst of popular interest, thanks in part to the high-profile heresies of Europe's great intellectual maverick Giordano Bruno.

On February 9, 1600, Bruno bowed on one knee before the Grand Inquisitor, after 6 years in papal custody. The charge was heresy, and the Inquisition had pronounced him guilty. When the executioners presented Bruno with a cross at the moment of his death, he waved it away. He thought he had already found his salvation.

Born in 1548, Bruno had trained as a Dominican friar in Naples, where he had studied and mastered the art of memory. He eventually forsook the monastery for a wandering life that took him through France, England, and Germany. Along the way he began teaching the art to interested lay students, including no less a personage than King Henri III of France. Bruno would later recall that when the king summoned him to court, he first "asked whether the memory which I had and which I taught was a natural memory or obtained by magic art; I proved to him that it was not obtained by magic art but by science."[13]

In truth, however, Bruno's version of the art contained a great deal of "magic." Bruno saw the practice not just as a tool for strengthening the memory but as a transcendental gateway to "innumerable worlds." He expanded the scope of the art beyond the usual doctrinaire topics of the monasteries, using it to integrate the classical wisdom of the Greeks, the magical religion of the Egyptians, ultimately penetrating, he believed, the highest truths of creation. In Bruno's rendition the art joins the lower world of physical reality with the incorporeal essences of the celestial sphere, for "it is by one and the same ladder that nature descends to the production of things and the intellect ascends to the knowledge of them."[14] In attempting to join heaven and earth, Bruno embraced an Aristotelian conceit: that the phenomena of the material world are expressions of inner essences, that things are, in a sense, symbols of themselves. It was, as Yates puts it, "a highly systematized magic."[15]

Bruno interpolated the old art into a new occult form of practice,

Memory wheel, from Giordano
Bruno's *De Umbris Idearum*,
1582.

claiming to have unlocked the deepest mysteries of the phenomenal
world thanks to a complex mnemonic device called the memory
wheel. The memory wheel relied on a series of ostensibly magic numbers, especially 30[16] and 150, with 150 images broken out into five
sets of 30 images each, all arranged in concentric circles, or wheels.

In a meticulous feat of literary reverse-engineering, Yates managed to decipher Bruno's dense text in sufficient detail to construct a
working model of the memory wheel—a feat that, as far as we know,
no one had attempted in 400 years. She describes how she believed
the mnemonic device must have operated:

> The lists of images given in the book are marked off in thirty divisions
> marked with these letters, each division having five subdivisions marked
> with the five vowels. These lists, each of 150 images, are therefore in-
> tended to be set out on the concentric revolving wheels. Which is what I
> have done on the plan, by writing out the lists of images on concentric
> wheels divided into thirty segments with five subdivisions in each. The
> result is the ancient Egyptian looking object, evidently highly magical,
> for the images on the central wheel are the images of the decans of the
> zodiac, images of the planets, images of the mansions of the moon, and
> images of the houses of the horoscope. The descriptions of these images
> are written out from Bruno's text on the central wheel of the plan. This
> heavily inscribed central wheel is the astral power station, as it were,
> which works the whole system.[17]

The system builds on wheel after concentric wheel, spinning out into innumerable combinations whose mastery demands extraordinary dedication and concentration. Bruno's path calls to mind the tantric practices of Tibetan Buddhism, which similarly rely on intricate visualizations and extreme feats of memorization as pathways to spiritual liberation. Bruno's "astral power station" was a prodigious piece of conceptual engineering, with its endless combinations of juxtaposed letters revealing layer upon layer of nested meaning. At the first level the wheel contains an inventory of empirical facts concerning the kingdoms of animals, vegetables, and minerals. Additional turnings of the wheel reveal new layers of abstraction, as the concentric circles expand to catalog the whole sweep of human achievement, encoding the names of mythical figures who represent the enabling technologies of civilization: Pyrodes, the inventor of fire; Aristeus, the discoverer of honey; Coraebus, the potter; and so on. The list then moves through more advanced technologies like glassblowing, surgery, writing (represented by our old Platonic friend Thoth), and up through the rarefied magical arts like necromancy, chiromancy, and pyromancy, and then to higher and higher degrees of celestial wisdom. It is a breathtakingly complete array of the known intellectual universe. And with a touch of authorial chutzpah, Bruno places himself squarely in his own cosmology, invoking himself as "Ior" (short for Iordano Bruno), the inventor of the "key."

Whereas the medievalists of the Thomist tradition treated the art of memory as a remedy for the failings of the human mind, Bruno saw it as a fruitional path, a means to put people in touch with their innate divinity. "If you contemplate this attentively," Bruno wrote, "you will be able to reach such a figurative art that it will help not only the memory but also all the powers of the soul in a wonderful manner."[18] Like the Gnostics, Bruno thought he had found a path of liberation that relied purely on training the mind, rather than on pious obedience to the top-down dictates of the Church.

While Bruno based his memory technique on the art of memory that would soon fall into disfavor among Renaissance scholars, his particular use of the technique anticipated the scientific method. By using the technique to articulate a system for classifying information about the natural and cosmological worlds and articulating the rules of that system in writing, he paved the way for the emergence of empirical methods that would soon transform Renaissance scholarship.

In Howard Bloom's parlance, Bruno would qualify as a first-rate diversity generator, a fount of alternative hypotheses who failed to survive the intergroup tournament—the Inquisition—and ultimately perished at the hands of conformity enforcers—the Church (see Chapter 1).[19] But despite Bruno's unfortunate demise, his ideas found their way into the mainstream of Renaissance thought, paving the way for the advent of the scientific method.

Ultimately, Bruno's practices amount to an aberration from the art of memory as it had been practiced beforehand. As historian Rhodri Lewis writes, "Bruno's ambitions—if not his achievements—were at variance with the history of mnemotechnique."[20] Throughout most of its history, the art of memory had been a practical tool for improving recollection; it was only in the latter years of the scholastic fascination that it began taking on mystical airs. After Bruno's execution, the monastic practice of the art of memory faded almost entirely from public view, but traces of its impact would linger for centuries to come. An Englishman named Robert Fludd wrote about the practice in the seventeenth century. Some scholars have even speculated that the art of memory went back underground into esoteric occult circles, as it had during the Dark Ages. Yates believes that Bruno's writings also embedded themselves into the secret practices of the Freemasons and Rosicrucians. Esoterica aside, however, the old medieval knowledge systems—with their cathedrals of imagery, theaters of memory, and books of mythological animals—were fast giving way to a new era of scientific reason. Soon, the old monkish ways would be all but forgotten, thanks in no small part to an Englishman well versed in the art of memory: Francis Bacon.

BACON'S WINDOW

The most striking feature of Francis Bacon's house in Gorhambury, England, was a lattice of stained glass windows, "every pane with severall [sic] figures of beast, bird and flower."[21] Bacon, who had studied the old art of memory in his youth, had taken great pains to create a physical facsimile of the old scholastic art in his house. Perhaps we can envision him gazing out his multicolored window, imagining the memory palaces he had visited in his monastic youth.

By the time Elizabeth I ascended to the throne in 1558, English intellectuals had started abandoning the mystery cults of the scholastics. The Cambridge-educated Bacon ultimately came to deride the old scholastic methods as overly stylized exercises in meaningless abstraction. His years in the monastery had given him a first-hand perspective on the futility of esoteric debates that seemed removed from practical problems: the medieval equivalent of the ivory tower syndrome. Along with Erasmus and other early humanist writers, he condemned the art of memory—in which he himself had trained—as a superfluous exercise that paled in comparison to an empirical style of reasoning based on direct observation and logical reasoning. "[W]e are certain that there may be had both better Precepts for the confirming and increasing *Memory*, than that Art comprehendeth," he wrote, "and a better Practice of that Art may be set downe than that which is receiv'd." He wrote of the art of memory, "it seemeth to me that there are better practices of that art than those received," deriding the monastic tendency to celebrate their elaborate memory feats as "points of ostentation."[22] He further derided the practitioners of the monastic art as a kind of intellectual gymnasticism practiced by "Tumblers; Buffones, & Iug[g]lers."

Despite his condemnation of the monastic art of memory, Bacon did not reject the technique altogether, but yearned for a "better Practice of that Art," stripped of scholastic excess. In his landmark *Novum Organon* ("New Tool of Reason"), he recommended the use of "artificial places in memory, which can either be places in the literal sense ... or familiar or famous persons, or whatever you like (provided that they are organized properly)."[23] Bacon longed for a new intellectual philosophy that rejected the cloistered model of scholastic learning in favor of practical inquiry into real-world problems. While he rejected the idle contemplations of the monastics, he nonetheless recognized the value of mnemonic techniques as a bridge toward a new way of understanding the natural world.

While history has remembered Bacon as one of the forebears of the scientific method, he did not envision himself as a "scientist" (the term did not yet exist). Rather, Bacon thought of himself as a natural philosopher, or even as a "magician." In the medieval sense of the term, a magician was not a conjurer or sleight-of-hand artist but an explorer of the phenomenal world, devoted to exploiting the laws of nature for practical use. Bacon practiced alchemy and saw no conflict between practicing magic and looking for empirical methods. "Toward the effecting of works," he wrote, "all that man can do is put together or part asunder natural bodies. The rest is done by Nature working within."[24] In this sense, magic is just another word for science. Elsewhere, Bacon wrote that "[t]he aim of magic is to recall natural philosophy from the vanity of speculations to the importance of experiments." The duty of a philosopher, as Bacon saw it, was not to reject magical traditions out of hand but to delve into them with fresh eyes and a critical perspective. "For although such things lie buried deep beneath a mass of falsehood and fable, yet they should be looked into . . . for it may be that in some of them some natural operation lies at the bottom."[25]

By invoking the power of observation to sift nature's truth from the "vanity of speculations," Bacon forged a new path of understanding the natural world, based not on faith in a divine truth but on the power of individual perception. He rejected monastic scholasticism as a form of mysticism that placed undue faith in divine revelation, preferring instead to trust the individual's powers of observation; Bacon belonged squarely to the Age of Reason. In 1620, Bacon introduced his most famous formulation of this new way of knowing in his greatest work, the *Novum Organum*.[26] Here he proposed nothing less than restructuring the enterprise of scholarship. The book laid the philosophical foundations for a process that would later become known as the scientific method, a radical departure from the scholasticism that sought pathways to truth through esoteric practices and belief in disembodied ideals. Bacon believed in the capacity of direct perceptual observation to reveal God's truth, rejecting appeals to external authorities like classical authors or even the scriptures. "I have taken all knowledge to be my province," he wrote—with no small display of authorial hubris—staking out an ambitious philosophical agenda in the form of a six-part approach to investigating the natural world.

The title page opens with a grand illustration depicting the words of the title rising above two ships sailing between the pillars of Hercules, symbolizing the limits of human knowledge in the ancient world. By invoking "the pillars of fate set in the path of knowledge," Bacon signaled his ambition to explore an entirely new kind of knowledge.

The book is an intellectual tour de force, a sweeping foray into a new mode of reasoning that would ultimately fulfill Bacon's ambition and reshape the trajectory of Western scholarship. Bacon proposed a new method of reason based on induction—reasoning from direction observation—and relying on an idealized system of scholarly collaboration that viewed knowledge as a cumulative enterprise. In other words, he favored networked communication between scholars over received top-down hierarchical modes of understanding, be they classical or ecclesiastical. "I do not endeavor either by triumphs of confutation, or pleadings of antiquity, or assumption of authority, or even by veil of obscurity, to invest these inventions of mine with any majesty," he wrote. Instead, he aspired to "present these things naked and open, that my errors can be marked and set aside before the mass of knowledge be further infected by them; and it will be easy also for others to continue and carry on my labours."[27] His vision of research as a collaborative process, subject to trial and error—rather than as the revelation of divine truths—marks the earliest expression of what we now recognize as the scientific method.

For all his belief in collaborative networks of scholarship, however, Bacon was no populist. He frequently voiced undisguised contempt for the common man, believing that the great uneducated masses posed a severe threat to the integrity of scholarship. Paradoxically, Bacon at once advocated the democratization of scholarship while espousing intellectual elitism. He believed that in order to achieve trustworthy results, scholars had to work to overcome the inherent human limitations that keep the majority of the population in the figurative dark. Bacon described these barriers to understanding as "idols," which he described as "the profoundest fallacies of the mind of Man" that spring "from a corrupt and crookedly-set predisposition of the mind. . . . For the mind of man . . . is rather like an enchanted glass, full of superstitions, apparitions, and impostures.[28] Bacon's idols include:

• *Idols of the Cave.* The problem of subjectivity. Each of us inhabits "a cave or den of his own, which refracts and discolors the light of nature." Our personal biases will always taint our perceptions. We might today say that the chemist sees chemistry in all things; the student of literature looks for narratives; the computer programmer looks for operable rules. Relying on our individual faculties alone can only lead us to imperfect, idiosyncratic versions of reality.

• *Idols of the Tribe.* The problem of human limitations. These are the inborn perceptual constraints of our human "tribe." He wrote, "human understanding is like a false mirror, which, receiving rays irregularly, distorts and discolors the nature of things by mingling its own nature with it." We cannot, for example, perceive the full spectrum of colors and sounds; but through the careful application of logical reasoning we can begin to compensate for our sensory limitations.

• *Idols of the Marketplace.* The problem of socially constructed meaning. Our understanding will always be warped by the vagaries of human language. "It is by discourse that men associate, and words are imposed according to the apprehension of the vulgar. And therefore the ill and unfit choice of words wonderfully obstructs the understanding." Words are imperfect vessels, pale approximations of direct experience.

• *Idols of the Theater.* The problem of belief. Mythologies, religious stories, or ideological convictions present enormous obstacles to understanding, like "so many stage plays, representing worlds of their own creation after an unreal and scenic fashion."

Only by renouncing received wisdom and superstitious beliefs, and refusing to take anything on faith, can we cultivate any hope of seeing things as they are.

Bacon's idols constitute a sweeping rebuke of the old medieval mind-set, predicated as it was on "superstitious" belief in the Word of God or the classical ideal of Truth. Bacon argued that the pursuit of scientific truth must be derived from direct observation of phenomena and a process he famously dubbed "induction," which requires meticulous observation and logical reasoning. In contrast to Aristotle's top-down system of ideal forms stemming from disembodied conceptual hierarchies (his Great Chain of Being), Bacon proposed a radical new system through which hierarchies of meaning emerged from the bottom up, through the collective effort of scholars creating conceptual building blocks of observed phenomena.

Bacon took an active and hopeful view of human agency, believing that the pursuit of empirical knowledge was a vehicle for human salvation. "Let us hope," he wrote, "that there may spring helps to man, and a line and race of inventions that may in some degree subdue and overcome the necessities and miseries of humanity."[29] Ultimately, Bacon's guiding philosophy was a steadfast conviction that "useful knowledge"—rather than the idealistic pursuit of Truth—would lead to humanity's salvation.

Bacon's pursuit of an empirical method would eventually lead him to formulate a new philosophical framework for classifying all of human knowledge. He postulated that all human intellectual pursuits revolve around three essential facilities: memory, reason, and imagination (or, in more familiar terms: history, philosophy, and poetry). Bacon hoped to expound on this framework in his great unfinished work *Instauratio Magna*. Nonetheless, this simple model would also prove to be one of Bacon's enduring legacies, influencing the thinking of information scientists for centuries to come. As we will see in later chapters, Diderot would embrace Bacon's scheme as the foundation for his great encyclopedia; Jefferson would later adopt it as the basis for organizing his own personal library, the foundation for the Library of Congress; and Melvil Dewey would acknowledge it as an influence on his decimal system.

For all of Bacon's subsequent historical impact, in his day his work met with a largely muted reception. His chief patron, King James I, appraised his work with a royal backhanded compliment, noting that he found his lord chancellor's work—like the peace of God—"passeth all understanding." Bacon acknowledged the density of his work, likening his undertaking to guiding readers through a "labyrinth." He never tried to sugarcoat the difficulty of finding a path to true understanding, an effort "presenting on every side so many ambiguities of way, such deceitful resemblances of objects and signs, natures so irregular in their lines, and so knotted and entangled," that the steps of the true method "must be guided by a clue," which Bacon envisioned as "a more perfect use and application of the human mind and intellect."[30]

WILKINS'S NEW WORD ORDER

On January 11, 1666, the great English diarist Samuel Pepys wrote of meeting with the well-known London bishop Dr. John Wilkins. Pepys had heard that Wilkins was working on an ambitious scheme to develop a "Universall [sic] Language," a new way of cataloging human knowledge. Wilkins had invited Pepys to contribute his knowledge of naval matters to the project, and Pepys eagerly answered the call. So too did many other prominent members of the newfound Royal Society, under whose auspices Wilkins had undertaken his project. John Ray assisted "in framing his Tables of Plants, Quadrupeds, Birds, Fishes &c. for the User of the universal Character." Other notable collaborators included botanist Robert Morison, naturalist Francis Willughby, and clergyman William Lloyd.[31] While the system would ultimately bear Wilkins's name, it was largely a collaborative effort.

In 1668 Wilkins published his landmark *Essay Toward a Real Character and a Philosophical Language.* Weighing in at a prodigious 454 folio pages, the *Essay* is divided into four sections: an introduction, the tables of "Universal Philosophy" that comprise the bulk of the work, the grammar of a new philosophical language, and finally a section explicating how the character and language work together. In the Universal Philosophy, Wilkins proposes classifying the phenomenal world into 40 basic categories, beginning with two top-level divisions—"General or universal notions," and "Special" things—which are then divided into 40 categories (see Appendix A for a complete list of Wilkins's categories). These categories are then subcategorized by "differences" and further by individual "species," for a total of 4,194 possible classifications. The system works by generating four-letter names based on the rules of the classification: the first two letters corresponding to the genus, the third letter (always a consonant) identifying the difference, and the fourth letter (always a vowel) identifying the species. For example, the genus *Zi* signifies "beasts"; within which the difference *p* refers to "rapacious dog-like beasts" (including, for example, both wolves and dogs); within which the final signifier *a* identifies the particular species, "dog." Thus, *zipa* means "dog."

Two Dutch scholars in the library of the University of Leyden, circa 1610, from William Andrews's *Curiosities of the Church: Studies of Curious Customs, Services and Records* (1891).

In an age of burgeoning secular scholarship, Wilkins believed the world desperately needed a new synthetic language capable of containing the growing surfeit of available data. He thought that the world's old natural languages had degenerated, becoming "inartificial and confused," and were poorly suited to accommodate the truth of God's creation. Older languages, he believed, were fundamentally flawed because of their haphazard development, by "that Curse in the Confusion of Tongues" that left them bedeviled with redundant and imprecise meanings. Like Bacon, Wilkins believed that human comprehension was limited by our preconceived notions about things (cf. Bacon's "Idols of the Marketplace"). To remedy the shortcomings of written languages, he set out to formulate a new system capable of describing such "natural truths as are to be found out by our own industry and experience," untainted by existing linguistic biases. As Wilkins scholar Rhodri Lewis puts it, "Wilkins believed that it was possible accurately to map the order of thought (and therefore of the things which this represented), and that it was possible to devise a language which might represent this."[32] To that end Wilkins set out to create a language "that should not signifie *words*, but *things* and *notions*." His classification, he hoped, would provide "a sufficient enumeration of all such things and notions, as are to have names assigned to them, and withal so to contrive these according to their order, that the place of everything may contribute to a description of the nature of it."[33]

For all its exhaustive ambition, Wilkins's scheme explicitly excluded many possible topics, including fictional and "complex" phenomena as well as place names, clothing, games, food, music, and, curiously, religious sects. He thought his language was best suited to describe simple, observable things and that more elusive concepts and ideas were best treated with "a more mixed and complicated signification."[34] Nonetheless, Wilkins believed that the truth of God's creation could be discovered primarily in observable nature, not through the received wisdom of the church. Elsewhere, he argued for the separation of scientific inquiry from religious doctrine, urging his contemporaries not to be "so superstitiously devoted to Antiquity as for to take up everything as canonical which drops from the pen of a

Father."[35] Wilkins saw his life's work as an endeavor to bring humanity closer to God by forsaking superstitious beliefs in favor of honest
intellectual striving.

For a time it looked as though Wilkins's ambitions might be realized. The book met with an enthusiastic public reception after its
initial publication. The Royal Society began using the system to organize its collections, and copies of the book circulated throughout Europe. Wilkins himself hoped the *Essay* was only a beginning; for the
language to reach its full realization, he thought, would require the
efforts of "a College or an Age." "I am not so vain," he wrote, "as to
think that I have here completely finished this great undertaking." He
hoped that the *Essay* would serve as an ontological beacon for future
generations.

Wilkins would doubtless have been dismayed to discover that,
centuries later, his life's great work is now best remembered not as the
birth of a universal language but as the butt of a literary joke. Today,
Wilkins is largely known as the target of Jorge Luis Borges's famous
satire, "The Analytical Language of John Wilkins." Taking stock of
Wilkins's system, Borges writes:

> Having defined Wilkins' procedure, we must examine a problem that is
> impossible or at least difficult to postpone: the value of the forty genera
> which are the basis of the language. Consider the eighth category, stones.
> Wilkins divides them into vulgar (flint, gravel, slate), middle-prized
> (marble, amber, coral), precious (pearl, opal), more transparent (am-
> ethyst, sapphire) and earthly concretions not dissolvable [*sic*] (pit-coal,
> oker and arsenic). Almost as surprising as the eighth, is the ninth cat-
> egory. This one reveals to us that metals can be imperfect (vermillion,
> mercury), factitious (bronze, brass), recrementitious (scoria, rust) and
> natural (gold, tin, copper). Whales belong to the sixteenth category; vi-
> viparous oblong fish.[36]

Borges went on to mock Wilkins's seemingly arbitrary classification with a modest taxonomic proposal of his own, masked as a fictional Chinese encyclopedia called *The Celestial Emporium of
Benevolent Knowledge.* Here, he proposed a wildly orthogonal system
for classifying animals as:

a. belonging to the Emperor
b. embalmed
c. trained
d. sloppy
e. sirens
f. fabulous
g. stray dogs
h. included in this classification
i. trembling like crazy
j. innumerable
k. drawn with a very fine camelhair brush
l. et cetera
m. just broke the vase
n. from a distance look like flies

Borges concluded that Wilkins's system was doomed to fail because "it is clear that there is no classification of the Universe not being arbitrary and full of conjectures. The reason for this is very simple: we do not know what the universe is." Much as Borges's essay deserves its fame, we must ask whether it was perhaps a bit uncharitable to the unfortunate Mr. Wilkins. Wilkins never saw himself as any kind of absolutist; he railed against the arbitrary top-down hierarchies of the church and saw his system as, after a fashion, a bottom-up endeavor. He was an empiricist, not an authoritarian. Paradoxically, Wilkins might even have appreciated Borges's joke.

TOWARD "SCIENCE"

Barely a century after Camillo had wowed his Venetian audience with his gearbox Theater of Memory, Europe had witnessed a period of remarkable intellectual fermentation. By the beginning of the eighteenth century, the old scholastic arts of the monasteries had faded to oblivion, supplanted by a new secular ethic of scholarship. The authority of the church had eroded to make way for a new mode of intellectual self-reliance best exemplified in the emerging scientific method and the dawning Age of Reason. Meanwhile, the ongoing caterwaul of publishing continued to fuel interest in a conceptual system capable of accommodating a growing tide of printed knowledge. The old wooden theaters, memory wheels, and artificial languages began to look like quaint relics of the bygone era of the monkish mind. While none of these systems would last, these pioneering efforts mattered less for what they actually accomplished than for the vision they suggested. These brilliant failed experiments in mnemo-technology pointed the way toward an even greater undertaking that would occupy philosophers for centuries to come: the quest for a universal classification.

8

The Encyclopedic Revolution

With the emergence of the scientific method and the rise of Renaissance secular scholarship, seventeenth-century Europe witnessed a scholarly publishing boom. Across the growing university towns and printing centers of Europe, writers and printers turned out a growing volume of books on all kinds of topics: poetry, philosophy, politics, the arts and the natural sciences, as well as traditional religious and devotional texts. Before 1500, European printers produced about 15 million to 20 million books (from a total of 30,000 to 35,000 different titles); in the century that followed, that number mushroomed to nearly 200 million (from 150,000 to 200,000 titles).[1] As books flooded the market, the burgeoning quantity of available information created the conditions for a new kind of book to emerge: the encyclopedia.

Today we think of encyclopedias as dull reference works, secondary sources relegated to school libraries or bundled with our computers on CD-ROMs. In the seventeenth century, however, the encyclopedia represented a major innovation: a new literary technology that promised to help readers cope with a surging tide of new information. Encyclopedias did more than just give users an easy reference source; this new technology also had revolutionary implications.

In 1624 the English playwright Thomas Heywood published an immensely popular book called the *Gunaikeion*, a proto-encyclopedia that purported to catalog all available information about his favorite subject: women. Inside this thick tome readers would find tales of brave queens, learned ladies, chaste damsels, Amazons, witches, and even a transgendered woman or two. Although Heywood's name graced the cover, the *Gunaikeion* was a compilation of material culled from other popular books of the day, condensed, as Heywood put it, into "a small Manuell, containing all the pith and marrow of the greater."[2] Like a kind of Renaissance hypertext, the book had no table of contents, no conceptual "top" or Aristotelian subject hierarchy. Instead, it presented its contents in a loose structure that left the reader plenty of discretion in choosing how to navigate the text.

In synthesizing a vast body of recorded knowledge on the subject of women, Heywood grappled with what literary scholars Crook and Rhodes call the "intractability of his subject matter." Rather than try to shepherd his fair subjects into a fixed classification, Heywood instead hit on a novel scheme: "I have not introduced them in order, neither Alphabetically, nor according to custome or president; which I thus excuse: The most cunning and curious Musick, is that which is made out of discords."[3]

The term "discords" seems like a useful rubric for the problem of organizing a large collection of information drawn from many disparate sources. In our era of distributed information systems, information architects struggle with the problem of imposing a workable order on an expanding body of information drawn from remote sources. Heywood anticipated this question long before anyone started using terms like "hypertext," articulating a system for organizing information that did not invoke a top-down hierarchical classification but emerged through a dialogue between author and readers—a kind of ad hoc network—working together to interpolate the contents of other books that had come before. As Heywood put it, his new book was "all mine and none mine. As a good hous-wife out of divers fleeces weaves one peece of Cloath, a Bee gathers Wax and

Hony out of many Flowers, and makes a new bundle of all . . . I have laboriously collected this Cento out of divers Writers."[4]

For example, when Heywood recounts the startling deeds of a woman who wrote an illustrated sex manual, he wonders whether she might best be classified a "poetess" or a "she-monster." Similarly, when he tells of the great Queen Semiramis, a brave and noble woman of antiquity, he lets readers gauge whether she might best be tagged as a valorous queen, a murderess, a transvestite, or a practitioner of bestiality.[5] Writing of Queen Elizabeth, Heywood sings her praises in polymorphous terms:

> Elizabeth, of late memory, Queene of England, she that was a Saba for her wisdome, an Harpalice for her magnanimitye . . . a Cleopatra for her bountie, a Camilla for her chastitie, an Amalasuntha for her temperance, a Zenobia for her learning and skill in language; of whose omniscience, pantarite, and goodnesse, all men heretofore have spoke too little.[6]

That process of condensation led Heywood to grapple with questions of classification and values. For example, in considering possible approaches to classifying historical events, Heywood writes: "Of History there be foure species, either taken from place, as Geography; from time, as Chronologie; from Generation as Genealogie, or from gests (deeds) really done, which . . . may be called Annologie: The elements of which it consisteth are Person, place, time manner, instrument, matter and thing."[7] Heywood seems to anticipate the kind of multidimensional classification that the great Indian librarian Ranganathan would propose centuries later in his famous Colon Classification (see Chapter 9 and Appendix D).

Heywood's attempts to liberate his text from fixed top-down categories, as Crook and Rhodes write, "throw into startling relief questions of classification and the logical disposition of knowledge in the period before the establishment of classical taxonomies from the late seventeenth through to the nineteenth centuries." Heywood does more than just call those taxonomies into question. He seems to suggest a prescient alternative to top-down systems of knowledge: a world in which readers actively participate in structuring the uni-

Cover plate of Heywood's *Gunaikeion*. Reproduced by permission of the University of Edinburgh Library, Edinburgh, Scotland.

verse of available knowledge, rather than following a classification imposed from on High. "The digressiveness of both hypertext and the *Gunaikeion* represents a departure from the kind of narrow, linear thinking that we traditionally characterize as male," write Crook and Rhodes, "and approximates more closely to ways of thinking and learning which in our present culture are considered by some to be the result of women's socialization."[8]

As one of the earliest examples of an encyclopedia-like volume, Heywood's popular work proved there was a poplar market for such synthetic works. Over the next 200 years, scholars would find the notion of a meta-book drawn from the contents of other books increasingly alluring. Ultimately, this quest would lead to whole new ways of thinking about the structure of human knowledge and eventually to the great Victorian quest for a universal classification. Those efforts, as we will see in the pages that follow, would eventually find themselves bogged down with increasingly rigid hierarchical constructs; but in their earlier incarnations, encyclopedias seemed to offer the hope of a new, flexible, reader-driven experience. Heywood's notion of a book whose structure is supplied at least in part by its readers, seems to foreshadow the self-organizing information ecosystem of the World Wide Web, which, like Heywood's women, seems to resist categorization.

DIDEROT'S ENCYCLOPEDIA

Well into the eighteenth century, most European households owned at most a single book, often a popular devotional text like the *Book of Hours*. Merchants might keep a small private bookshelf with a few volumes, while scholars and clergy might maintain slightly larger private libraries. There was no such thing as a public library. For all the expansion of publishing, most people could not afford many books; they were still expensive commodities. In such a constrained market, the idea of a book culled from other books held out a tantalizing value proposition.

As printed books continued to proliferate across Europe, authors and publishers started to expand their ambitions. By the eighteenth century a few scholars, inspired in part by Bacon's quest for a unifying philosophical framework, had started to pursue the idea of a great "universal" encyclopedia. History's greatest encyclopedist was Denis Diderot, a Frenchman who adopted Bacon's classification as the foundation for his monumental *Encyclopédie ou Dictionnaire Raisonné des Sciences, des Arts et des Métiers* ("Encyclopedia or Dictionary of the Sciences, the Arts, and the Professions"), published in a succession of volumes from 1751 to 1772. A massive collection of 72,000 articles written by 160 eminent contributors (including notables like Voltaire, Rousseau, and Buffon), Diderot created a compendium of knowledge unrivaled in any previously published work.

The new encyclopedia was more than just a collection of previously published scholarship. Diderot took the unprecedented step of trying to capture folk knowledge from common tradespeople, devoting an enormous portion of the encyclopedia to knowledge about everyday topics like cloth dying, metalwork, and glassware, with entries accompanied by detailed illustrations explaining the intricacies of the trades. The encyclopedia gave folk knowledge roughly equal billing with the traditional domains of literary inquiry: scripture, scholarship, and politics. While publishing this kind of "how-to" information may seem unremarkable today, in the aristocratic literacy culture of eighteenth-century France such a mingling of high and low cultures constituted a blunt political statement. By granting craft knowledge a status equivalent to the high written culture of statecraft, scholarship, and religion, Diderot took a epistemological step toward revolution. At the time, most lower-class people remained illiterate, and whatever trade knowledge they held still passed primarily through the close-knit social networks of family traditions, apprenticeships, and trade guilds. Almost none of that information had ever been recorded, and even if it had, it certainly would have held little or no interest for the powdered-wig habitués of Parisian literary salons. In according tradespeople such respect, Diderot was sounding a clarion call in favor of the common worker.

Today, we may find it difficult to imagine how the act of publishing information about cloth dying could possibly foment political upheaval. In eighteenth-century France, however, Diderot's work

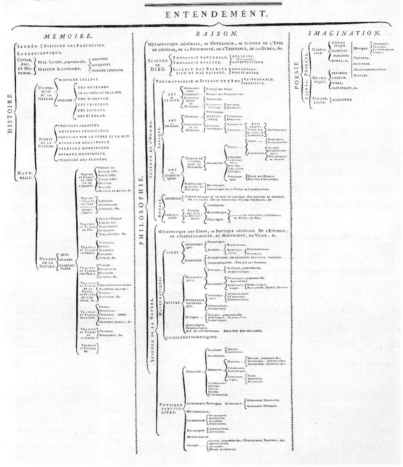

Outline of Diderot's *Encyclopédie*.

caused enormous consternation among the privileged classes. Pope Clement XIII castigated the work. King George III of England and Louis XV of France also condemned it, anticipating the political consequences of providing the common folk with such easy access to knowledge that had previously been sealed away. In 1759 the French government ordered Diderot's publisher to cease publication, seizing 6,000 volumes, which they deposited (appropriately enough) inside the Bastille.

Diderot died 10 years before the revolution of 1789, but his credentials as an Enlightenment encyclopedist would serve his family well in the bloody aftermath. When his son-in-law was imprisoned during the revolution and branded an aristocrat, Diderot's daughter pleaded with the revolutionary committee, citing her father's populist literary pedigree. On learning of the prisoner's connection to the great encyclopedist, the committee immediately set him free.[9]

Diderot's *Encyclopédie* provides an object lesson in the power of printed texts to disrupt old political and religious hierarchies. In synthesizing information that had previously been dispersed in local oral traditions and craft networks, he created a new system that challenged old aristocratic assumptions about the boundaries of scholarship. Just as the networked movement of the French Revolution was powered in large part by the free flow of documents through the revolutionary social network, Diderot drew on the networks of folk expertise to craft a new kind of book that presented an epistemological challenge to the aristocracy.

Today, the encyclopedia is reemerging as a disruptive information technology. In recent years the Wikipedia project—a Web-based encyclopedia that allows anyone to publish and edit entries—has sparked a fervent debate in scholarly circles. With more than three million entries in more than 100 languages, it is already far larger than any other encyclopedia ever created. Wikipedia's success has sparked a heated controversy in traditional academic and publishing circles. Questions of authority and credibility inevitably swirl around it. Critics argue that Wikipedia's lack of quality controls leaves it vulnerable to bias and manipulation, while its defenders insist that openness and transparency ensure fairness and ultimately will allow the system to regulate itself. There also seems to be a deeper tension at work, between traditional forms of top-down editorial authority and the bottom-up ethos of the Web. Like Diderot's *Encyclopédie*, the Wikipedia is stirring tensions between established interests— academic scholars and publishers—and a rising populist sentiment. While Wikipedia is unlikely to spell the demise of traditional scholarship, it serves as a telling example of the power of "books about books" to challenge existing institutional systems. The Web, like the printing press, seems poised to augur long-term social and political transformations whose effects we are only beginning to anticipate. And once again, the humble encyclopedia may prove the most revolutionary "book" of all.

AFTERMATH

Three hundred years after Gutenberg, the printing press had permanently altered Europe's social, political, and intellectual landscape. Ever since Luther posted his theses on the church door, the spread of printing had left a trail of upheaval in its wake. Popular literacy put an enormous strain on old institutional hierarchies. The Vatican had lost its iron religious and political grip, the French government had fallen, and England and Scotland were feeling the first rumblings of the Industrial Revolution. Meanwhile, across the Atlantic, the printing press had provided the essential platform for the world's first "document nation"[10]: the United States. The Gutenberg revolution had fomented widespread political upheaval around the world.

For scholars, the old monastic ways had fallen into disrepute, and learned readers struggled to develop new secular frameworks to contain the growing sprawl of published knowledge. Despite the best efforts of Renaissance philosophers and encyclopedists, the volume of printed information was outstripping the ability of any one system to keep up, as a burgeoning collection of books and manuscripts threatened to overwhelm all available ontologies. By the end of the eighteenth century, the problem would come to a head in the domain where it all began: taxonomy.

9

The Moose That Roared

Ay, in the catalogue ye go for men;
As hounds, and greyhounds, mongrels, spaniels, curs,
Shoughs, water-rugs and demi-wolves, are clept
All by the name of dogs: the valued file
Distinguishes the swift, the slow, the subtle,
The housekeeper, the hunter, every one
According to the gift which bounteous nature
Hath in him closed.

Shakespeare, *Macbeth*

In 1787 Thomas Jefferson took delivery in his Paris hotel of the complete skeleton, skin, and antlers of a 7-foot-tall American Moose. The moose had journeyed across the Atlantic, packed in salt, and then traveled overland from Le Havre to Paris in a horse-drawn wagon. By the time it arrived at Jefferson's hotel, the animal was in sorry shape. Its skin was sagging, and its hair was falling out. But the thing would serve its purpose well enough. Jefferson, then in Paris as ambassador to France, arranged to have the decomposing quadruped placed on public display in the front entrance to his hotel.[1] Parisians flocked to see the strange spectacle. Jefferson hoped that one particular Parisian—the famous Comte de Buffon—would take note of his specimen.

With this curious stunt, the sage of Monticello cast his vote in a raging scientific debate then captivating Europe's intellectual class. The problem of reconciling the New World with the Old, as we will see shortly, led to a wave of scientific conflicts that would reverberate for centuries. The moose marked Jefferson's entrée into a taxonomic feud that would have lasting consequences for the future of science, shaping the trajectory of worldwide information systems for centuries to come.

To understand the importance of Jefferson's moose to the subsequent history of information science, we must step back 50 years to early eighteenth-century Sweden, where in 1735 a young botanist named Carolus Linnaeus published his landmark *Systema Naturae*, a treatise on the classification of plants. Pursuing his lifelong passion for plant life (as a child he had been nicknamed the "little botanist"), Linnaeus had pursued an ambitious program of collecting information about the plant world and proposing a new systematic framework for describing the natural world, based on his own private studies and on his firsthand experience documenting new plant life while working with the Royal Society of Science. From this project Linnaeus would emerge as the "father of taxonomy," the first scientist to propose what we would now consider a modern biological classification system.

The eighteenth century was a period of intense research and discovery in the natural world, with scholars discovering thousands of new plants each year. The spread of printing and the rise of the scientific method had fueled a boom in scholarly publishing, as biologists (or "natural historians," as they would have called themselves) found the means to share their findings with a growing audience of scholarly peers. Cataloging and sharing their observations, eighteenth-century biologists began to create their own idiosyncratic systems to organize their findings. Absent a unifying conceptual framework, however, much of that work was effectively wasted. Scholars communicated with each other through a vast ad hoc network, publishing books and treatises as they discovered and cataloged new plants in a vast scientific free-for-all. Students of the natural world lived in a Babel of varying naming conventions, assigning Latin words to animal species almost entirely at random. Those names changed frequently as manuscripts changed hands. The hippopotamus—an animal that almost no Europeans had actually seen—went variously by the names river horse, sea horse, behemoth, river paard, and water elephant.[2] And those were just the English names.

The lack of a common classification system made it all but impossible for scientists to build on each other's work. Instead, each scientist labored in a kind of personal echo chamber. Recognizing the problem, philosophers over the years had proposed several attempts at universal classification systems. Joseph Pitton de Tournefot grouped 10,000 species into 689 natural genera. English naturalist John Ray sorted all known plant species into two groups—monocots and dicots. Some naturalists preferred to use Conrad Gesner's sixteenth-century classification. But none of these systems ever caught on.

By the eighteenth century, publishers were turning out numerous works about the natural world. As naturalists clamored for attention from the growing public readership, the problem of classification was coming to a head. To make matters worse, a stream of fresh data was pouring in from the New World. Travelers were returning from the European colonies with reports of new plants and animals hitherto unheard of: corn, squash, beans, tobacco, tomatoes, cranberries, strange new animals like bison, and variations on existing species like the aforementioned moose. There was even a new "species" of New World human beings to contend with: Where did they fit into the tree of life? European naturalists struggled to make sense of the New World.

Linnaeus's *Systema Naturae* articulated a simple but powerful system for classifying living things. The system turned on a nested hierarchy, consisting of top-level kingdoms, which in turn were divided into classes, orders, families, genera, and species. For example, within the plant kingdom he identified 24 classes, each grouped according to the characteristics of the plants' stamens. Every class was subsequently divided into 65 orders, based primarily on the number and orientation of its pistils. Ultimately, his system would encompass more than 7,700 plant and 4,400 animal species.

In the centuries that followed, scientists have expanded Linnaeus's framework to include as many as 17 levels of hierarchical descriptors, notably adding the phylum (a division between kingdoms and classes) and additional subcategories. But in its original incarnation, the Linnaean system bore a striking resemblance to the folk taxonomies (see Chapter 2) that preceded it. This was no accident. While

Section of the table of the Animal Kingdom from Carolus Linnaeus's first edition of *Systema Naturae* (1735).

Linnaeus's Classification

Level	Example
Kingdom	Animals
Class	Mammals
Order	Primates
Family	Hominidae
Genus	Homo
Species	Homo sapiens

traditional histories of science tend to give Linnaeus credit as the author of his system, in fact he drew on earlier folk traditions. What sets his system apart was his willingness to embrace folk conventions rather than try to assert his own idiosyncratic vision. Linnaeus intuitively recognized the wisdom of crowds. The subsequent success of his system stems from its roots in our evolutionary heritage. The durability of Linnaean taxonomy may have a great deal to do with the epigenetic rules governing folk taxonomy: hierarchical categorization of five to six levels deep, binomial naming conventions, and a "real name" or psychologically primary category. The genius of Linnaeus's system owes not just to its transparency, but to its intuitive resonance with the epigenetic rules governing folk taxonomies. For many naturalists the Linnaean system simply feels "right."

Whereas earlier schemes had stalled at two or three levels of hierarchy, Linnaeus seems to have hit on the precise structure of taxa that occurs among tribal societies. This should come as no surprise; Linnaeus drew heavily on these systems that had persisted through oral transmission since ancient times. Aristotle's naturalist works were already widely known, providing a foundational work for naming conventions (the standard binomial convention of genus-species derives from Aristotle), but his Great Chain of Being provided only a one-dimensional hierarchy; it did not provide a unifying theoretical system. Meanwhile, the old folk taxonomies had always persisted in local communities, but while they shared a rough conformity, they were also highly heterogeneous.

Linnaeus's system succeeded by incorporating aspects of folk taxonomies and Aristotelian classification and by articulating an easily understood system that relied not on the mental prowess of individual researchers but on a precise rule set. This rule set in turn lent itself to systematization and to a division of scientific labor. The hierarchical information system enabled an organizational hierarchy to take shape around it. Linnaeus created a team of researchers or, as he called them, "apostles," to work under his guidance in fleshing out his classification; each apostle worked to complete a particular piece of the taxonomic puzzle.

By providing a rule set that other scientists could follow, Linnaeus paved the way for modern biology. Linnaeus himself allowed that his system was "artificial," using as it did an arbitrary construct of Linnaeus's own devising—the classification of plants according to "male" and "female" characteristics. Linnaeus even used the terms "husband" and "wife," invoking a matrimonial metaphor that echoes social kinship relations.[3] In fact, Linnaeus hoped someday to supplant his own system with a more "natural" classification that more accurately revealed God's order and spent most of the rest of his career pursuing that elusive goal.

Today, Linnaeus ranks as the uncontested historical founder of modern biological classification. But his ascendance did not come easily. Linnaeus had a powerful rival on the scientific world stage: the French Comte de Buffon, the man who inspired Jefferson to send for his moose.

BUFFON'S "NATURAL" TAXONOMY

George-Louis Leclerc, Comte de Buffon, was, like Linnaeus, a botanist who had also worked as a royal gardener. And like Linnaeus he became fascinated with classifying flora and fauna. But unlike Linnaeus, Buffon eschewed strict hierarchies in favor of seeking a "natural" system more reflective of God's will.

From 1749 to 1788, Buffon published his monumental *Histoire naturelle*, a compilation of information about known species. The work was a best-seller by eighteenth-century standards. Issued in 44 volumes (eight of which were published posthumously), the work became a standard text in European intellectual circles. Inspired by Pliny, author of the 37-volume encyclopedia of the natural world, Buffon rejected earlier Renaissance humanist attempts at reconciling Holy Scripture with observations about the natural world. Instead, Buffon proposed a strictly secular framework predicated on the deist view that God was more of a primal architect who set natural processes in motion, rather than the "hands-on" creator of each individual being.

Buffon believed that humans' propensity for classifying the natural world stemmed from the inherent inadequacy of human perception. In his view the world existed more as a continuum of life forms; fixed categories were simply the insecure projections of feeble human minds. Buffon had little use for Linnaeus's detailed classification system. He dismissed the work as an uninspired collection of tables.

Buffon's opposition to the Linnaean system of classification, which was
based on a narrow set of "essential" anatomical features, would lead him
to develop an alternative system. He considered schemes that would take
into account an animal's physiology, ecology, functional anatomy (e.g.,
flying vs. swimming), behavior and geography. This approach ultimately
proved unwieldy, but it did make him sensitive to patterns often ignored
by Linnaean taxonomists.[4]

It is not easy to see today who was the more "modern" of the two.
While Linnaeus believed in the fixity of species, Buffon was convinced
that species were constantly changing; he regarded Linnaean classification as too confining and arbitrary to reflect the true state of the
natural world. In this sense, Buffon's approach directly presaged Darwin; indeed, Darwin would later acknowledge his debt to Buffon.

In the eighteenth century, Buffon's ideas seemed radically new.
While Linnaeus believed that animal species reflected ideal forms that
allowed for limited variation that did not change over time, Buffon
believed that animals did indeed change in response to their environment, although each animal came preprogrammed with a *moule
intérieur* (interior mold) that shaped their development. Since he believed that the natural world was constantly changing, Buffon saw
that "artificial" classification systems like Linnaeus's failed to allow
for this variation. Buffon found the Linnaean system overly constrain-
ing, and thought that deriving classification from the characteristics
of sexual organisms seemed too one-dimensional, failing to account
for the richness and variety of nature. Instead, Buffon wanted to classify animals by their "communities of origin."

Buffon was, in other words, an opponent of hierarchical systems.
He approached classification from the bottom up, assigning classifications based on empirical observation rather than top-down categories. Most importantly, he believed that these classifications could
change over time.

The scholarly rivalry between Linnaeus and Buffon spilled over
into personal animosity. Linnaeus chose to name a particularly foul-
smelling plant *Buffonia*. While history has relegated Buffon's theory
largely to obscurity, in its day the system commanded an influential
following among Europe's learned classes. The struggle between

Buffon's and Linnaeus's classifications swirled as one of that age's most active public debates.

Buffon's theory held one important corollary: that because species changed over time, they could also "degenerate" under adverse conditions. The discovery of such degenerate species would mark a resounding affirmation of his theory. Buffon believed he had found just such evidence in the form of the strange specimens coming back from the New World. In the *Histoire,* he wrote:

> In America, therefore, animated Nature is weaker, less active, and more circumscribed in the variety of her productions; for we perceive, from the enumeration of the American animals, that the numbers of species is not only fewer, but that, in general, all the animals are much smaller than those of the Old Continent. No American animal can be compared with the elephant, the rhinoceros, the hippopotamus, the dromedary, the camelopard [giraffe], the buffalo, the lion, the tiger, &c.[5]

Further, he noted that the New World appeared to have fewer species altogether—additional proof of that continent's intrinsic inferiority. Given the paucity of species and the apparent deteriorated state of existing specimens, the New World was therefore (his theory went) an intrinsically "degenerate" place.

Which brings us back to Jefferson's moose. As the recently appointed ambassador to France, Jefferson served as booster in chief for the young republic among the Parisian diplomatic set. He squarely faced the challenge Buffon had thrown down. Buffon's doctrine of American degeneracy undercut the young country's international standing. It was, Jefferson wrote, "within one step" of predicting that European immigrants would also degenerate in the New World. If true, what self-respecting European would consider picking up and relocating to such a place?

Jefferson had an especially keen fascination with the natural world. He had personally cataloged all the known plant species in the New World, compiled the 101 species of Virginia birds, filled his home in Monticello with an enormous collection of animal skulls and plant seeds, and kept exacting records of natural events around his home:

wind, temperatures, and 50 years' worth of data on the annual spring-time appearance of bugs and birds. Indeed, Jefferson was one of the primary contributors to the incoming flow of naturalist reports from the New World. His personal correspondence is peppered with disquisitions on naturalist topics ranging from philosophies of taxonomy to the genitalia of the mole.

In his *Notes on the State of Virginia*, Jefferson went to great lengths to disprove Buffon's contention that American animals were smaller (and therefore inferior) to their European counterparts. Jefferson castigated Buffon's theory of classification as a "no-system." He castigated Buffon as "the great advocate of individualism in opposition to classification. He would carry us back to the days and to the confusion of Aristotle and Pliny, give up the improvements of twenty centuries, and co-operate with the neologists in rendering the science of one generation useless to the next by perpetual changes of its language."[6]

Jefferson embraced the Linnaean classification system, which he felt "offered the three great desiderata: First, of aiding the memory to retain a knowledge of the productions of nature. Secondly, of rallying all to the same names for the same objects, so that they could communicate understandingly on them. And Thirdly, of enabling them, when a subject was first presented, to trace it by its character up to the conventional name by which it was agreed to be called." While Jefferson did not assert the Linnaean system to be intrinsically more accurate or true than other possible systems, he felt that its legitimacy derived largely from the sheer weight of its popularity.

> I adhere to the Linnean because it is sufficient as a ground-work, admits of supplementary insertions as new productions are discovered, and mainly because it has got into so general use that it will not be easy to displace it, and still less to find another which shall have the same singular fortune of obtaining the general consent. During the attempt we shall become unintelligible to one another, and science will be really retarded by efforts to advance it made by its most favorite sons. . . . And the higher the character of the authors . . . and the more excellent what they offer, the greater the danger of producing schism.[7]

Jefferson's argument came in the corpse of that moose. It stood at least a third taller than its continental cousin. This was clearly no "degenerate." It was a tangible refutation of Buffon's theory of American degeneracy and an implicit endorsement of Linnaean classification. Jefferson presented the moose to Buffon personally, along with a copy of his *Notes on the State of Virginia,* in which Jefferson demonstrated that domesticated animals were consistently larger in America than in Europe, and made a compelling case for biodiversity by demonstrating that America harbored four times more species of quadrupeds than Europe. Buffon was sufficiently impressed with Jefferson's argument that he promised to revise his theories. Unfortunately, Buffon died before completing the task.

Jefferson's endorsement of Linnaean classification would not mark the last time the gentleman from Monticello influenced the course of information science. Jefferson's legacy as a naturalist has long since faded in the shadow of his great contributions as a statesman—as president, vice president, and author of the Declaration of Independence and the Virginia Statute of Religious Freedom. Jefferson, however, prided himself first and foremost on being a naturalist. He is said to have considered it a higher honor to have been named president of the American Philosophical Society than to have been elected vice president of the United States. "Nature intended me for the tranquil pursuits of science," he once wrote, "by rendering them my supreme delight."

JEFFERSON'S LIBRARY

Almost 30 years after he left Paris, Jefferson would again make a final grand gesture with lasting effects on the structure of information systems. In the autumn of 1814 (after he had retired from the presidency), the British sacked Washington, destroying much of the federal government's physical infrastructure, including its nascent library. Just as previous wars had left burning libraries in their wake (see also Alexandria, the Aztecs, and the Chinese emperor Shi Huangdi), the British had tried to burn down the young nation's intellectual capital.

As Washington recovered from the British attack, Jefferson

penned a letter to his longtime friend Samuel H. Smith, then serving as chairman of the congressional Library Committee. Jefferson offered his entire personal library as a replacement for the Library of Congress.

Jefferson had amassed an enormous collection, much of it during his tenure in Paris, where he scoured local bookstores and established standing orders with book dealers in Amsterdam, Frankfurt, Madrid, and London. "[S]uch a collection was made as probably can never again be effected," wrote Jefferson. By 1814 Jefferson's library ranked among the largest private book collections in the world: 6,500 volumes, consisting of "what is chiefly valuable in science and literature generally, [it] extends more particularly to whatever belongs to the American statesman. In the diplomatic and parliamentary branches, it is particularly strong." His collection embodied a monumentally important transfer of knowledge between continents.

Fifty years in the making, Jefferson's library at Monticello constituted a formidable intellectual warehouse. Among the volumes Jefferson prized most were Milton's *Paradise Lost*, Sir Isaac Newton's *Optics*, works by Thomas More and Alexander Pope, numerous histories, and a 10-volume gardener's dictionary. He also had 20 copies of the Bible and two of the Koran.

Congress accepted Jefferson's offer but not without a bout of partisan intellectual wrangling. "The grand library of Mr. Jefferson will undoubtedly be purchased," wrote the *Boston Gazette*, "with all its finery and philosophical nonsense." Massachusetts Rep. Cyrus King, in high Puritan dudgeon, insisted that the collection be purged of "all books of an atheistical, irreligious, and immoral tendency." After a bout of acrimonious debate, the gentleman from Massachusetts eventually withdrew his objection. In this small gesture he may well have influenced the course of history.

Finally, Jefferson loaded his library on 10 wagons packed with pine bookcases for the trip from Monticello to Washington. "I hope it will not be without some general effect on the literature of our country," he later wrote.

While Jefferson's library was impressive in size, far more interesting was its complex semantic structure. At the time, libraries typically

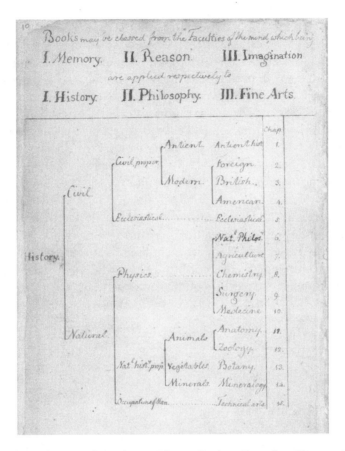

A page from Thomas Jefferson's 1783 Library Catalog. Reproduced by permission of the Massachusetts Historical Society, Boston, MA.
(See Appendix B for the full classification scheme.)

arranged their books by alphabetical order. In describing his own collection, Jefferson explained to Librarian of Congress George Watterston that he had abandoned the popular convention and chosen as his philosophical reference point "Lord Bacon's table of science," a hierarchical classification scheme that divided the whole of human knowledge into three broad categories: Memory (history), Reason (philosophy), and Imagination (fine arts).

Jefferson modified the scheme to suit his own needs, developing a permuted classification system that would sometimes classify books by subject, sometimes by chronology, "& sometimes a combination of both." It is worth noting that Jefferson's scheme, like so many other hierarchical classification systems, extends five levels deep, echoing the structure of ancient folk taxonomies.

Like Aristotle, Jefferson had created a great personal library, cataloged it, and then donated it as the foundation for a budding national library. And just as Aristotle's own library catalog, coupled with his writings on natural classification, would reverberate long after his passing, Jefferson exerted a similar influence on the intellectual underpinnings of the United States of America. He rarely receives the credit he deserves as a forefather of information science. Jefferson's decisions—embracing Linnaean taxonomy and Baconian empiricism over the competing theories of Buffon and others—set the stage for the information architecture of the young republic.

10

The Industrial Library

A library book . . . is not, then, an article of mere
consumption but fairly of capital.
Thomas Jefferson to James Madison, September 1821

In 1909 a Boston gentleman named Edmund Lester Pearson remarked on the proliferation of a new apparatus fast becoming a fixture in library reading rooms: the card catalog. "As these cabinets of
drawers increase in number," he wrote, "it seems as if the old joke
about the catalogues of the Boston Public Library and Harvard University meeting on Harvard Bridge might become literally true."[1]

The image of catalogs colliding seems an apt metaphor for the
bibliographical boom that was sweeping the library world. The Industrial Revolution had spawned more than factories, textile mills,
and Marxists. It had also transformed the economy of the written
word. New steam-driven mechanical presses were stamping out thousands of pages an hour, powering the rise of great publishing houses
that turned out books and newspapers in mass quantities, catering to
a growing market of newly literate readers (thanks to another industrial innovation: public education). Novels, magazines, pamphlets,
and all manner of printed artifacts sluiced through the literary mills.
Books became industrial products, even commodities.

Libraries struggled to keep pace. Before the nineteenth century
was out, they too would find themselves transformed into industrial-
ized institutions. Preindustrial libraries had been little more than gen-

teel reading rooms, staffed by learned gentleman curators who looked after modest collections of hand-bound leather volumes. Some university libraries employed a "professor of books," a descendent of the medieval *armarius*, to help guide the bookish student, but there were few "librarians" in the modern sense. Public libraries were all but unheard of; most libraries belonged to universities, learned societies, or private citizens (although some cities boasted private subscription-based libraries for upper-crust society men, like the Boston Athenæum). Those few libraries with collections large enough to warrant a catalog usually maintained an alphabetical list of holdings in leather-bound book catalogs. These were typically little more than inventories, designed to keep track of the collection and allow readers to locate a specific book on the shelf.

The industrialization of the printing press and the rise of a growing literate populace exerted severe pressures on these formerly placid institutions. In 1800 the library of the British Museum (precursor to the modern British Library) held 48,000 volumes. By 1833 the collection had quintupled to more than a quarter million.[2] As collections grew, libraries found it increasingly difficult to maintain their old leather-bound catalogs. Faced with rapidly growing collections, libraries inevitably started to mirror the industrial methods that were causing the disruption. Faced with processing backlogs and bulging catalogs, they succumbed to the inexorable logics of industrialization, seeking operating efficiencies, standardizing roles, and normalizing their data. As the nineteenth century progressed, the effects of industrialization would transform the enterprise of the library from a bookman's craft into a bibliographical assembly line.

Today, if you walk into almost any library, you will find what is still, at its core, a nineteenth-century institution. The primary feature of most libraries is still a set of long shelves populated by industrially printed books, organized according to a proscribed hierarchical system of call numbers, maintained by specially trained workers laboring in a highly regimented organizational system. The old card catalog may have given way to computer terminals, but the underlying organizational and ontological structures of the modern library have hardly changed at all. Librarians still follow cataloging practices that originated in the 1850s; library organizations are notoriously top-down, hierarchical, and process-oriented operations. And like steel mills, factories, secondary schools, and other institutional offspring of the nineteenth century, libraries are struggling to reinvent themselves in a postindustrial age.

To appreciate the legacy of the industrial library—and why it has proved such a durable fixture even in our digital age—we must look to where the revolution began: Great Britain.

In 1831 the British Museum hired Anthony Panizzi as its new assistant keeper of printed books. By this time there were already early rumblings of the industrial printing boom. Books were streaming in and so were readers. In 1759 the library had attracted five visitors a month. A century later there were 180 visitors a day. Changing conditions seemed to demand a radical rethinking of the library operation. Fortunately for the British Museum, the man they had just hired was no stranger to radical causes.

A lawyer by training, Panizzi had fled Italy after escaping arrest for his membership in a secret revolutionary group struggling to liberate Italy from the grips of the Austrian empire. After a dramatic getaway, Panizzi traveled all over Europe before landing in England. Although he would spend the rest of his life in exile, Panizzi never lost his revolutionary disposition. The fiery young Italian appears to have struck quite a figure among his staid British colleagues. One of his early biographers, Louis Fagan, describes him as "tall, thin and of dark complexion; in temper somewhat hot and hasty, but of calm and even judgment. . . . He must have been most diligent in his pursuit of knowledge, losing no opportunity of study, for he is described as constantly engaged in reading, even while walking from his house to the office."[3] In the years that followed, the energetic Panizzi would stir up more than his share of trouble with the British establishment, bringing his revolutionary zeal to bear in forming a new, highly politicized philosophy of librarianship and leaving behind a legacy of committed, socially engaged librarianship that still resonates today.

By the time Panizzi arrived, the British Museum's library catalog was in desperate need of an overhaul. In 1810 the printed catalog had run to 7 volumes; when Panizzi took over in 1831, it had bulged to 48 volumes, overflowing with inserts and scribbled errata. When the museum's commissioners asked their young hire to begin work on revising the catalog, they may have thought they were assigning a rote task to a junior employee. But Panizzi, the exiled radical, surprised everyone by coming back to propose the most ambitious revision to the catalog since Callimachus.

Panizzi saw the incoming flurry of books as more than just an inventory problem. He saw the makings of a larger opportunity for the cause of education and literacy. He wanted to reconceive the catalog in a new populist spirit. He began by introducing a subject catalog. While great libraries of the past had cataloged books by subject, no one had ever tried to create Panizzi's kind of comprehensive classification. He created a new schedule of tiered subject headings, a carefully constructed classification system that reflected the universalist ambitions of the British Empire at the height of its power. "Some would argue [the subject headings] were too ambitious," writes Elaine Svenonius, "that there was no need to construct elaborate Victorian edifices since jerrybuilt systems could meet the needs of most users most of the time."[4] But the introduction of subject headings at all marked a major philosophical step toward opening up the catalog to a broader audience.

In addition to subject headings, Panizzi introduced an important innovation that would allow the catalog to reveal the relationships between particular books. Panizzi explored a sophisticated and nuanced approach to modeling the implicit links between books, recognizing that "a book is a particular edition of a work, a part of a complex web of editions and translations, and that catalog users should be able to see these relationships even as they search for a particular book."[5] He felt the old catalog was too limited, linear, and one-dimensional, proposing instead a new, intricate set of rules for identifying additional "meta" information such as editions, publishers, dates, and places of publication. He introduced a total of 91 rules, covering a vast array of bibliographical scenarios. For example, he introduced the distinction between a "book" and a "work"—that is, between the physical edition and the intellectual property encoded within. That distinction marks a major conceptual leap in the practice of cataloging. By recognizing the dual nature of books as both physical objects and, separately, conveyors of meaning, he introduced an important layer of abstraction. Now librarians could separate the process of identification—locating a particular book on the shelf—and integration—situating the intellectual contents of a book within the topical cosmos of the larger collection. The great Library of Congress cataloger Seymour Lubetzky would later characterize Panizzi's insight as recognizing "the dichotomous character of the book, which, extrinsically, is a separate physical entity, an artifact unrelated to any other, but, intrinsically, a record of human thought and experience."[6] Panizzi's 91 rules would become the foundation for the Anglo-American Cataloging Rules, still in widespread use today.

While Panizzi's painstakingly detailed rules may seem abstruse and esoteric—the stuff of bureaucratic make-work—Panizzi saw his rules as anything but quotidian. For him the rules embodied the fulfillment of a higher political purpose. Creating a more usable catalog was no exercise in ontological hairsplitting; it was, in fact, an act of revolution. He wanted to open the library up beyond its traditional audience of privileged men of letters to attract a new class of common readers who initially might know little about books. "I want the poor student to have the same means of indulging his learned curiosity," he wrote, "of following his rational pursuits, of consulting the same authorities, of fathoming the most intricate inquiry as the richest man in the kingdom." He took this populist credo a step farther, arguing that Britain owed as much to its citizens. "I contend that the government is bound to give the most liberal and unlimited assistance in this respect."[7] Like Diderot, Panizzi was a devout populist willing to stake out a provocative social agenda.

Panizzi's radical vision did not sit entirely well with the British literary establishment. Soon after he introduced his rules, he met with a stout backlash from some of the library's most eminent patrons. One influential reader, Sir Nicholas Harris Nicolas, wrote a withering attack on the new catalog for *The Spectator*, deriding the "exotic capriccios" of the young Italian librarian. Particularly galling to many of the library's longtime readers was Panizzi's insistence on a new procedure for requesting books from the shelves. Previously, readers had simply scribbled book titles on any handy piece of paper and handed it to a desk clerk. Panizzi insisted that readers now had to fill out a printed form, requiring them to consult the catalog to request books by call number (or "pressmarks," as they were then known). This trifling bit of bureaucratic process creep sparked a small outrage among some of the library's more prominent patrons. "We know the inconvenience attending this obligation is felt by many literary men," wrote Nicolas, "whose time is of value to them. . . . [N]o more should be expected of a Reader than to specify the book he wants by its title, and that all besides belongs to the librarian." Panizzi seemed to be putting the burden on readers, but in truth he was actually trying to make the structure of the library more transparent, so that readers could mine the collection for themselves.

Panizzi's ambitious catalog took far longer than expected to produce, further angering his opponents. Literary worthies like Thomas Carlyle railed against the project: "Elaborate catalogues are not what we require," he wrote. At hearings before the Royal Commission, Carlyle fretted that the library would flounder without a simpler and more quickly produced catalog and that it would become "a Polyphemus without any eye in his head." Carlyle, it should be noted, harbored a personal animus toward Panizzi. He felt that the library staff had failed to support him effectively while he was doing research at the library, and he took his grudge out on Panizzi. Panizzi informed Carlyle that he had received the same level of support as every other user of the library. That came as an outright affront to the famous man, and Carlyle was incensed. He was no ordinary reader, after all; he was the most famous writer in England. Despite the ongoing public criticism, the library commissioners stood by Panizzi, eventually forbidding the library trustees from interfering with the library's cataloging decisions—and thus ensuring the transformation not just of the British Museum library but of all libraries.

Panizzi's catalog, born of the industrial age, would usher in a new era of democratic access to libraries worldwide. When the catalog was finally published in the 1850s, it became enormously popular as a reference work in its own right. The first edition sold 5,000 copies; a subsequent revision was published in 20,000 copies—a testament to

the unprecedented public interest in the new catalog. For all its tribu-
lations, Panizzi's catalog would go down as a landmark in the history
of library science. Walk into any public library today and you can still
see the visible echoes of Panizzi's revolution at work.

CUTTER'S CLASSIFICATION

As the industrial wave extended across the Atlantic, American libraries experienced the same growing pains as their British counterparts.
Unlike the established great libraries of Europe, America's libraries
had no lingering aristocratic class to contend with. From the outset a
populist ethos would guide the development of American library
catalogs.

In Boston the great American cataloger Charles Ammi Cutter
pioneered a new way of cataloging books for the public. A devout
populist and egalitarian, Cutter believed that the highest purpose of a
library catalog should be to serve "common usage," a philosophy that
stood in stark contrast to the predominant European view (Panizzi
notwithstanding) that library catalogs existed primarily to serve the
needs of scholars. Like Panizzi, Cutter viewed his library calling as the
fruition of a higher purpose. But Cutter was no political firebrand; he
saw cataloging as more of a spiritual pursuit. A former divinity student, Cutter envisioned himself as one of the "humble servants of the
Gospel of learning, of knowledge, of science" and espoused his commitment to the "pastoral side of librarianship."[8]

First as a librarian at Harvard and later at the Boston Athenæum,
Cutter introduced a series of innovations. Like Panizzi, Cutter embraced subject cataloging as the key to liberating the contents of the
catalog and making them accessible to the common reader. He recognized that unlike scholarly readers, many public library patrons did
not arrive with lists of specific book titles; rather, they often came
with nothing more than a vague question in mind. The library, then,
would succeed or fail based on the usability of its subject catalog.

In his *Rules for a Dictionary Catalog*, Cutter proposed a new multidimensional catalog system, which he dubbed the Expansive Classification System. It was more sophisticated than Panizzi's system. It

provided a mechanism for describing books by author, title, and sub-ject, but its main feature was an elaborate multitiered subject scheme. Cutter's system drew distinctions between high-level "classes" (like, say, history) and "individual subjects" (say, the history of the Peloponnesian War). Using this system, librarians would assign call numbers using letters of the alphabet in one- or two-letter combina-tions, each letter or combination of letters representing a particular subject; more granular topics could be assigned using sequences of numbers. For example, WP83 stood for United States Painting: "W" for Fine Arts, "WP" for Painting, and "83" for United States.

Cutter's Expansive Classification

A	Reference; General works
B	Philosophy
BR	Religion
C	Christianity, Judaism
D	Ecclesiastical history
E	Biography
F	History
G	Geography
H	Social Sciences
I	Sociology
J	Government, Politics
K	Law
L	General science; Physical sciences
M	Natural history
N	Botany
O-P	Zoology
Q	Medicine
R	Useful Arts
S	Engineering; Building
T	Manufacturing
U	Military
V	Recreation (sports, theater, music)
W	Fine arts
X	Languages
Y	Literature
YF	Fiction
Z	Book arts; Bibliography

Cutter's system also recognized the practical limitations of a one-size-fits-all system, acknowledging that different-sized libraries called for different cataloging solutions. He designed his system to scale up or down by releasing it as a seven-tiered system, with the lowest level of classification appropriate for small libraries and the seventh level for large research collections. Despite his hope for a system that would work equally well for small public libraries and large academic collections, Cutter would see his scheme eclipsed by the subsequent success of the Dewey Decimal System, which became the established standard for public libraries. But Cutter's framework lives on in the form of the Library of Congress catalog, also the de facto standard for academic libraries, which use a two-letter scheme derived directly from Cutter's work. Today, academic library catalogers still assign "Cutter numbers" to new books.

In addition to his breakthrough cataloging work, Cutter introduced a technical innovation that would soon take hold in libraries worldwide: the card catalog. While he did not invent the card catalog,[9] he recognized its value and advocated it as a logical replacement for the traditional bound catalog. Cutter developed his own makeshift card catalog for the Boston Athenæum. The device would soon gain a wider following, thanks to the energetic efforts of Cutter's friend and eventual rival, Melvil Dewey.

DEWEY'S DISMAL DECIMALS

While Cutter ranked as perhaps the preeminent librarian of his day, his historic contribution has long since been overshadowed by Dewey, whose eponymous decimal system is now in use at almost every public library in the United States (and many abroad). While most nonlibrarians know of Dewey only by virtue of his ubiquitous call numbers, the man's legacy casts a long shadow over the whole enterprise of modern librarianship. Almost single-handedly, Dewey exerted a profound influence over the trajectory of American libraries. He founded the first library school at Columbia, cofounded (with Cutter) the American Library Association, and set in motion a process of standardization that would enable the great expansion and influence of libraries in American life. Paradoxically, his industrious efforts on behalf of American libraries were predicated in no small part on curtailing the power of librarians.

One of his most visible achievements, the standardized card catalog, serves as a perfect metaphor for Dewey's legacy. Dewey saw the catalog, like the library, as in essence a great machine. By standardizing its operations—introducing interchangeable parts, establishing consistent standards and practices, and normalizing variations—he saw the hope for a more perfect system. Catalog cards, like librarians, would function as distributed cogs in a great national system of Dewey's devising.

Dewey was obsessed with efficiency. He even changed his name from "Melville" to "Melvil" as a time-saving gesture and briefly even changed his last name to "Dui." He once scolded his secretary for wishing him a good morning, admonishing her for such a frivolous use of time that could otherwise have been spent doing work.

In hopes of recruiting more pliant librarians willing to follow directions and conform to his desire for implementing a centralized scheme, Dewey actively encouraged the recruitment of women into the profession. He believed that women were more likely to acquiesce to implementing his system rather than devising their own (Dewey was, by modern standards, an unreconstructed chauvinist). However offensive such sentiments might strike many of us today, his strategy seems to have worked, at least in part: Today women make up the overwhelming majority of American librarians.

Dewey's relentless efforts to create a unified national library system, magnified by his considerable ambition, would prove a potent mix that yielded lasting consequences for American libraries. Dewey's obsession with efficiency and his strong bent for hierarchical management made him an ideal agent of the industrial age. While his energetic efforts exerted a lasting impact on libraries—many of them salutary—his hyper-controlling personality exerted an unfortunate influence over the subsequent history of American librarians, who have long struggled with excessive bureaucratization and a process-centric work culture that regularly leaves libraries struggling to adapt in a world of fast-changing information technologies. Dewey's tireless efforts may have ultimately yielded many public benefits but they proved a mixed blessing for librarians, many of whom spend their careers chafing under the often stultifying management culture that Dewey played a large part in fostering.

When Dewey introduced his cataloging system for the first time in 1876, he tried to attract interest by touting its economic benefits. "The usefulness of these libraries might be greatly increased without additional expenditure," he wrote, "for with [the Dewey Decimal System's] aid, the catalogues, shelf lists, indexes, and cross-references essential to this increased usefulness, can be made more economically than by any other method which he has been able to find."[10] For American libraries to move forward, Dewey believed, they had to abandon idiosyncratic local practices and adopt common standards. The economic argument was apparent on its face; the continuing explosion of printed books demanded efficiency and promised libraries the opportunity to expend their resources on public service rather than maintaining homegrown catalogs. The adaptation of national standards promised a simple economy of scale. By supplanting the unpredictable judgment of willful librarians with the logic of a centrally administered system, libraries could function more efficiently, expanding their reach by yielding some of their autonomy. It was a classic industrial value proposition, straight from the factory floor: constricting individual autonomy in service of the greater ideal of productivity.

In its original incarnation the Dewey Decimal System called for organizing books into nine top-level "classes," each with a corresponding beginning number (1 for Philosophy, 2 for Theology, and so on). Each class was further subdivided into ten "divisions," which in turn were subdivided into 1,000 distinct headings. The system's original divisions included:

0	GENERAL
100	PHILOSOPHY
200	THEOLOGY
300	SOCIOLOGY
400	PHILOLOGY

500	NATURAL SCIENCE
600	USEFUL ARTS
700	FINE ARTS
800	LITERATURE
900	HISTORY

(See Appendix C for the complete Dewey classification.)

The top-down determinism of the Dewey Decimal System has drawn its share of critics, who deride the classification as overly simplistic and riddled with cultural bias. Nowhere are its biases more explicit than in its self-evident favoritism toward Christianity. For example, within the Theology class, divisions 200-280 are devoted to Christian denominations, while Judaism and Islam must make do with a single number each (296 and 297, respectively). Dewey, in his own defense, readily admitted that his system was far from perfect. "Theoretically, the division of every subject into just nine heads is absurd," he wrote. "Practically, it is desirable."[11]

Whatever its shortcomings, the Dewey Decimal System has proved remarkably resilient over the years. Although it undergoes periodic revision, its basic contours have remained unchanged for more than a century. It remains the standard in public libraries throughout the United States (and in many other countries). While many academic libraries use the more complex Library of Congress Cataloging system, the Dewey system has outlasted numerous competing systems. It has also survived the transition from the old card catalog to the new online catalogs now in service at most public libraries.

While physical card catalogs have all but disappeared from most libraries, the imprint of Dewey's industrial library lives on. Most electronic catalogs are in truth simply digitized card catalogs, employing the same bibliographic standards (known in library circles as the MARC format) and cataloging techniques devised for the old card catalogs. The seemingly modern Internet-connected online catalog is a living relic of the nineteenth century.

In recent years Web pundits have invoked Dewey's catalog as an exemplar of the kind of anachronistic, top-down, institutional ontology the Internet so effectively subverts. While Dewey's system surely represents a vestige of industrial age mind-set, it is somewhat unfair to dismiss it as simplistically hierarchical. Although the system does provide seemingly rigid categories, it also allows for access through multiple points of entry, such as cross-referenced subject headings; and critics who deride the one-dimensionality of its numbering scheme tend to overlook the fact that the system actually does provide multidimensional access. But the system's enduring strength lies in its simplicity and transparency. Almost anyone can grasp the system; it is easy to implement and easy to use. Like the most successful products of the industrial age, it enjoys mass appeal. As we move into the digital era, however, the value of mass appeal is starting to diminish.

In an era of networked systems, rigid hierarchies are becoming less practical than fluid systems able to adapt to the needs of emergent communities. The industrial virtues of mass appeal and transparency are ceding ground to the digital virtues of flexibility and reconfigurability. On these counts, Dewey's system falls short. In the age of the Internet search engine, the Dewey catalog looks increasingly anachronistic, and almost certainly pressure will continue to mount on libraries to reengineer their old industrial ontologies.

As entrenched as the Dewey system may now seem, it competed with alternative cataloging systems throughout the late nineteenth and early twentieth centuries. Cutter never liked the system, arguing that "its notation would not afford that minuteness of classification which experience taught me to be needed in our library. I did not like (and I do not like) Mr. Dewey's classification."[12] In addition to Cutter's system, other classifications like the Bliss system, the Universal Decimal Classification (see Chapter 11), and the Library of Congress system all vied for the attention of libraries—indeed, all of them are still in use somewhere in the world. These systems all shared a similarity of approach, relying on a set of descriptive cataloging rules and a hierarchical schedule of subject headings. They also shared the same fundamental limitation: a reliance on proscriptive subject cataloging. In other words, they relied on the efforts of librarians to identify and anticipate the universe of possible subjects. As the universe of available subjects continued to expand, however, this labor-intensive approach began to show cracks in its conceptual seams.

RANGANATHAN'S FACETS

In the 1930s the visionary Indian librarian Shiyali Ramamrita Ranganathan proposed an entirely new approach to cataloging. While his system would fail to catch on, his idea has since proved portentous. As the librarian at Madras University and a prolific writer on library theory (he coined the term "library science" in 1931), Ranganathan wrote a series of books outlining a new model of cataloging known as faceted (or analytico-synthetic) classification. Faceted classification allows for more nuance and specific categories than simple hierarchical subject schemes, by supporting descriptions based on multivalent characteristics, rather than on a single top-down deterministic list of subjects. Ranganathan's Colon Classification (see Appendix D) described a framework by which any document could be broken down in terms of five facets: personality, matter, energy, space, and time. These facets could then be combined and interpolated to describe any piece of information in almost endlessly reconfigurable ways.

For example, a faceted classification of a book about management of the London stock exchange until 1975 might look like this:

Facet	Description	Examples
Personality	Primary attribute	Economics
Matter	Physical characteristics	Stock Exchanges
Energy	Processes or actions	Management
Space	Location	London
Time	Period or duration	1975

Using the faceted system, subject entries could then be generated by taking any of the major facets as a starting point and interpolating the other facets as qualifiers. It is literally multifaceted. The above example might appear in a catalog in any of the following ways:

Economics.
Stock Exchanges. Management. London. 1975.

Stock Exchanges.
Economics. Management. London. 1975.

Management.
Economics. Stock Exchanges. London. 1975.

London.
Economics. Stock Exchanges. Management. 1975.

1975.
Economics. Stock Exchanges. Management. London.

The system thus allows for a multidimensional subject classification that assumes no particular orientation on the part of the user. Using Ranganathan's system, any item can be described in a highly specific way yet without imposing a deterministic subject hierarchy. It is a bottom-up classification, rather than a top-down ontology.

Despite its limited real-world track record, Ranganathan's model has exerted a significant influence, especially on the development of the Library of Congress Subject Headings, which support a limited implementation of faceted classification. In recent years, faceted classification has also acquired considerable cachet in computer programming circles, largely because it lends itself so easily to relational database implementations. At the University of California at Berkeley's School of Information, researchers have developed a system called Flamenco that allows users to search and browse a collection of 35,000 images from the fine arts collection cataloged by using hierarchical faceted metadata. Commercial software companies like Endeca are marketing Web-based software tools that apply the theory of facets to practical knowledge management applications. Ranganathan's vision has proved particularly well suited to Web-based search applications because it lends itself to the kind of iterative querying on which so many Web users have learned to rely.

While Ranganathan enjoys a resurgent reputation among software developers and remains widely admired by librarians, his original Colon Classification failed to catch on. The system has never been fully implemented outside India but remains a kind of Platonic object for many librarians and information scientists. Perhaps the simplistic hierarchies of the Dewey and Cutter systems, for all their ontological limitations, exert a deeper psychic pull, invoking our ancient reliance on hierarchical information systems. Could the epigenetic rules of classification (see Chapter 2) dispose us toward simpler top-down systems, even as our rational minds recognize the evident superiority of the endless reconfigurability of facets?

INFORMATION AS "SCIENCE"

As libraries continued to proliferate in the early twentieth century, many of them also became more specialized. A new breed of narrowly focused libraries began to appear: newspaper libraries, business libraries, biology libraries, and so forth. At the beginning of the twentieth century, a new professional field of "special libraries" began to emerge. While Victorian-era librarians concerned themselves almost exclusively with the organization of books, special librarians saw their roles in a different light, less as book curators and more as active participants in organizational ecologies of information. In 1915 the American librarian Ethel Johnson wrote: "The main function of the general library is to make books available. The function of the special library is to make information available."[13] In 1909 a group of these librarians banded together to form the Special Libraries Association. One of its early members, Aksel G. S. Josephson, predicted that eventually librarians "might come to the point where special libraries will not even have whole books, but only such parts of many books as it needs, treating books as well as periodicals on the principle of documentation."[14] That principle, predicated on liberating the contents of books from the confines of their physical volumes—harkening back to Panizzi's original distinction between the book and the work—anticipates the promise of the digital era, the liberation of texts from their physical confines. A new term began to gain currency: "documentation."

The so-called documentalist movement marked the beginnings of a trend that would unfold over the coming century. Library workers were recasting their traditional responsibilities to take on a more active role in the production of intellectual capital. They no longer saw themselves as cogs in an industrial machine like Dewey's but instead as what we might today call "knowledge workers." In 1910, Arthur D. Little librarian Guy E. Marion articulated this emerging vision in his article "The Library as an Adjunct to the Industrial Laboratory" in which he describes the nontraditional "specific nature of the laboratory library" as trafficking in an ever-shifting mix of "textbooks, specialists' pamphlets, trade catalogs, reference works, maps, etc." The mission of the special library extended beyond the acquisition of data from outside the organization, however; these libraries were also deeply involved in collecting data from inside the organization. "[T]here is a vast bulk of data which we may properly call acquired." Internal reports, employee correspondence, laboratory test results, technical reports, and client communications all added up to "the accumulated results of the internal life of the laboratory itself. In fact, this acquired data is unquestionably for the laboratory library the most valuable part of the information."[15]

This emerging role as an information clearinghouse augured a shift of organizational focus for libraries, bringing them directly into the value chain of the industrial enterprise. The emerging special libraries were no longer passive institutions but were now active participants in the production of information. As the twentieth century progressed, innovations like microfilm and punchcards soon opened the door to new ways of working with information. On the eve of the digital age, the documentalists had started to anticipate the transformations that would soon reshape the industrial world.

TOWARD A VIRTUAL LIBRARY

In 1883 Cutter wrote a futuristic essay entitled "The Buffalo Public Library in 1983." Imagining what a library might look like in 100 years, he envisioned readers sitting at desks equipped with "a little keyboard" through which they could connect with a central electronic

catalog, ordering books from the stacks by punching in a call number. He even foresaw networks of libraries connected by a
"fonographic foil" that would enable them to communicate tele-
graphically, accessing each other's collections so readily that "all the
libraries in the country . . . are practically one library."[16] He missed
the mark by less than a decade.

11

The Web That Wasn't

So much has been written about the World Wide Web that it scarcely seems productive to try to say anything new about what may be the most documented—and self-documenting—phenomenon in human history. After less than two decades, Tim Berners-Lee's invention already ranks with Gutenberg's press as a technology of epochal importance. Some futurists have even suggested that the emergence of the Web signals an event of evolutionary significance for our species. While it is still much too early to divine the Web's ultimate impact, there is no question that Tim Berners-Lee's invention has already established itself a world-changing technology.

The Web's astonishing ascent has also lent it an aura of historical inevitability, as if the past century's advances in computing somehow pointed to it all along. If the theory of natural selection teaches us anything, however, it is that evolution rarely runs in a straight line. Just as the fossil record is littered with false starts, dead ends, and unexpected adaptations, so the history of human information systems is largely a story of unpredictable outcomes. Writing emerged as a form of bookkeeping, after all; it took thousands of years for people to start writing stories. At this early stage of Web history, it seems impossible to forecast its ultimate effects. We might do well to remember, however, that throughout human history the information technologies that mattered most rarely left halcyon outcomes in their wake; for the most part, they left trails of wrenching disruption: burned-out libraries, once-civilized nations regressing into illiteracy, and episodes of blood-curdling violence. For all the populist optimism surrounding today's Web, a happy ending is far from guaranteed.

While the Web's long-term trajectory may be impossible to project, we can look for clues to its near future by mining its recent history. Just as the Gutenberg revolution effectively started well before Johannes Gutenberg invented his printing press, so the Internet revolution is really the culmination of a series of precursor events. As far back as the 1890s, inventors were already developing new mechanical approaches to coping with a growing flood of published data. Those experiments percolated for the next several decades with occasionally promising results, but more often leading to frustrating dead ends. As the modern computer industry took shape in the years following World War II, however, computer scientists began developing new hypotheses that broke from the old physical reference points of libraries, catalogs, and indexes to map out a new kind of virtual information space that could take advantage of the emerging digital medium.

Taken together, these early networked technologies not only shed light on how the Web came to be, but they also present alluring visions of how things might have turned out differently. By exploring the history of the "Web that wasn't," we can find glimpses of a Web that might have been and, perhaps, clues to a Web that may yet be.

THE FORGOTTEN FOREFATHER

One rainy afternoon in 1968 a young Australian graduate student named Boyd Rayward stepped into an abandoned office in the Parc Leopold in Brussels, Belgium. Inside, he discovered "a cluttered, musty, cobwebbed office into which the rain leaked—and one day flooded—causing the attendant then on hand to have a kind of epileptic seizure."[1] Piled high to the ceiling were dusty stacks of books, files, and manuscripts: the intellectual flotsam of a seemingly disorganized old scholar.

The previous occupant, Paul Otlet, had been dead for nearly 25 years. A bibliographer, pacifist, and entrepreneur, Otlet in his heyday had been feted as a great man, enjoying the company of Nobel laureates and even playing a role in the formation of the League of Nations. But by the time of his death in 1944, he had lived long enough to see his reputation fade to near-obscurity, witness the failure of his greatest ambition, and suffer the final humiliation of watching the Nazis cart away and destroy much of his life's work. When he died a few months before the end of war, hardly anyone noticed. So ended the legacy of the Internet's forgotten forefather.

In 1934, years before Vannevar Bush dreamed of the Memex and decades before Doug Engelbart and Ted Nelson pioneered the possibility of hypertext information retrieval, Otlet had already delivered a stunningly prescient prophesy of a new kind of networked, multimedia-rich information space:

> Here, the workspace is no longer cluttered with any books. In their place, a screen and a telephone within reach. Over there, in an immense edifice, are all the books and information. From there, the page to be read . . . is made to appear on the screen. The screen could be divided in half, by four, or even by ten, if multiple texts and documents had to be consulted simultaneously. . . . Cinema, phonographs, radio, television: these instruments, taken as substitutes for the book, will in fact become the new book, the most powerful works for the diffusion of human thought. This will be the radiated library, and the televised book.[2]

Otlet imagined a day when users would access databases of recorded information from great distances by means of an "electric telescope," retrieving facsimile images to be projected remotely on a flat screen. At the center of this electronic nexus, Otlet imagined a new kind of scholar's workstation: a moving desk shaped like a wheel, powered by a network of hinged spokes beneath a series of moving surfaces. The machine would let users search, read, and write their way through a vast mechanical database. This new research environment would do more than just let users retrieve documents; it would also let them annotate the relationships between them, "the connections each [document] has with all other [documents], forming from them what might be called the Universal Book."

Otlet's vision rested not just on communications technology but on brilliant insights into the possibility of stitching otherwise discrete bits of information together, creating semantic relationships that would allow users to navigate from one resource to another across an electronic network. In 1934 the notion of networked documents was still so novel that no one had a word to describe such relationships, until Otlet invented one: "links." He envisioned the whole endeavor as a great "*réseau*": a web.

Otlet's idea relied on a new classification framework that, he believed, could succeed where other "universal" classifications had failed. Generations of philosophers had tried to solve the problem of universal classification—including Bacon, Diderot, and Wilkins—in the nineteenth century. The industrialization of printing, coupled with the advent of cheap binding materials, had spurred an explosion in publishing no less disruptive than the advent of Gutenberg's press 400 years earlier. Faced with an onslaught of new texts, nineteenth-century scholars and bibliographers had wrestled again with the problem of classification. Catalogers like Panizzi, Dewey, and Ranganathan had made great headway in systematizing subject headings, laying the foundations of modern library and information science. With the profusion of printed books, the prospects for a viable universal catalog were growing dim.

In 1895 Otlet and Henri La Fontaine established the *Repertoire Bibliographique Universel*, an ambitious attempt at developing a master bibliography of the world's accumulated knowledge. Otlet recognized from the beginning that the success of the project would depend on the scalability of its classification system. After evaluating the popular systems then in use, including the Dewey Decimal System and Panizzi's scheme for the British Museum, Otlet realized that they all shared a fatal flaw: They were designed to guide readers as far as the individual book—but no further. This was an epiphany with potentially revolutionary implications.

Ranganathan had voiced the ethos of modern cataloging when

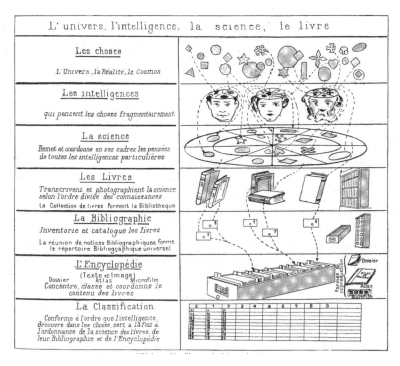

Illustration from Otlet's *Traité de documentation* (1934).

he said, "every reader his or her book, and every book its reader." But once book and reader were matched, they were left pretty well to their own devices. Otlet wanted to go a step further. He wanted to penetrate the boundaries of the books themselves, to unearth the "substance, sources and conclusions" inside. Taking Dewey's system as his starting point, Otlet began developing what came to be known as the Universal Decimal Classification (UDC), now widely recognized as the first—and one of the only—full implementations of a faceted classification system. While Ranganathan deserves credit as the philosophical forbearer of facets, Otlet was the first to put them to practical use. Today, the UDC comprises over 62,000 classes, and has been translated into over 30 languages (one reason for its popularity outside the United States).

In addition to a set of Main Tables for subject headings, the UDC supports a series of Auxiliary Tables allowing for the addition of facets. These tables provide notations for place, language, and physical characteristics and for marking relationships between topics using a set of connector signs such as "+," "/," and ":". The UDC's capacity for mapping relationships between ideas—for constructing the "social space" of a document—provides a dimension of use not supported in other purely topical classification schemes. As the Universal Decimal Classification Consortium puts it:

> UDC's most innovative and influential feature is its ability to express not just simple subjects but relations between subjects.... In UDC, the universe of information (all recorded knowledge) is treated as a coherent system, built of related parts, in contrast to a specialised classification, in which related subjects are treated as subsidiary even though in their own right they may be of major importance.[3]

In 1910, in the wake of the Brussels world's fair, Otlet and La Fontaine created an installation, called *Mundaneum*, at the *Palais du Cinquantenaire* of the *Palais Mondial*. Originally envisioned as the centerpiece of a new "city of the intellect," the *Mundaneum* was to be the hub of a utopian city that housed a society of the world's nations. Otlet successfully lobbied the Belgian government to provide a new home for the *Mundaneum*. Not coincidentally, the Belgian government had just launched a lobbying campaign to host the nascent League of Nations's new headquarters. Hoping to help his country take center stage in wooing the new organization, Otlet managed to secure a wing of a government building in Brussels to incubate his operation, assembling a vast "documentary edifice" that eventually comprised over 12 million individual index cards and documents. At the time the index card represented the latest advance in information storage technology: a standardized, easily manipulated vessel for housing individual nuggets of data. So, Otlet's *réseau* began taking shape in the form of an enormous collection of index cards, arranged in a sprawling array of cabinets.

The effort met with early success, even attracting a healthy mail-

FONCTIONS DU TRAVAIL SCIENTIFIQUE

ⒶCONSERVATION DE LA SCIENCE
[DOCUMENTATION UNIVERSELLE]
1. AU CENTRE
(BIBLIOTHEQUE
BIBLIOGRAPHIE
ENCYCLOPÉDIE
MUSÉE
2. RÉSEAU D'OFFICES DE DOCUMENTATION

ⒷDIFFUSION DE LA SCIENCE
a) UNIVERSITÉ INTERNATIONALE
b) PROPAGANDE SCIENTIFIQUE ET OPINION PUBLIQUE
1. UNIVERSITÉ CENTRALE
2. TOURS UNIVERSITAIRES

ⒸRECHERCHES SCIENTIFIQUES
1. LABORATOIRES CENTRAUX
2. SECTIONS INTERNATIONALES DANS LES LABORATOIRES NATIONAUX

ⒹUNIFICATION

ⒺPUBLICATIONS
1. PUBLICATIONS INTERNATIONALES
2. SECTIONS ÉTRANGÈRES ET COMPARÉES DANS LES PUBLICATIONS NATIONALES

ⒻDISCUSSIONS SCIENTIFIQUES
ASSOCIATIONS ET ACADÉMIES
1. ASSOCIATIONS INTERNATIONALES
2. SECTION DE RELATIONS INTERN DANS LES ASSOCIATIONS NATIONALES

ⒼAPPLICATIONS DE LA SCIENCE

ÉTATS (U.S.A.) FRANCE / EUROPE / CENTRALE / ANGLETERRE &c
0 1 2 3 4 5 6 7 8 9

GÉNÉRALITÉS — PHILOSOPHIE — THÉOLOGIE — SOCIOLOGIE — PHI LOL — SCIENCES NATUR ELLES — SCIENCES APPLIQUÉES — BEAUX-ARTS — LITTÉRATURE — HISTOIRE GÉOGRA PHIE

"L'organisation mondiale du Travail intellectuel," from Otlet's *Traité de documentation* (1934).

order business, in which users submitted search queries for a fee (27 francs per 1,000 cards retrieved). The service attracted more than 1,500 requests a year on subjects ranging from boomerangs to Bulgarian finance. But by 1924 the Belgian government had lost patience with the project, especially after the newly formed League of Nations chose Geneva over Brussels as its headquarters—thus robbing the *Mundaneum* of one of its primary raisons d'etre. Otlet had to relinquish his original location, moving the *Mundaneum* to a succession of smaller quarters, even landing briefly, ignominiously, in a parking garage. After a series of fiscal struggles and management missteps, Otlet finally faced the difficult but unavoidable choice of shutting down the operation in 1934. A few years later Nazi troops stormed in and carted it all away, to make way for an exhibition of Third Reich art.

After Otlet's death in 1944, what survived of the original *Mundaneum* was left to languish in an old anatomy building of the Free University in the *Parc Leopold*, all but forgotten for three decades, until Boyd Rayward found his way into Otlet's old office. Over the ensuing half-century, more than 70 tons of its original contents were destroyed. Finally, in the mid-1990s a group of volunteers began resurrecting Otlet's original vision, hoping to preserve and refurbish the original *Mundaneum*. In 1996 the new *Mundaneum* opened in Mons, Belgium, to preserve Otlet's legacy and his vision of the "Universal Book." While today's *Mundaneum* serves primarily as a museum and learning center rather than as a working incarnation of Otlet's original plan, the new institution does an admirable job of perpetuating his legacy and reminding us of Otlet's premonitory vision of a worldwide networked information environment.

In a bitter irony, the *Mundaneum*'s 1934 closure coincided almost exactly with the publication of Otlet's masterwork, the *Traité de documentation*, a manifesto crystallizing 40 years' worth of writing and research into the possibilities of networked information structures. Rayward describes the *Traité* as "perhaps the first systematic, modern discussion of general problems of organising information." With the faceted philosophy of the UDC as backdrop, the *Traité* posited a universal "law of organization" declaring that no document could ever be fully understood by itself, but that its meaning becomes clarified through mining its relationship with other documents. "[A]ll bibliological creation," he said, "no matter how original and how powerful, implies redistribution, combination and new amalgamations."[4]

While that sentiment may sound postmodernist in spirit, Otlet was no semiotician; he simply believed that documents could best be understood as three-dimensional things, with the third dimension being their social context: their relationship to place, time, language, as well as other readers, writers, and topics. Otlet believed in the possibility of empirical truth, or what he called "facticity"—a property that emerged over time, and through the ongoing collaboration between readers and writers. In Otlet's world each user would leave an imprint, a trail, which would then become part of the explicit history of each document.

Vannevar Bush and Ted Nelson would later voice strikingly similar ideas about the notion of associative "trails" between documents. Distinguishing Otlet's vision from the later ideas of Bush, Nelson, and Berners-Lee is the conviction—long since fallen out of favor—in the possibility of a universal subject classification working in concert with the mutable social forces of scholarship. Otlet's vision suggests an intellectual cosmos illuminated by both objective classification and the direct influence of readers and writers: a system simultaneously ordered and self-organizing and endlessly reconfigurable by the individual reader.

Jorge Luis Borges's fictional Library of Babel was a place containing "all the possible combinations of the twenty-odd orthographical symbols . . . the translation of every book in all languages, the interpolations of every book in all books." For Borges the universal library was a literary conceit. For Otlet it was an achievable dream: an "edifice containing all the books and the information together with all the resources of space needed to record and manage them." Otlet also recognized the practical importance of "search and retrieval performed by an appropriately qualified permanent staff." Substitute the word "Google" for "permanent staff," and Otlet's vision starts sounding a lot like the World Wide Web.

While it would be an exaggeration to claim that Otlet exerted any direct influence on the later development of the Web, it would be no exaggeration to say that he anticipated many of the problems bedeviling the Web today: the explosion of published information, the limitations of fixed documents, and the opportunities for scholarship that open up when readers can penetrate the "meta" content surrounding a document to get at the contents inside. In the Web's current incarnation, individual "authors" (including both individuals and institutions) exert direct control over fixed documents. Each document is essentially a fait accompli, with its own self-determined set of relationships to other documents. It takes a meta-application like Google or Yahoo! to discover the broader relationships between documents (usually through some combination of syntax, semantics, and reputation). But those relationships, however sophisticated the algorithm, remain largely unexposed to the end user, never becoming an explicit part of the document's history. In Otlet's vision those pathways constituted vital information, making up the third dimension of social context that made his system so potentially revolutionary.

Would Otlet's Web have turned out any differently? We may yet find out. The explosive growth of socially driven Web applications—like secondlife.com, MySpace.com, Flickr.com, and del.icio.us—suggest that many Web users are clamoring for social context, relying less on formal ontologies than on socially constructed information spaces. At the same time, many of these social systems suffer from problems of fluidity and instability; they are moving targets. Otlet's vision holds out a tantalizing possibility: marrying the determinism of a top-down classification system with the bottom-up relativism of emergent social networks.

In Otlet's last book, *Monde,* he articulates a final vision of the great *réseau* that might as well serve as his last word:

> Everything in the universe, and everything of man, would be registered at a distance as it was produced. In this way a moving image of the world will be established, a true mirror of his memory. From a distance, everyone will be able to read text, enlarged and limited to the desired subject, projected on an individual screen. In this way, everyone from his armchair will be able to contemplate creation, as a whole or in certain of its parts.

MEMEX REDUX

While Otlet's *Mundaneum* vanished like a mirage in the wake of World War II, a similarly ambitious vision of automated information retrieval was percolating across the Atlantic. In 1945 Vannevar Bush[5] published his seminal essay, "As We May Think," in *The Atlantic Monthly*, sketching the contours of a fictional machine dubbed the Memex. Bush envisioned the device as a scholar's workstation, providing access to large collections of documents stored on microfilm, allowing users to read, write, and annotate documents and—most importantly—to forge "associative trails" between them. Written in the age before digital computers, Bush's essay painted a provocative and inspiring vision of an entirely new kind of machine.

Bush's imaginary device captured the popular imagination right away. Excerpts and feature stories appeared in the *Associated Press, Life,* the *New York Times,* and elsewhere. Even after the initial swell of popular interest subsided, the ideas that Bush suggested would per-

Alfred D. Cimi's rendering of the Memex in *Life*, September 10, 1945. Caption read: "MEMEX in the form of a desk would instantly bring files and material on any subject to the operator's fingertips. Slanting translucent viewing screens magnify supermicrofilm filed by code numbers. At left is a mechanism which automatically photographs longhand notes, pictures and letters, then files them in the desk for future reference."[6]

colate for decades. Today, computer scientists still genuflect reflexively to the inspiration of the Memex. Yet Bush's vision remains surprisingly misunderstood, even by many of those who claim to embrace it. "It is strange that ['As We May Think'] has been taken so to heart in the field of information retrieval," writes Ted Nelson, "since it runs counter to virtually all work being pursued under the name of information retrieval today."[7] Indeed, Bush's essay in some ways reads as an indictment of everything that was about to go wrong with the computer industry.

While Bush's essay now ranks as one of the canonical texts in computer science—inspiring generations of programmers and, as we shall see later in this chapter, directly influencing the evolution of the World Wide Web—the essay's fame has in some ways overshadowed

Bush's real intellectual legacy. "As We May Think" has cast such a long historical shadow that it now obscures much of Bush's subsequent thinking and writing about the Memex, most of which now languishes in out-of-print obscurity. Bush would have no doubt recognized the bitter irony that most of his best writing is nowhere to be found on the Web, persisting only on the shelves of the old-fashioned physical libraries he spent much of his career trying to automate out of existence.

The deeper history of the Memex suggests a vision far more provocative than the original microfilm-based device he proposed in 1945. It is not just a story about an innovative idea for managing documents; it is a parable of how a great American engineer turned into cautionary prophet, warning against the influence of corporations on the trajectory of computer science, of the predominance of mathematical and logical models of computing over what he considered a more natural biological approach, and even, in Bush's later writing, espousing provocative and sometimes controversial views on topics like ESP and the coevolution of human brains and machines. None of these themes would emerge until after the publication of "As We May Think."

To understand the broader implications of the Memex, we need to begin by looking at Bush's earlier experiences in the real world of nonimaginary machines. By the time he started musing about the Memex in the late 1930s, Bush had already designed a series of analog computers dating back to the 1920s, including the successful Differential Analyzer, a room-sized machine that employed a complicated array of gears, cams, and shafts to solve complex mathematical problems like differential equations. While other engineers were probing the possibilities of computing with electrical circuits, Bush took a different, almost nineteenth-century, approach, modeling his invention after Charles Babbage's famous gear-driven Difference Engine. Bush's computer did not rely on electrical circuits to perform calculations; instead it only used electricity to power a set of gear shafts that did the actual math. The thing was a kind of turbocharged abacus.

In 1933 Bush published a long-overlooked essay in *Technology Review* entitled "The Inscrutable 'Thirties." Until this point in his career, he had been a prolific inventor and engineer, publishing a string of dry technical papers and patent filings. Now, he began to carve out a more ambitious role for himself as a kind of technological Jeremiah, forecasting the future trajectory of technology by trying to identify long-term predictive trends. Bush scholars Nyce and Kahn describe the essay as "a literary satire, an ironic description of the present seen from an imaginary future when an appreciation of the 'difficulties surrounding a former generation' would lead the reader to marvel that so much was accomplished with so little."[8] Bush conjures up the character of a harried professor of the 1930s, contending with, among other things, a slow-moving car and a primitive environment for conducting scholarly research:

> The library, to which our professor probably turned, was enormous. Long banks of shelves contained tons of books, and yet it was supposed to be a working library and not a museum. He had to pore over cards, thumb pages, and delve by the hour. It was time-wasting and exasperating indeed. . . . The idea that one might have the contents of a thousand volumes located in a couple of cubic feet in a desk, so that by depressing a few keys one could have a given paper instantly projected before him, was regarded as the wildest sort of fancy.[9]

Bush saw libraries as one of the great unsolved technical challenges of his age, a domain that suffered from unfortunate neglect largely because so much of the nation's technological agenda was driven by corporate interests. While Bush was by no means opposed to corporations in principle, he recognized that corporations were exerting a growing influence on the development of computing that left less and less room for the kind of human-centered, individualistic computing he envisioned. In later years, Bush would lament that the computer revolution had left libraries altogether behind. "The great digital machines of today have had their exciting proliferation because they could vitally aid business, because they could increase profits. The libraries still operate by horse-and-buggy methods, for there is no profit in libraries."[10]

The dream of a digital library was still a long way off in the mid-1930s, when Bush began work on a new kind of computing device, this time designed not for mathematical problem solving but for retrieving bits of information from a storehouse of data. His new Rapid Selector relied on the then-state-of-the-art storage technology of microfilm, allowing users to sift through large collections of documents from a single "terminal" with a projection screen housed in a large desk (unbeknownst to Bush, German inventor Emanuel Goldberg had designed a strikingly similar photoelectric microfilm selector in 1927[11]). The machine, Bush wrote, "rapidly reviews items on a roll of film, selecting out desired items in accordance with a code. . . . In order to select items from a film, the roll is placed in the machine, a set of indices are placed in accordance with the code of the desired items, and the film is run through rapidly." It was, essentially, a hopped-up microfilm reader with a built-in indexing facility.

By the late 1930s Bush had built four Rapid Selectors with funding from NCR and Kodak, but they were all plagued with technical problems; they were painfully slow and prone to malfunction. The available technology simply could not keep up with Bush's evolving vision. It was during this period that he began to set his sights farther out on the horizon, rather than limiting his vision to the realm of the merely feasible.

In 1939 Bush drafted an essay provisionally entitled "Mechanization and the Record," in which he penned almost the entire contents of "As We May Think." The essay sprang in part from Bush's experience as an administrator at MIT, where he witnessed firsthand the growing sprawl of scientific publications threatening to overwhelm the enterprises of science and engineering.

> There is much evidence that we are becoming bogged down today, as specialization extends and research is quickened. There is a growing mountain of research results; the investigator is bombarded with the findings and conclusions of thousands of parallel workers which he cannot find time to grasp as they appear, let alone remember; specialization becomes increasingly necessary for genuine progress, and effort [sic] to bridge between disciplines correspondingly superficial. Still we adhere rather closely, in our professional efforts, to methods of revealing, transmitting, and reviewing results which are generations old, and now inadequate for their purpose.[12]

He went on to describe his proposed solution, revealing an almost complete vision of the Memex fully 6 years before he published "As We May Think." With war on the horizon, however, Bush shelved his essay to focus on the more imminent threats facing the country. During the War, Bush applied his work on the Rapid Selector to a new machine custom-built for the Navy, the Comparator. The war provided him with the impetus to work through the technical kinks that had hamstrung the old Rapid Selector; by the war's end, he had devised a fully functioning information retrieval device. As Bush began winding down his military career, he looked forward to bringing his machine into civilian deployment. "When peace returns," he wrote, "it ought to be applied to something." Turning his eye toward the most challenging information retrieval problems he could find, Bush approached the Federal Bureau of Investigation (whose fingerprint files were sprawling out of control), then the U.S. Patent Office (whose labyrinthine approval and record-keeping processes seemed to make it a ripe candidate for automation), and finally the Library of Congress, whose sprawling collection of books and documents presented an alluring test case.

Once again, the realities of technological constraints and institutional bureaucracies thwarted realization of his plans. The Library of Congress experiment proved at best a mixed success. Partly due to technical limitations (the mechanical film-reading apparatus performed more slowly than expected) but primarily due to the limitations of the manual indexing process, the project sputtered. In the process, Bush developed a crucial insight that would pave the way for the Memex: an antipathy toward manual indexing and toward librarians, who Bush increasingly saw as overly attached to manual processes and a potential obstacle to the user-driven information environment he envisioned.

In 1945 Bush dusted off his 1939 essay and revised it to produce "As We May Think," publishing it first in *The Atlantic Monthly* and later in *Life*. The essay crystallized Bush's first 12 years of thinking about how an ideal information retrieval device would work. The most frequently quoted passage in Bush's essay crystallizes his prophetic vision:

Wholly new forms of encyclopedias will appear, ready-made with a mesh of associative trails running through them, ready to be dropped into the Memex and there amplified. The lawyer has at his touch the associated opinions and decisions of his whole experience, and of the experience of friends and authorities. The patent attorney has on call the millions of issued patents, with familiar trails to every point of his client's interest. The physician, puzzled by a patient's reactions, strikes the trail established in studying an earlier similar case, and runs rapidly through analogous case histories, with side references to the classics for the pertinent anatomy and histology. The chemist, struggling with the synthesis of an organic compound, has all the chemical literature before him in his laboratory, with trails following the analogies of compounds, and side trails to their physical and chemical behavior. The historian with a vast chronological account of a people, parallels it with a skip trail which stops only on the salient items, and can follow at any time contemporary trails which lead him all over civilization at a particular epoch. There is a new profession of trailblazers, those who find delight in the task of establishing useful trails through the enormous mass of the common record. The inheritance from the master becomes, not only his additions to the world's record, but for his disciplines the entire scaffolding by which they were erected. Thus science may implement the ways in which man produces, stores and consults the record of the race.[13]

The Memex would consist of five interlocking parts: (1) a microfilm document collection; (2) a workstation capable of displaying documents on a projection screen[14]; (3) a mechanism for adding images to the microfilm store; (4) a code input mechanism for identifying and selecting individual records, or groups of records; and (5) associative trails, the conceptual linchpin of the system.

Drawing on his experience with the failures of the Rapid Selector, Bush insisted on the inefficiency of human indexing systems. "Our ineptitude in getting at the record is largely caused by the artificiality of systems of indexing," he wrote. "One has to use rules as to which path will locate [data], and the rules are cumbersome."[15] The basic problem facing contemporary scholarship, as he saw it, was an expanding corpus of literature that "extended far beyond our present ability to make real use of the record."[16] The problem boiled down to, in his view, "the matter of selection," the ability of readers to sift through the available literature, find the most relevant materials, and retrieve them quickly for consultation. He believed that the practice of filing references alphabetically or numerically or by hierarchical classes of subjects forced the reader to operate within a set of cumbersome rules that required enormous cognitive overhead. The journey between documents—central to the scholar's mission—required a constant process of zooming in and out. "Having found one item," he wrote, "one has to emerge from the system and re-enter on a new path."[17]

Like Otlet, Bush sought to liberate the contents of books from the confines of physical volumes, breaking down the old hierarchy of the codex book in favor of a new kind of intertextuality that allowed for direct links between documents, removing the mediating filter of an external index. This kind of internal linking constituted a radical alternative to the deterministic indexing systems then (and still) prevalent in the scholarly publishing world, offering readers a fast path from one document to another. Otlet had called it a "link." Bush called it an "associative trail." He described it as a model of "selection by association, rather than by indexing." By association he meant allowing authors (and readers) to insert explicit linkages between documents in a collection. "This is the essential feature of the Memex," he wrote. "The process of tying two items together is the important thing." Using associative trails, the user could forge a personal trail through any number of documents, creating an exteriorized representation of an internal thought process that other users could later see. "Thus he goes, building a trail of many items. Occasionally he inserts a comment of his own, either linking it to the main trail or joining it by a side trail to a particular item. . . . He inserts a page of longhand analysis of his own. Thus he builds a trail of his interest through the maze of materials available to him." Like ants leaving pheromone signals for their peers, the scholar could thus create a pathway for others to follow. The associative trail, then, represented a new kind of stigmergy.[18]

Bush's vision differed from Otlet's in two important respects. Otlet's system relied not just on readers' associations but on the reinforcing framework of a formal classification scheme. Bush eschewed formal classification as needlessly artificial; indeed, he harbored a certain contempt for librarians and social scientists, believing instead that expert scientists could do a better job of self-organizing their own output than a troop of bibliographic bureaucrats. And unlike Otlet, Bush never envisioned the possibilities of penetrating the contents of the documents themselves. Otlet's "links" worked within documents, whereas Bush's "trails" worked only at the higher level of document references, never penetrating the texts themselves.[19]

While Otlet managed to construct a working model of his idea in the *Mundaneum*, Bush never actually imagined the Memex as a functioning device. "No memex could have been built when that article appeared," Bush later acknowledged. It was from the beginning a conceptual stalking horse, more relevant as a philosophical guidepost than as a blueprint for an actual machine. Indeed, one could speculate that had the machine ever actually been built, its impact might actually have been reduced. With its microfilm reels, photographic copying plate, and forehead-mounted camera, a real-world Memex would today strike most of us as a Rube Goldberg contraption, a historical curiosity rather than the inspirational object it has become.

For all the legions of computer scientists who have since purported to embrace the Memex, few comprehend the depth of Bush's antipathy toward the subsequent trajectory of the computer industry. While Bush's Memex has often been associated with the rise of the modern computing industry, Bush never saw his machine as a tool for business. "I proposed a machine for personal use rather than the enormous computers which serve whole companies," he wrote. "I suggested that it serve a man's daily thoughts directly, fitting in with his normal thought processes."[20] Instead, large computer companies have often co-opted his vision in service of big-business agendas.

Paradoxically, even though Bush achieved his greatest results working in large governmental and academic institutions, he was a great believer in individual freedom and saw institutions primarily as the guarantors of environments in which individual genius could thrive. Bush's focus on the individual user ran directly counter to the main trajectory of computing well into the 1970s, when the first personal computers began to emerge. Throughout most of this period, large so-called mainframe computers operated in the back room, executing programs in support of deterministic business or scientific processes. Only a handful of specially trained operators ever had much contact with the machines. In the 1970s, so-called minicomputers gave individual offices and departments their first chance to interact directly with computers. The personal computer revolution of the late 1970s and 1980s brought more people into direct contact with computers, but even the modern personal computer is in many ways a descendant of the old command-and-control, militaristic systems. Behind the friendly graphical user interfaces and consumer-friendly marketing messages of the modern PC lie the vestige of exactly the kind of machine Bush did not want to build: a calculating machine, populated by hierarchical information systems like files and folders. Bush's "associative trails" are nowhere to be found in the modern PC. As Nelson puts it, "Bush rejected indexing and discussed instead new forms of interwoven documents."[21]

Even the modern World Wide Web, which does echo certain aspects of his vision, fails to fulfill Bush's larger aspiration for a participatory scholarly research environment. Web browsers are ultimately unidirectional programs, designed primarily to let users consume information from a remote source. To the extent that users can create information through a Web browser, they must do so through the mediation of that remote source. As an authoring tool, the Web browser is all but impotent. The Memex was always envisioned as a two-way authoring environment, allowing users to create new information as readily as they could consume existing information. This is not to say that the Memex is necessarily an entirely superior concept. Bush envisioned the Memex as a powerful stand-alone machine, while the Web works by virtue of a distributed network, lending it the advantages of robustness and scale. And while the Memex may have anticipated the idea of hypertext, it was by no means a true hypertext system. Bush wanted the machine to link individual frames of a microfilm; but given its mechanical limitations, it could not penetrate any deeper into the body of the text to, for example, insert links between individual words or sentences. But Bush's model did enjoy one enormous advantage over the kinds of hyperlinks that prevail across today's Web: His links were permanent. By contrast, Web hyperlinks are notoriously evanescent.

While the 1945 model Memex continues to influence developers today, few of Bush's present-day apostles know anything of his later work. In 1945 Bush had spent only a few years thinking about the Memex. "In the quarter-century since then," he later wrote, "the idea has been with me almost constantly, and I have watched new developments in electronics, physics, chemistry, and logic to see how they might help to bring it to reality. That day is not yet here, but has come far closer."[22]

Bush's subsequent vision for the Memex reveals a far more provocative vision, influenced not just by changing technological realities but by the evolution of Bush's own ideas about how computers should work. In particular, Bush developed a fascination with biological models of computing, as a potential alternative to the mathematical and logical models that have since predominated. "A great deal of our brain cell activity is closely parallel to the operation of relay circuits," he wrote. "One can explore this parallelism and the possibilities of ultimately making something out of it almost indefinitely."[23] Unlike digital computers, which rely on linear sequencing and the indexing of documents in hierarchical file structures, "the brain does not operate by reducing everything to indices and computation," he wrote.

> It follows trails of association, flying almost instantly from item to item, bringing into consciousness only the significant. The trails bifurcate and cross, they become erased in disuse, and emphasized by success. Ultimately, the machine can do this better. Its memory will be far greater and the items will not fade. Progress along trails will be at lightning speed. The machine will learn from its own experience, refine its own trails, explore in unknown territory.[24]

The notion of a Memex that learns, adapting to user behavior along the way, suggests fascinating possibilities of machine-human symbiosis and new ways of thinking about information environments. Today, most of us experience personal computers as fixed entities, with hierarchical folders and a familiar set of programs. Our computers are not so far removed from the dumb terminals of the mainframe era. They know very little about us. Bush's vision suggests the possibility of smarter machines that could anticipate our needs and adapt themselves to our behaviors, like good servants.

Bush also tried to adapt his vision to the changing technological landscape. After the publication of his original essay, Bush recognized that the advent of digital computers made his analog mechanical device seem increasingly anachronistic. Although he never mastered the intricacies of digital computing, he did begin to revise his theories to account for the evolving development of computer technology. In 1958 Bush wrote a sequel to his original essay, entitled "Memex II," which was never published during his lifetime.[25] Recognizing that microfilm was a soon-to-be-defunct technology, he envisioned a new kind of memory apparatus using biological crystals. Bush also envisioned the possibility of networking large remote collections of data, of letting users dial in to a Memex from afar. In his final years, he even speculated on the possibility of ESP arising as human brains and external storage devices began to coalesce. He believed that a long-term symbiosis between human brains and computing equipment would lead to the coevolution of new neural pathways in the human brain.

These provocative musings seem all the more prescient today, but Bush's reputation has been largely limited to his comparatively primitive 1945 vision. While Bush's subsequent thinking remains largely forgotten, "As We May Think" touched off a wave of innovation that still reverberates more than 60 years later.

GARFIELD'S PROTO-GOOGLE

In the 1950s, a young library science student named Eugene Garfield took Bush's 1945 essay as his inspiration to explore a new way of facilitating access to scientific journals. His work ultimately led him to create a methodology known as citation ranking, a tool for assessing the impact of scholarly articles by tracking the frequency of bibliographic citations. Depending on the relative frequency of citations, an article would acquire a higher influence ranking, which would in turn lend more weight to whatever documents it cited. The technique, used most powerfully in the influential Science Citation Index, provided a way of ranking the impact of scholarly journal articles. By measuring the cumulative impact of citations, it allowed scholars to assign a collective weight of importance to any given article. The tool effectively circumvented the old manual indexing systems that once predominated in the sciences. The Science Citation Index would go on to exert a sweeping influence on the trajectory of scientific research, becoming the de facto authority in determining the importance of scientific articles and an essential fixture in every science library. At many academic science libraries, a subscription to "SCI" constitutes the single biggest line item in the acquisitions budget.

Inspired by Bush's vision of associative trails, Garfield's notion of citation ranking would in turn inspire two young graduate students at Stanford, Larry Page and Sergey Brin, who extrapolated Garfield's work to the problem of Web search results. In their white paper, "The Anatomy of a Large-Scale Hypertextual Search Engine,"[26] they outline a new algorithm based on Garfield's idea: Pagerank. That algorithm lives at the heart of their search engine: Google.

Google, for all its success, does not necessarily embody the greatest triumph of Garfield's theory. In fact, Google's approach proves both the power and the limitations of citation analysis. Because it tries to be all things to all people, Google inevitably turns the Web into a kind of worldwide popularity contest, often at the expense of smaller, more focused communities of interest. As Paul Kahn puts it, "Link-node models work best on small units."[27] As such, it is particularly well suited for weighing the impact of literature within smaller, focused communities like scientific specialties, where the literature consists mainly of research papers containing references to other papers within a well-defined domain of knowledge. When the same mode of analysis is applied to the great public Web, however, problems of context inevitably surface. Without the structured conventions of a scientific paper, the Web presents more difficult problems of determining context and the "aboutness" of a particular domain. Google's brute-force algorithm in some ways represents a step backward from the more focused, special-purpose research environment that Garfield (and Bush) envisioned.

THE MOTHER OF ALL DEMOS

Bush's essay would find another enthusiastic disciple in Doug Engelbart, who read the essay as a young Navy radio technician in the Philippines. "As We May Think," Engelbart later recalled, would become the philosophical guidepost for his entire career. On returning from the Navy, Engelbart set his professional sights on exploring the kinds of networked information retrieval tools that Bush had envisioned. He would go on to develop a series of breakthrough technologies that would shape the course of the personal computer: the mouse, the graphical user interface, and a dramatically new kind of computer system that owed a deep debt to Bush's vision.

In 1962 Engelbart published a report entitled "Augmenting Human Intellect: A Conceptual Framework," in which he described his proposed framework for machine-assisted intelligence. Written during his tenure at the Stanford Research Institute (SRI) for his project sponsors in the Air Force, the report lays out Engelbart's vision for how an "augmented" human intellect might work. His report was at once a practical blueprint and a philosophical treatise. "By 'augmenting human intellect,'" he wrote, "we mean increasing the capability of a man to approach a complex problem situation, to gain comprehension to suit his particular needs, and to derive solutions to problems." But Engelbart was not referring to the mathematical problems that had preoccupied computer scientists up to that point. He explicitly geared his solution to audiences that had traditionally had no truck with computers: diplomats, executives, social scientists, lawyers, and designers, as well as scientists, like biologists and physicists, who were then not typically using computers. His vision was expansive. "We do not speak of isolated clever tricks that help in particular situations. We refer to a way of life in an integrated domain where hunches, cut-and-try, intangibles, and the human 'feel for a situation' usefully co-exist with powerful concepts, streamlined terminology and notation, sophisticated methods, and high-powered electronic aids."[28] It was, at root, a deeply human-centered vision of computing.

The whole framework rested on a carefully considered model of how humans process information, recognizing that in order to make an information system useful it must involve breaking down information into atomized nuggets of information that map as closely as possible to the processes of human cognition. "The human mind neither learns nor acts by large leaps," he wrote, "but by steps organized or structured so that each one depends upon previous steps."[29] Engelbart identified the linchpin of the entire system as a series of "process hierarchies" that would enable the system to encode units of information that could be atomized into discrete units of semantic meaning that could then be recombined in endless possible reconfigurations. "Every process of thought or action is made up of sub-processes," he wrote. "Let us consider such examples as making a pencil stroke, writing a letter of the alphabet, or making a plan . . . although every sub-process is a process in its own right, in that it consists of further sub-processes." In turn, each of these process hierarchies forms a building block in a larger repertoire of higher-level hierarchies that Engelbart dubbed a "repertoire hierarchy." For example, "the process of writing is utilized as a sub-process within many different processes of a still higher order, such as organizing a committee, changing a policy, and so on."[30] Each of these routines then formed a discrete hierarchical process, which could then be stitched together in any number of possible combinations: networks of hierarchies. The entire framework rests on this conceit.

Working with a team of developers at SRI, Engelbart brought his vision to working reality in the form of a prototype system dubbed the oN-Line System (NLS). Given SRI's institutional priorities and military funding, it is perhaps not surprising that the system placed a special emphasis on facilitating organizational workflow, or what Engelbart called "asynchronous collaboration among teams distributed geographically" (what software developers today would call "groupware"). NLS equipped its users with a set of tools that today we would consider rudimentary: a simple word processor, a tool for sending messages to other users, and a basic system for building associated links between documents. The user manipulated a cursor on the screen using a wooden box with wheels attached to the bottom, attached by a wire to the computer. Engelbart's team originally called it a "bug" but later christened it with a name that stuck: mouse.

In 1968 Engelbart showed a working prototype of his new tool to a public audience at the San Francisco Civic Auditorium. In later years the event would go down in Silicon Valley lore as "the mother of all demos." For many of the 1,000 San Francisco audience members that night, his presentation proved nothing short of an epiphany. Perhaps some of them may have felt something like the curious pagans who first encountered Saint Augustine on the beach wielding his illuminated Gospel. These people had witnessed something profoundly new that they did not entirely understand, a strange vision so powerful they sensed it might soon change everyone's life for good.

Today, many of us may find it difficult to understand just what a radically different vision Engelbart presented that night. In our age of networked personal computers, cell phones, and digital cameras, it requires a backward cognitive leap to conjure the world of 1968, when computers were still churning out punch cards and tape reels, relegated to back-office tasks managing payrolls, counting election results, and solving complex equations for NASA. Most people had never seen a computer.

More than a few members of that audience became enthusiastic converts to the digital revolution. Historians of computer science often invoke Engelbart's demo as the seminal event in the personal computing revolution. NLS found its most immediate successor in a series of projects at the new Xerox PARC (Palo Alto Research Center), a think tank founded with the mission of researching "the architecture of information." Indeed, several of Engelbart's former associates left SRI to join the PARC team. The legacy of PARC on the subsequent development of the personal computer is difficult to overstate. In the 1970s, PARC researchers for all intents and purposes invented today's windows-style graphical desktop, bit-map displays, and even the Ethernet protocol. When a young Steve Jobs visited PARC to see the work in progress, he came away with a vision that would later take shape as the Macintosh (which in turn provided the conceptual foundation for Microsoft Windows).

Engelbart's vision also inspired any number of people outside the mainstream computer industry: people like Stewart Brand, a former Merry Prankster who would go on to found the distinctly hypertext-like Whole Earth Catalog and Whole Earth Review, whose alumni Kevin Kelly and Howard Rheingold would go on to play instrumental roles in the early days of the *Wired* era. Paradoxically, the staid, buttoned-down, military-funded Engelbart found his greatest following in the burgeoning 1960s counterculture. Over the coming years, Engelbart's influence would reverberate throughout the grassroots computer movement that would ultimately unleash the PC revolution.

SLOUCHING TOWARD XANADU

In the mid-1960s a young Harvard sociology student named Ted Nelson took his first computer class. He was fascinated by the first-generation computing machines but found the emerging discipline of computer science profoundly dissatisfying. At the time, academic computing was strictly the province of mathematicians, logisticians, and scientists. With a few notable exceptions like Harvard's pioneering Russian-English machine translation project, humanists rarely ventured anywhere near the things. It was a far cry from Bush's vision of an individualized computing experience modeled after the human brain. In the early days of academic computing, mathematicians ran the show.

Soon after he encountered the Harvard computer labs, Nelson started to harbor a gut feeling that the computer scientists had it all wrong. They insisted on approaching computers as glorified calculators. To Nelson, an idealistic young social scientist, a computer "was not a mechanical, a numerical device, it was not a mathematical device, it was not an engineering device, it was an all-purpose machine! . . . Computer was a bad name for it. It might just as well have been called an oogabooga box."[31]

At Harvard, Nelson discovered the germ of an impulse that would propel him into a lifelong pitched battle against the dominant institutional forces of the computer industry. In 1965, he wrote an academic paper entitled "A File Structure for the Complex, the Changing and the Indeterminate." In that paper, he coined a term that has lasted: "hypertext." Nelson would later write, "By 'hypertext,' I mean nonsequential writing—text that branches and allows choices to the reader, best read at an interactive screen. As popularly conceived, this is a series of text chunks connected by links which offer the reader different pathways."[32] That paper voiced his earliest inklings of a new kind of computing environment designed not for computer scientists but for readers and writers.

Known today as the conceptual father of hypertext, Nelson has spent most of his career on the fringe of academic respectability (a position he still enjoys today). A self-described "rogue intellectual," operating mostly outside the mainstream of universities and the computer industry, he nonetheless enjoyed an influential following among a small cult of early programmers.

Computer scientists Gillies and Cailliau describe Nelson as a Hitchcock-like figure. Just as the great director knew almost nothing about the technical details of filmmaking—he rarely even looked through the camera viewfinder—Nelson somehow managed to shape the course of the entire computer industry while knowing little about their technical operation.[33] Perhaps it was his love of filmmaking that inspired Nelson to name his pet project "Xanadu," just as Orson Welles had named the fictionalized Hearst Castle in *Citizen Kane.*[34]

As a child, Nelson remembers reading a magazine called *Flair,* a publication that featured "little doors and windows throughout the magazine you could pop through. You could open the door and you could see something on the next page," he recalls. "I loved that! And so it was obvious that you could get around linearity in these ways but you were always limited physically. The mind could imagine much richer spaces."[35] For Nelson that childhood template helped guide his thinking about what networked information spaces could be.

Along with Engelbart, Nelson took inspiration from the vision Bush outlined in "As We May Think." But while Engelbart pursued his ideas from within the institutional mainstream, Nelson worked on the fringes, assembling an ad hoc team of programmers to help bring his vision to fruition. Whereas Engelbart tailored his efforts toward teams collaborating on projects, Nelson was more interested in the solitary user. "The fundamental difference between my wonderful and very great stepfather Douglas Engelbart and myself," Nelson says, "is that he wanted to empower working groups and I just wanted to be left alone and given the equipment and basically to empower smart individuals and keep them from being dragged down by group stupidity."[36] In this sense, Nelson is a more direct descendant of Bush, who also advocated for a vision of individual-centered computing.

Nelson was (and is) a devout maverick, intent on shaking up institutional hierarchies with a vision of liberating the individual from suffocating organizational strictures. In Howard Bloom's parlance, Nelson would qualify as a Diversity Generator, a free-wheeling change agent who relentlessly probed the boundaries of the status quo. Whereas Engelbart embraced the notion of hierarchy as the essential building block of his system, Nelson railed against hierarchies of all kinds. "From earliest youth I was suspicious of categories and hierarchies," Nelson wrote, and in his books he railed against the establishment at every turn, dispensing vitriol at two favorite targets: the modern university and the computer industry. "If you are not falsely expecting a permanent system of categories or a permanent stable hierarchy, you realize your information system must then deal with an ever-changing flux of new categories, hierarchies and other arrangements which all have to coexist."[37]

If Engelbart's ideas were a revelation, Nelson's were a revolution. Excoriating the soul-crushing effects of a modern university system that "imbues in everyone the attitude that the world is divided into 'subjects'; that these subjects are well-defined and well-understood; and that there are 'basics,' that is, a hierarchy of understandings."[38] He dismissed professors as "feudal lords" (the Duchess of History, the Count of Mathematics) and went on to vent much of his literary spleen against what he perceived as the professional class of the computer industry. He argued that technologists had created an insular culture for themselves, forming a "polite conspiracy" with humanists based on what he considered a faulty understanding of what computers really were. "Their shared false notion of computers is that they are Inhuman, Oppressive, Cold, Relentless; and that they somehow Reduce Everything to Mathematics."[39] Nelson's aim was to liberate computers from the back office and to transform the whole understanding of what computers were. In this aim, it must be allowed, the computer industry has effectively thwarted his efforts.

Like a latter-day Ruskin, Nelson railed against the central system orientation that then pervaded the computer industry (and, many would argue, still does), with its growing layers of professional specialization. Nelson objected vehemently to the emergence of a "priesthood" with a "punch card mentality" that asserted its dominion over the new field with increasing layers of specialist vocabulary, relentlessly excluding nonspecialists, a phenomenon he deemed "the creeping evil of Professionalism, the control of aspects of society by cliques of insiders." Nelson sets out to demystify—and debunk—the institutional computer industry, laying out his new vision of computing centered around the individual, not the organization. Nelson christened himself a "systems humanist."

His books, notably *Computer Lib, Dream Machines,* and its sequel *Literary Machines,* have in retrospect taken on a visionary glow. But at the time they went all but ignored among mainstream scholars and the computer industry. In keeping with his revolutionary ideals, Nelson wrote in an over-the-top style, employing a mishmash of exotic metaphors, kinetic drawings, and occasionally vituperative diatribes against mainstream institutions that lend his writing a countercultural, occasionally raving quality. His outlandish style may deter some readers from recognizing the occasional bursts of genius that percolate throughout his work.

The sheer intensity of Nelson's writing presents an imposing barrier to close reading. To wade into a Ted Nelson book is to immerse oneself in turbocharged rhetoric. His language is peppered with wildly inventive words: "zippered lists," "window sandwiches," "indexing vortexes," "part-pounces," "tumblers," "humbers," and "thinkertoys." That none of these terms have come close to entering the common parlance testifies to Nelson's secure position on the fringe of the mainstream. But Nelson did invent one word that stuck: "hypertext."

Computer Lib, released as a reverse-bound, upside-down companion volume to his better-known *Dream Machines,* finds Nelson at his ranting, idiosyncratic best. Presaging the *Wired* era by 20 years, *Dream Machines* attracted a cultlike following with its radical alternative vision of computing, outrageous and provocative presentation style, and unapologetic skewering of the institutional model of com-

puting. The book offered readers a technotopian vision of a new
world powered by computers but ultimately putting hands in the individual creator. Here Nelson coined his famous maxim, "Everything
is intertwingled," and the book itself seems to reflect that ethos. The
text makes every effort to resist linear reading, broken out in a series
of cascading chunks and nested diagrams—all delivered in Nelson's
signature frenetic voice—evoking the nonlinear quality of "hypertext"
that Nelson, at this point, was still only dreaming about. Bound as an
oversized manifesto, with three columns of typewritten text inter-
spersed with hundreds of Nelson's hyperkinetic pencil sketches, the
whole volume has a handmade, mimeographed quality. It almost
seems to evoke the nineteenth-century Arts and Crafts ethic, resem-
bling nothing so much as a handmade book. Inside this antic book is
a searing vision of what computers could be.

While today the popular conception of hypertext has been shaped
by the working reality of the World Wide Web, Nelson originally articulated a sweeping vision that went far beyond the simplistic model
of one-way hyperlinks. Nelson envisioned three basic flavors of
hypertext: "ordinary" hypertext, consisting of notational links and
references to other documents (roughly the equivalent of a URL in a
modern Web page); "stretchtext," wherein documents would incorporate entire sections of text by allowing one document to directly
access the contents of another and to easily expand one document
directly into another; and "collateral hypertext," which would facilitate person-to-person sharing of content, in which two versions of a
document could open on one screen, with a facility for reviewing
multiple versions of a document over time. The book also postulates
a range of possible semantic relationships going well beyond simple
text linking—hypergrams, hypermaps, and "branching movies"—
suggesting the possibility of using networked computers to share not
just documents, but visceral and sensory experiences. These various
permutations of hypertext would also roll up into higher-order collections of knowledge about a particular topic: "fresh hyperbooks,"
or original works about a particular topic; "anthropological
hyperbooks," containing collected references to other hyperbooks,
like annotated bibliographies; and "grand systems," consisting of "'ev-

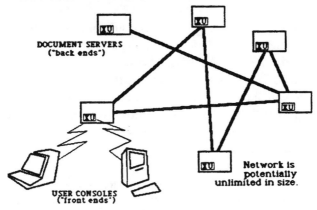

Illustration from Ted Nelson's *Literary Machines.*

erything' written about the subject, or vaguely relevant to it, tied together by editors."

Nelson envisioned all of these threads coming together in a single, unified system he dubbed Xanadu, after Samuel Taylor Coleridge's opium-fueled vision of Kublai Khan's imaginary pleasure dome. Imagining his own Xanadu as "a new form of software with potentially revolutionary implications," Nelson imagined an environment supporting an enormous range of tasks: word processing, file management, e-mail, and the ability to create vertical views of information drawn from a wide repository of sources. Twenty years before the Web emerged into the popular consciousness, Nelson outlined a staggeringly ambitious vision:

> [A] world wide network, intended to generate hundreds of millions of users simultaneously for the corpus of the world's stored writings, graphics and data.... The Xanadu system provides a universal data structure to which all other data structures will be mapped ... a fast linking electronic repository for the storage and publication of text, graphics and other digital information; permitting promiscuous linkage and windowing

among all materials; with special features for alternative versions, historical backtrack and arbitrary collaging.[40]

In 1981 Nelson would expand on his vision of Xanadu in *Literary Machines*, a sequel to *Dream Machines* that would ultimately provide the direct inspiration for the World Wide Web (a debt readily acknowledged by Tim Berners-Lee). By this time Nelson had spent 7 years working with a team of programmers to prototype a real-world implementation of Xanadu. The experience had given him an opportunity to refine his vision and articulate a more detailed vision of how the system would actually work:

> The Xanadu system, designed to address many forms of text structure, has grown into a design for the universal storage of all interactive media, and, indeed, all data. . . . From this you might get the idea that the Xanadu program is an enormous piece of software. On the contrary: it is one relatively small computer program, set up to run in each storage machine of an ever-growing network.[41]

This vision of a small program (which today we might call a "browser") resident on the user's computer interacting with "storage machines" (which today we would call "servers") provided the essential blueprint for the operation of the World Wide Web.

However, Nelson's vision reverberated far beyond the mechanics of client-server networked computers. He also proved eerily prescient in anticipating a series of potential concerns with implementing a hypertext environment, such as privacy, copyright, archiving, and version control—all problems very much in evidence in today's implementation of the Web.

Xanadu has taken on mythical proportions in the literature of computer science. Despite several attempts, the product has never successfully launched (most recently the rights had been acquired by Autodesk). But Nelson soldiers on, most recently as a fellow at the Oxford Internet Institute, where he continues to pursue his inspired and idiosyncratic vision of an alternative universe of humanist computing. Despite his outsize influence on the evolution of the Web, Nelson remains surprisingly little-read today. *Dream Machines* has long been out of print; copies now fetch $300 or more (I was fortunate enough to find a dog-eared copy kept under lock and key at the San Francisco Public Library). While Nelson has worked with large corporations and institutions in trying to bring his vision to life, his colorful style and virulent antiestablishmentarianism seem to have guaranteed his status as a committed outsider.

In the struggle between networks and hierarchies, Nelson has cast his lot squarely on the side of the network, insisting on a purely bottom-up model of information storage and retrieval, absent familiar hierarchies like files and folders, and liberated from the control of the computer priesthood that he has devoted his career to confronting.

Perhaps Nelson's hopes for a humanist vision of computing amounts to tilting at windmills. For all its promise of individual creativity and liberation, the control of today's Web ultimately rests in the hands of corporate and governmental entities. While many scholars have decried the commercialization of the Web, however, perhaps we can take some solace in knowing that every major information technology in human history has taken hold primarily due to commercial impetus. Writing emerged at the hands of merchants; the printing press spread not because of the Gutenberg Bible but on the strength of a booming business in religious indulgences and contracts; so it should perhaps come as no surprise that adoption of the Web has been fueled largely by commercial interests. But Nelson's work still resonates as an inspired, if at times hyperventilated, alternative vision of a humanist computer environment.

OTHER XANADUS

While Nelson and his band of idealistic programmers were pursuing their vision outside the institutional mainstream, the burgeoning computer industry was growing mainly at the behest of large organizations like banks, insurance companies, the government, and the military. Computers lived in the so-called back office, tended by specialized information technology staff—Nelson's "priesthood"—who typically had little direct contact with the front office marketing, sales,

and management staff. Corporate computing followed a strictly hierarchical model, in which systems architects would carefully mediate
the requirements of the front office into structured documents that
formed the basis for rigid, deterministic programming regimens designed to maximize efficiency and minimize risk. Information flowed
in tightly controlled channels. The age of the desktop PC was still
over the horizon.

The command-and-control model of enterprise computing fueled the industry's growth in the postwar era, but during the late
1960s and 1970s an alternative vision of human-centered computers
began to percolate. In Palo Alto, California, a group of former
Engelbart disciples came together at the legendary Xerox PARC, a
research and development facility that Xerox founded in 1970 with
the express mission of creating "the architecture of information." That
group's accomplishments, including the graphical user interface,
WYSIWIG (What You See Is What You Get) text editing tools, the
Ethernet protocol, the laser printer, and the pioneering Alto personal
computer, have been amply chronicled elsewhere.

By the early 1980s, many universities began to experience the
emergence of two separate computing cultures: the administrative
information technology (I/T) infrastructure of the formal organization that handled the payroll, ran the online library catalog, and pro-
cessed billing, payments, and course registrations. These were
Nelson's "priests." Typically working behind an organizational
firewall, the I/T department usually maintained its own battery of
mainframes and minicomputers. End users, in this culture, still used
green-screen "dumb" terminals, but all the actual computing happened behind closed doors. Meanwhile, in the computer labs, faculty
offices, and dorm rooms, students and faculty were starting to build
their own computing infrastructure, often operating outside the administrative I/T department. Whereas in the 1970s and 1980s everyone had shared space on the campus mainframe, now the two cultures
were beginning to diverge: minicomputers and mainframes for the
administration and Unix workstations and personal computers for
the academics. Students and faculty started using PCs and sharing
information with each other.

Across the continent, another group of researchers explored the possibilities of networked information retrieval in an academic setting. In the late 1960s Andries van Dam led a research team at Brown University in producing the first working prototype of an interactive hypertext system on a commercially available mainframe, the IBM 360/50. Inspired by a chance meeting between van Dam and his Swarthmore contemporary Ted Nelson at the 1967 Spring Joint Computer Conference, the system came to be called the Hypertext Editing System (HES). Nelson helped van Dam formulate requirements for the system, designing the hypertext features and contributing a set of interconnected patents on electroplating. Eventually, Nelson became disappointed with the project's emphasis on paper printout capabilities (by Nelson's own account, the Brown researchers viewed him as a "raving" and "flaming" intruder), and he left Brown to pursue his hypertext vision in the form of his new Xanadu project. Nonetheless, HES marked an important early validation of Nelson's vision: It proved that a hypertext environment could work in practice. Meanwhile, van Dam went on to build a series of pioneering hypertext systems that would ultimately be used by thousands of people around the world.[42]

The original HES system had two equally important goals: (1) to support individual authors in the process of creating documents or other work products; and (2) to explore the notions of nonlinear information structures that Ted Nelson had dubbed hypertext. These goals arose out of the needs of a user community that wrote papers on typewriters and had no interest in working with the teletype-driven text editors that programmers used to write programs at the time. Nelson's vision of hypertext suggested a new way of working with ideas that would be free of the linear constraints imposed by the then-ubiquitous paper media.

HES ran on standard hardware and software (IBM 360/50 OS/MFT with a 2250 graphics display terminal), combining nonhierarchical and flexible document structures with the first true non-line-oriented word processing system. The Brown team envisioned HES as a research system, intended to explore notions of document structures and text editing; as such it did not immediately come into wide use on campus, especially since it was quickly replaced by research on its successor, FRESS, a system designed to overcome the limitations of HES, extend its strengths, and incorporate lessons learned from Doug Engelbart's NLS. Nonetheless, IBM released it as part of its Type Three Library of customer-generated applications. Years later van Dam would receive a letter from a NASA program manager, informing him that HES had been used to produce Apollo documentation that went to the Moon.

In 1967, almost as soon as HES was deployed, van Dam and his team envisioned a more accessible tool, one that could be employed across campus. The result was the File Retrieving and Editing SyStem (FRESS). Once again, the team had designed a computing environment as both a process and a product. When HES development started, van Dam hadn't known about Engelbart's work with NLS, but by the time FRESS development was under way he did. Consequently, FRESS was a response to both the experience with HES and the insights gained from NLS, both positive and negative.

FRESS was a multiuser, device-independent system. It ran on equipment ranging from typewriter terminals and glass teletypes to high-end vector graphics terminals with light pens. The system was designed to support online collaborative work, the writing process, and document production. It had bidirectional links, macros, metadata in the form of both display and textual keywords, and a notion of document structures that in some sense paralleled programming structures, although it lacked fully conditional branching, multiple windows, view specifications, structured links that allowed documents and document views to be dynamically structured on the fly, and dynamic access control mechanisms that accommodated conflicting demands on the same information corpus.

Users could include two kinds of links: "tags" pointing to another part of the same document, such as an annotation or footnote, and "jumps" that provided bidirectional links between documents. Developed in the years before the computer mouse became a common feature, the system at first allowed users to manipulate objects using a light pen and a foot pedal ("point and kick," to borrow Gillies and Caillieau's pun).

As primitive as the system might have seemed—with its foot pedals, green screen, and text-only readouts, FRESS was in some ways more sophisticated than today's Web. Links worked in both directions—a link from one document to another would always invoke a reciprocal link going the other way. If someone linked to your document, you would know about it. For example, a class of students could annotate a set of documents, adding their own links, and view whichever links they wanted to see from their peers. FRESS also provided a facility for keyword annotations, allowing readers to search and filter by subjects and to assign names to discrete blocks of text for later research. The ability to assign free-form keywords—now often referred to as "tagging"—allowed users to begin creating their own idiosyncratic meta structure for document collections. Thus, readers could view each other's annotations, and even filter by reader—a major step toward what Bush called "associative trails."[43]

FRESS also marked the first experiment with hypertext in the classroom. Brown offered two experimental courses—one on energy, another on poetry—in which students conducted all of their reading, writing, and postclass discussion online. Class dialogue followed the now-familiar threaded discussion format, with commentary threads attached to the related document or resource. Students wrote three times as much as in offline classes, and got better grades than their peers in a control group; class participation proved much higher than in physical classrooms, as quiet wallflowers felt comfortable piping up in the online arena. After the classes wound down, the system maintained the hypertext "corpus" of information that each class had created.[44]

The early Brown experiments proved enormously influential, allowing nonspecialist users to read and write documents online without understanding how to program a computer. Although including the term "hypertext" in the name may have been a stretch—as Nelson points out, the system had few truly hypertext capabilities beyond document linking—it marked an important milestone in the history of computing. And if nothing else, it lent an institutional imprimatur to the possibilities of hypertext in the academy.

In the years leading up to the emergence of the Web, Brown's early work on HES and FRESS would provide the foundation for an even more ambitious effort—IRIS Intermedia—which was the most fully fledged hypertext environment to emerge before the Web, indeed a work whose collaborative and interactive authoring capabilities have yet to be equaled by the Web. The Institute for Research on Information (IRIS) was founded in 1983 with grants from the Annenberg Foundation and IBM. Its 20-person staff began work on creating a new kind of scholarly computing environment dubbed Intermedia. Led by Norm Meyrowitz and Nicole Yankelovich, the team began work on an ambitious interactive hypertext environment.

The authoring environment provided users with a suite of interlinked tools for text editing, vector graphics, photo editing, and video and timeline editing. By allowing users to create collections of interlinked original material online, the system allowed users to create a "web" of knowledge about any topic. To keep track of the relationships between objects, Intermedia stored links in a central repository database—an approach with great advantages for ensuring the integrity of links but one that ultimately precluded the system from scaling beyond a relatively limited local deployment.

The Intermedia development team pioneered a number of innovative software features that now seem commonplace: e-mail with hyperlinks, collaborative authoring tools, and "live" objects that could be updated dynamically across multiple applications. Most importantly, the system allowed for bidirectional links, so that any document would "know" which documents pointed to it (one of the present-day Web's notable shortcomings is its lack of such a backtracking feature). The system also allowed for links to point to multiple resources simultaneously, using so-called link anchors. Perhaps the most important distinction between Intermedia and the modern Web stemmed from Intermedia's roots as a scholarly tool: Every document in the system was editable; the system was designed as much for writing as for editing. "The tools you used to create documents were the same tools you used to link them together,"[45] recalls Yankelovich. In contrast to Intermedia's read–write tools, today's Web browser works only as a reader, designed to consume rather than create.

Intermedia constituted a landmark in the history of hypertext. It also proved to be ahead of its time. Despite a string of early successes, by the early 1990s the IRIS team encountered difficulties securing funding for an ambitious second-phase project to be known as the Continents of Knowledge. The National Endowment for the Humanities turned down the institute's grant request, questioning why scholars in the humanities should need computers.[46] By the time IRIS closed its doors in 1994 the institute had dwindled down to a small team of three headed by director Paul Kahn. By this time many key staffers had left for higher-paying jobs at private-sector computer companies.

It seems a bitter irony that such a promising hypertext experiment shut its doors on the eve of the Web revolution. While Intermedia failed to survive into the Web era, the project left a trail of important scholarship. One of the earliest and most enthusiastic advocates of Intermedia was Brown University professor George P. Landow, who would go on to write important theoretical texts like *Hypertext* and *Hyper/Text/Theory* that brought a critical eye to the philosophical implications of hypertext. Describing one IRIS project, a collection of materials about Tennyson's "In Memoriam," Landow described how teaching the text in a hyperlinked environment brought out its networked qualities, by capturing "the multilinear organization of the poem," and describing how "using the capacities of hypertext, the web permits the reader to trace from section to section several dozen leitmotifs that thread through the poem."[47] In his 1992 book *Hypertext,* Landow articulated a vision that unified the literature of the nascent hypertext movement with the aims of contemporary literary scholarship. Invoking both Ted Nelson and theorist Jacques Derrida, Landow penned an elegant jeremiad arguing for a new model of authorship, insisting that "we must abandon conceptual systems founded upon ideas of center, margin, hierarchy, and linearity and replace them with ones of multi-linearity, nodes, links, and networks."[48] He goes on to explore the deep parallels between hypertext—with its emphasis on the decentering of the text and reduction of authority—with contemporary trends in literary theory, notably the work of Foucault and Derrida. Landow even goes so far as to argue for reconstituting our ideas of authorship:

The Intermedia system, circa 1989 (courtesy of George P. Landow).

> In reducing the autonomy of the text, hypertext reduces the autonomy of
> the author. Lack of textual autonomy, like lack of textual centeredness,
> immediately reverberates through conceptions of authorship. . . . Simi-
> larly, the unboundedness of the new textuality disperses the author as
> well.[49]

Echoing Nelson's call to break down the rigid structures of institutional hierarchy—albeit in a more sober academic voice and from a
position lodged squarely inside the academy—Landow recognizes the
politics inherent even in the seemingly simple act of creating a footnote, a transaction predicated on "divisions of text that partake of
fixed hierarchies of status and power." If footnotes are replaced by
hyperlinks, that power relationship becomes more fluid and nego-
tiable, and the authority of texts now derives not from the author's
act of subordination but from the reader's own constantly shifting
perspective. "Hypertext linking situates the present text at the center
of the textual universe, thus creating a new kind of hierarchy."[50] This

new democratization of texts, in which the "marginal" work steps on to a level playing field with privileged texts, meshed nicely with postmodern notions of "deconstruction," dissolving the illusion of the authoritative writer and creating a new teleology of literature, with readers and writers engaged on more equal footing.

Invoking Derrida's vision of a new form of hieroglyphic writing, Landow intimated that networked hypermedia authoring might provide a remedy to the linear, sequential, hierarchical model of thinking that had taken deep root in the culture in the form of the printed book. During the age of print, the relentless march toward linear sequencing of text had effectively suppressed what hypertext scholar Gregory Ulmer calls "the pluridimensional character of symbolic thought."[51] Hypertext seemed to hold the promise of a remedy for the linear constrictions of the printed text: postmodernism made manifest.

Landow has gone on to write provocatively about the changing nature of authorship, exploring the inherent economic impetus behind authorship. As technology changes the economics of publishing, it inevitably changes the status of authors. Today, writers "exist in a cyborg relation with a complex technology that affects us more than we affect it."[52] Arguably, however, this relationship is nothing new; technologies have always shaped peoples' behavior at a macro level often masked by the powerful subjective sensations of individuals. Landow admits that by taking such a provocative stance, "I horrify a lot of people in literature and the humanities."[53]

THE WEB THAT WAS

Throughout the 1980s and early 1990s, the hypertext movement quietly gathered steam, spawning other early experimental environments like Apple's Hypercard, Perseus, and early Internet information-sharing applications like the Wide Area Information Server. None of these systems achieved widespread use, but each contributed to a growing wave of interest in a new humanist mode of computing that took advantage of the possibilities of hypertext.

One application that gained an enthusiastic following in the years leading up to the Web was Gopher, originally developed as a campus information system for the University of Minnesota by Mark McCahill and Farhad Anklesaria. Named for the university's mascot (and for its ability to "fetch" information), Gopher functioned as a large distributed menu system, enabling content owners to publish content in a unified browsing environment. Gopher presented users with a series of nested menus in simple lists of linear text. Each text link pointed to an object within the directory tree, which might be stored locally on the host machine or—a glimmer of the Web—on a remote computer accessible over the Internet. While the system followed a strictly hierarchical model, allowing navigation between resources only through nested menus, it nonetheless may have paved the way for the evolution of the Web by setting in motion a process of linking documents across disparate geographical locations. Gopher proved enormously popular in the academic computing labs of the early 1990s and, although largely forgotten today, almost certainly played a role in seeding popular interest in the notion of remote file sharing. By 1993 a thriving Internet subculture had emerged in campus computing environments.

Paradoxically, this computing subculture would never have emerged had it not been for the U.S. Department of Defense, which had funded development of the Internet since the late 1960s. Working under the auspices of the ARPANET project, pioneering engineers such as Vinton G. Cerf and Robert B. Kahn created distributed networking protocols like Transmission Control Protocol/Internet Protocol (TCP/IP) that would ultimately form the backbone for the modern Internet. In 1985 the National Science Foundation created NSFNet, the first national network specifically designed to support institutions of higher education. Other countries opened up similar academic networks, taking advantage of the open Internet technical standards to create a worldwide network capable of handling e-mail and exchanging files between servers distributed around the globe.

In the years before the National Science Foundation opened the Internet up to commercial use in 1991, an enthusiastic group of dedicated hackers, university staff, and scientific researchers were busily experimenting with new tools for sharing, retrieving, and organizing information online. At the CERN laboratory in Switzerland, a young researcher named Tim Berners-Lee was working on a new software tool that would soon reverberate around the world.

Ted Nelson had predicted that the future of hypertext would spring not from large institutions or top-down computing initiatives but from innovation by free-thinking individuals. Berners-Lee was about to prove him right.

As a child, Tim Berners-Lee's family had owned a copy of an old nineteenth-century English almanac entitled *Enquire Within Upon Everything*. In sensible Victorian prose, the book contained a compendium of useful tidbits on a host of seemingly unrelated topics. As the editor of the 1875 edition wrote, "Whether you wish to model a flower in wax; to study the rules of etiquette; to serve a relish for breakfast or supper; to plan a dinner for a large party or a small one; to cure a headache; to make a will; to get married; to bury a relative; whatever you may wish to do, make, or to enjoy, provided your desire has relation to the necessities of life, I hope you will not fail to *Enquire Within*."[54] When Berners-Lee released his first version of his prototypical information-sharing tool in 1980, he decided to call it Enquire. Unfortunately for historians of the Web, all traces of this early proto-Web application disappeared in a calamitous hard drive crash. Undeterred, Berners-Lee started from scratch on developing a new incarnation of his hypertext information retrieval tool. In 1989 he released his program under a new name: WorldWideWeb.

The rest is not quite history.

As of February 2006, there were more than 20 billion Web pages residing on more than 78 million Web sites around the world. An estimated 1.2 billion people have now used the Internet at least once. In less than two decades the program that took shape on Tim Berners-Lee's desktop has circled the globe and changed the lives of a huge swath of the planet's population. As the Web has worked its way into the fabric of humanity's cultural, economic, and political lives, networked information retrieval has radically reshaped the contours of our old institutional hierarchies. The Web has forced dramatic transformations inside many corporations, posed challenges to the author-

Screen shot of Tim Berners-Lee's original WorldWideWeb environment running on the NEXT platform (courtesy of CERN).

ity of the press, and completely transformed the way many people interact. Old fixed systems like library catalogs, controlled vocabularies, and manual indexes seem increasingly problematic in the digital age; new fluid systems like Web search engines and collaborative filtering tools seem to be displacing them. Once again, old hierarchies are giving way to emergent networks, with long-term effects that we cannot entirely foresee.

Ted Nelson, who arguably started it all, has disavowed the current Web as an ill-conceived perversion of his original idea, a simplistic implementation of "chunking hypertext," the most rudimentary form of hypertext. Staying true to his iconoclastic form, Nelson issued a defiant polemic on his personal Web site, presented in unadorned ASCII text:

I Don't Buy In

The Web isn't hypertext, it's DECORATED DIRECTORIES!

What we have instead is the vacuous victory of typesetters over authors, and the most trivial form of hypertext that could have been imagined.

The original hypertext project, Xanadu®, has always been about pure document structures where authors and readers don't have to think about computerish structures of files and hierarchical directories. The Xanadu project has endeavored to implement a pure structure of links and facilitated re-use of content in any amounts and ways, allowing authors to concentrate on what mattered.

Instead, today's nightmarish new world is controlled by "webmasters", tekkies unlikely to understand the niceties of text issues and preoccupied with the Web's exploding alphabet soup of embedded formats. XML is not an improvement but a hierarchy hamburger. Everything, everything must be forced into hierarchical templates! And the "semantic web" means that tekkie committees will decide the world's true concepts for once and for all. Enforcement is going to be another problem :) It is a very strange way of thinking, but all too many people are buying in because they think that's how it must be.

There is an alternative.

Markup must not be embedded. Hierarchies and files must not be part of the mental structure of documents. Links must go both ways. All these fundamental errors of the Web must be repaired. But the geeks have tried to lock the door behind them to make nothing else possible.

We fight on.[55]

Nelson's angry dismissal undoubtedly springs in part from personal disappointment at the Web's ascendance over his own vision for Xanadu, which now seems relegated to the status of a permanent historical footnote. Nonetheless, he correctly identifies many critical limitations of the Web: the evanescence of Web links, the co-opting of hypertext by corporate interests, and the emergence of a new "priesthood" of programmers and gatekeepers behind the scenes who still exert control over the technological levers powering the commercial Web.

Even the Web's own inventor, Tim Berners-Lee, has written despondently over its current state. Like Nelson, Berners-Lee originally envisioned a two-way authoring environment, in which browsers would function as both clients for reading documents and tools for writing new ones. However, such a democratic ethos ultimately runs counter to the profit motives of commercial software companies, which have a strong vested interest in treating users as consumers rather than creators.

For all its limitations, however, the Web's colossal success serves as a ringing vindication of its forefathers' vision. While it may be far from perfect, the Web has proved to be an enormously important democratizing technology. It is a profoundly humanist medium, open, accessible, and largely populated by nonprogrammers who have found ways to express themselves using a panoply of available technologies. The explosion of blogging, photo sharing, and other forms of personal expression testify to the viability of a computing environment populated not by "priests" of the computer but by ordinary citizens.

The Web's popularity has proved a mixed blessing for the original hypertext visionaries. While its success has vindicated their vision, it has also effectively limited the research horizons for many otherwise promising paths of inquiry. While the two decades before the Web saw a flurry of innovation and hopeful experimentation in networked information systems, the current dominance of Web standards has created a technological monolith that seems to preclude further experimentation.

As the Web continues to grow, however, its structural weaknesses are coming into stark relief. The sheer fluidity of Web pages makes it all but impossible to create fixed reference points; the lack of archiving functions leaves much of the Web in a state of perpetual amnesia; hyperlinks work in only one direction, making it difficult for the owner of a document to identify incoming links; and Web browsers are still designed primarily as tools of consumption, not creativity. At a more visceral level, the Web still carries the legacy of print: "pages" remain the dominant metaphor on the Web, a two-dimensional construct that seems woefully inadequate to support the range of possible interactions that networked computers could support. Internet theorist McKenzie Wark has suggested that we need "a new spatial architecture for dealing with text,"[56] echoing the sentiments of many earlier hypertext theorists. Perhaps our centuries of reliance on the familiar form of the printed book will make the page metaphor difficult to dislodge, or perhaps some new system will yet emerge to break the conceptual stranglehold of a basic form that has remained essentially unchanged since the age of papyrus.

Twenty years after Johannes Gutenberg invented his printing press, a bare handful of people in Germany and France had ever seen a printed book. Less than 20 years after its invention, the World Wide Web has touched billions.

12

Memories of the Future

And new philosophy calls all in doubt,
The element of fire is quite put out;
The sun is lost, and the earth, and no man's wit
Can well direct him where to look for it.
And freely men confess that this world's spent,
When in the planets, and the firmament
They seek so many new; they see that this
Is crumbled out again to his atomies
Tis all in pieces, all coherence gone;
All just supply, and all relation.
John Donne, "An Anatomy of the World"

Today, we stand at a precipice: between the near-limitless capacity of computer networks and the real physical limits of human comprehension. More than a billion people have now used a Web browser. Soon, millions of children in developing countries will start using $100 laptops to connect with each other online.[1] In an era when almost anyone can publish—and millions do—digital technology has fueled an unprecedented surge of individual expression. In the legions of bloggers, artists, politicians, journalists, and everyday citizens taking advantage of the Internet's ease of communication, we are witnessing the rise of vast populist networks threatening the power of old institutional hierarchies. The recent success of pop philosophy books like *The Tipping Point* and *The Wisdom of Crowds* seems to attest further to the appeal of the new populism, suggesting a growing faith in an emergent order guided not by an elite class of philosophers but by the will of the people.

Whether or not the most utopian visions of digital populism ever come to fruition, we are already witnessing social, political, and cultural change on a scale comparable only to the greatest previous axial periods in the history of technology. During the Ice Age information explosion, the new technologies of symbolism allowed previously loose-knit social groups to form larger tribal organizations; in ancient Sumeria, the advent of writing allowed traders to broaden their circles of trust and pave the way for the first bureaucracies; in medieval Europe, the continent's great descent into illiteracy and the subsequent renewal of oral culture provided the catalyst for the literary innovations of the medieval scriptoria; centuries later, the violent disruptions of the Gutenberg era brought mass literacy into conflict with the older folk traditions that had predominated outside the cloisters, resulting in a series of transformations that still reverberate today. All of these developments had one thing in common: They all triggered conflict between literacy and orality.

With the rise of the Internet, we may be witnessing a similar phenomenon taking shape today. Many of our familiar digital communication tools like e-mail, instant messaging, and blogs may seem, on the surface, like just another form of writing. But if we look closely at how people use these tools, we can see that many of these new modes of communication bear at least as much resemblance to the spoken word as to traditional forms of writing. The conversational tone of e-mail, the shorthand familiarity of instant messaging, and the loose rhetorical style of many blogs seem to suggest the casual rhythms of speech. Of course, large parts of the Internet still consist of traditional literary artifacts like books, newspapers, essays, dissertations, and so forth. But as more and more people get online, their interactions feel increasingly like a vast, far-flung conversation. Ultimately, the Internet's popularity may have less to do with a renewed public love of reading and writing than with our deep-seated need to talk.

As Steven Pinker points out, most children learn to write only with great difficulty; but we are born babblers, the "talking ape."[2] Until recently, most people on earth remained illiterate (and today more than one in five people still cannot read[3]). But almost every one of us is a natural talker. So perhaps it should come as no surprise that our most durable information systems—mythologies, religions, and various forms of practical know-how—have persisted not by dint of libraries, indexes, or taxonomic systems, but largely through word of mouth. Books and other forms of writing come and go, it seems, but the lineage of the spoken word gives us an unbroken connection to the deep past.

Today, we may be witnessing the latest manifestation of that ancient disposition toward spoken language. Linguist Walter J. Ong coined the term "secondary orality" to describe the parallels between electronic media and earlier oral cultures. While electronic media do not exactly mimic the dynamics of the spoken word, they nonetheless recall many of the same forms. Secondary orality is "post-literal," as Ong puts it, inasmuch as it is predicated on literacy, allowing for the mediation of spoken culture through the technology of the written word. Unfortunately, our understanding of how oral cultures really operate remains sketchy, thanks to a longstanding disdain for oral tradition among the literate scholarly class. Traditional scholarship—itself a product of literacy—has invariably elevated writing over the "primitive" culture of the spoken word. As a result, the study of oral traditions has until recently received scant attention from serious scholars. "Despite the oral roots of all verbalization, the scientific and literary study of languages and literature has for centuries, until quite recent years, shied away from orality," writes Ong. "Texts have clamored for attention so peremptorily that oral creations have tended to be regarded generally as variants of written productions or, if not this, as beneath serious scholarly attention."[4] While generations of academic scholars have devoted their careers to the study of the written word, only a handful of researchers have opened serious lines of inquiry into the study of orality. As a result, our understanding of the effects of electronic media on culture remains partial at best, and at worst egregiously biased toward the written word.

Today, we are witnessing the reemergence in electronic form of oral patterns that have been hiding in plain sight for generations. So deeply ingrained is our cultural disposition toward literacy, however, that many of us fail to recognize the oral characteristics of electronic media. Today, writers inevitably tend to describe the Web in terms of "publishing" or, like H. G. Wells, to compare it to a vast library. And while the Web does indeed support new kinds of publishing, it is also a place to "talk."

Ong suggests that the difference between oral and literate cultures boils down to a few core distinctions: Oral traditions are additive rather than subordinative, aggregative rather than analytic, empathetic and participatory rather than objectively distanced, and situational rather than abstract. The written word also enables individuals to transcend the limits of subjectivity. As Ong puts it, "Abstractly sequential, classificatory, explanatory examination of phenomena or of stated truths is impossible without writing and reading."[5] Writes Ong, "To say writing is artificial is not to condemn it but to praise it. Like other artificial creations and indeed more than any other, it is utterly invaluable and indeed essential for the realization of fuller, interior, human potentials." This is the paradox of literacy: It enables us to externalize our experiences and share those experiences with utter strangers, while simultaneously fostering deeper and deeper levels of introspection. "Technologies are not mere exterior aids but also interior transformations of consciousness, and never more than when they affect the word." And while technology inevitably relies on artifice, "artificiality is natural to human beings."[6]

Perhaps it should come as no surprise, then, that so many people have taken to the Internet, an artificial technology that lends itself to both "oral" and literate forms of expression. Often both modes coexist with each other. To take a familiar example, many commercial Web sites—like Amazon.com—offer independent reviews to accompany their product listings. Typically, these come in two flavors: "expert" reviews, usually licensed from publications, and customer-written reviews contributed by users. Frequently, these reviews appear side by side, yet separately. Customer reviews seem to fit Ong's criteria of an oral medium; they acquire value additively and aggregatively—that is, we look at the cumulative customer ratings for a product more than an individual review; they are empathetic—usually written in the first-person—and participatory, insofar as they invite conversation. Editorial reviews, by contrast, bear the hallmarks of literate culture: they are subordinative—that is, presuming a voice of authoritative judgment—analytic and objectively distanced, and abstract (usually written in the third person). These two forms—the oral and the written—coexist, yet they never quite meet. Most readers easily make the distinction between the two forms, and they may award more authority to the individual editorial review over the individual customer review. But the cumulative "oral tradition" of the customer reviews as a whole may often carry more weight than the individual editorial review.

The distinction between oral and literate cultures surfaces not just in the editorial content of Web sites, but increasingly at deeper structural levels as well. Many Web sites now support "social tagging" or other user-driven mechanisms for allowing visitors to organize the contents of a Web site. Popular sites like YouTube, Flickr, and de.licio.us give users a measure of control over how they organize the contents of the sites, allowing users to "tag" entries with keywords of their own choosing. The result is an emergent classification—sometimes called a "folksonomy"[7]—that, while typically flawed, allows users a great deal of flexibility and control over the information at hand. Over time, users typically reach a rough consensus over how a particular object should be categorized, and an emergent structure begins to take shape. A few sites, like Amazon.com, have tried to reconcile these bottom-up systems with more traditional top-down organizational models, with mixed results. The tension between oral and literate cultures seems to resist a smooth reconciliation.

At the level of organizational dynamics, the tension between literacy and orality manifests as a polarity between "fixity" and "fluidity" (to borrow John Seely Brown and Paul Duguid's terms). Examples of fixed systems include books, filing systems, taxonomies, and ontologies: the static instruments of literacy. Fluid systems include e-mail, instant messaging, and chat rooms: the shifting miasma of the new orality. Fixed systems beget hierarchies, while fluid systems lend themselves to the social motility of networks. In recent years, many corporations have embraced the mantra of flattening their organization charts to become more responsive in the face of technological change. Even such hidebound bureaucracies as the U.S. Army are working to transform themselves into "edge organizations,"[8] driving decision-making responsibility away from the old command-and-control centers and toward the outer rim of the organization, in an effort to enable individuals to take better advantage of new communications technology. In the process, organizations large and small are undergoing radical and disruptive change.

Fixity and fluidity can and do coexist, however. "While it's clear that self-organization is extraordinarily productive, so too is formal organization," write Brown and Duguid. "Indeed, the two perform an intricate (and dynamic) balancing act, each compensating for the other's failings. Self-organization overcomes formal organizing's rigidity. Formal organization keeps at bay self-organization's tendency to self-destruct."[9] In other words, hierarchies and networks do not necessarily have to stand in opposition; they may not only coexist, but ultimately prove consilient. As Kevin Kelly puts it in his 1994 book *Out of Control*:

> In the human management of distributed control, hierarchies of a certain type will proliferate rather than diminish. That goes especially for distributed systems involving human nodes—such as huge global computer networks. Many computer activists preach a new era in the network economy, an era built around computer peer-to-peer networks, a time when rigid patriarchal networks will wither away. They are right and wrong. While authoritarian "top-down" hierarchies will retreat, no distributed system can survive long without nested hierarchies of lateral "bottom-up" control. As influence flows peer to peer, it coheres into a chunk—a whole organelle—which then becomes the bottom unit in a larger web of slower actions. Over time a multi-level organization forms around the percolating-up control: fast at the bottom, slow at the top.[10]

While the tension between hierarchies and networks may in the long run prove complementary, in the short term the results can look a lot like chaos. Today, the old hierarchies of the literate world are reeling from a collision with the chaotic energies of oral culture. This is more than just a clash of epistemologies; it is a conflict with potentially revolutionary implications. Throughout most of human history, the top layers of the institutional hierarchy have always belonged to the literate elite. Without a lettered class there would have been no Sumerian temples, no library at Alexandria, no monastic scriptoria. Even after the Gutenberg revolution, only a tiny handful of people actually produced written documents, let alone whole books. Today, however, the planet has more readers and writers than ever before, and increasingly they are connected to each other on the Internet.

The long-term results of such a dramatic technological shift may be impossible to predict, but in the near term one thing seems plain enough: As people find their way online, they seem to coalesce into small groups.

Before the age of television, many historians believed that the spread of literacy signaled the forward march of technological progress, in which human civilization was moving inexorably forward toward higher degrees of social complexity. In this view, the spread of information technologies helped smaller communities coalesce into larger entities: bands into tribes, tribes into city-states, city-states into nations, nations into empires, and so on. Culture and technology propelled each other forward. Recent history, however, seems to support an alternative view that in our modern technological era human culture may not be moving unidirectionally at all, but rather multidirectionally. The notion of inevitable progress toward hierarchical complexity began to fracture in the 1960s, with the rise of the great modern liberation movements: civil rights, the antiwar movement, feminism, sexual liberation, gay rights. All of these social movements also happened to coincide with the spread of electronic media. Suddenly, women, minorities, homosexuals, and other previously marginalized groups had access to technologies that provided new windows into the culture at large. Televised images provided a unifying reference point that encouraged like-minded individuals to seek each other out. Small, self-organized communities emerged around common causes and shared values. In each of these cases, spontaneous networks emerged as individuals began to communicate with each other, thanks in large part to the facilitative power of electronic media. As these spontaneous networks joined together, they began to challenge the existing institutional power structures. Black citizens demanded the vote; women demanded equal rights; homosexuals demanded legal equality. The same dynamic played out in smaller groups as well, as the cultural convulsions of the 1960s brought wave after wave of spontaneous bottom-up challenges to the traditional top-down establishment. The success of these self-organized movements seemed to call into question the unidirectional progression from smaller to large units of social organization. Instead, it seemed, the age of electronic media was leading not to the forward march of civilization, but rather to social and cultural fragmentation. That trajectory toward social atomization would accelerate further with the advent of the personal computer and, later, the Internet.[11]

The 1960s liberation movements provided the social backdrop for the emergence of the personal computer industry. The first-generation PC hackers, many of whom traced their lineage to Doug Engelbart's 1968 San Francisco demonstration (see Chapter 11), aligned themselves with the countercultural values of the hippie movement, embracing an ethos of personal empowerment in contrast to the old top-down, command-and-control systems of the mainstream military–industrial computing industry.[12] Ted Nelson—the philosophical godfather of the Web—always portrayed himself as an ardent antiestablishmentarian. For the early programmers the PC represented a vehicle for personal liberation from the oppressive control of hierarchical institutions.

As PCs moved into the workplace in the 1980s, they triggered a struggle between self-directed "power users," who wanted to take advantage of their increasingly powerful desktop computers, and old guard information technology departments that continued to insist on centralized control (a tension that still carries over to this day in many large organizations). That simmering tension would finally boil over when the Internet started allowing those users to network with each other directly, bypassing the old command-and-control systems. For many old-guard organizations, the results proved nothing short of paroxysmic. As the Internet gave employees more avenues for reaching out to each other—via the Web, e-mail, or instant messaging—they started to coalesce into spontaneous, self-organizing groups that often bore little resemblance to the formal structure of the organization chart. Decades after the liberation movements of the 1960s had peaked, the same revolutionary ethic was echoing in the corridors of corporate power. Organizations found themselves forced to change in response to the emerging technology. Fueled by the growth of personal computing and network technology, many organizations have since had to come to terms with an ongoing transfer of power, away from the old central planning hierarchies and toward increasingly self-organized groups of individuals.

Meanwhile, across the Internet, new communities are constantly emerging, dissolving, and reforming. This burgeoning network activity does not spell the end of institutional hierarchies, however. As we have seen over and over again, hierarchies and networks are constantly spawning each other. One instructive contemporary example comes from Wikipedia, the ambitious public Internet encyclopedia that in a few short years has grown to encompass millions of entries written by thousands of individual users. For all its populist appeal, Wikipedia's sheer growth has forced it to develop a set of hierarchical control systems, instituting a governing organization and approval processes to exert a measure of top-down regulation over the sprawling bottom-up activity of its contributors. As the network has grown, a new governing hierarchy emerged.

Large-scale bottom-up systems like Wikipedia remain the exception, however, as Internet users continue to congregate in small groups that often take shape outside of traditional institutional containers. While this tendency toward self-organization might seem like an effect of the Internet's democratic architecture, such behavior also harkens back to our deepest rooted social instincts. For most of our species' history, human beings have interacted in small, tightly woven communities: families, villages, guilds, and other social groups whose members were bound by ties of direct kinship or close personal affiliation. Only in the past few thousand years have people allowed themselves to be governed by institutional bodies. On the scale of evolutionary history, institutions remain a short-lived hypothesis. Yet for tens of thousands of years, human beings have interacted as social animals, following unwritten norms strengthened by kinship, reinforced by the limbic responses that strengthen our personal relationships, and transmitted through the spoken word. Today, we are seeing those instincts returning to the fore, as people adapt new technologies to invoke the ancient emotional circuitry that carried us through the age before symbols. The future of memory may lie not in our heads but in our hearts.

Appendix A

John Wilkins's Universal Categories

General; namely those Universal notions, whether belonging more properly to Things; called TRANSCENDENTAL
    GENERAL. I
    RELATION MIXED. II
    RELATION OF ACTION. III
    Words; DISCOURSE. IV
Special; denoting either
    CREATOR. V
    Creatures; namely such things as were either created or concreated by God, not excluding several of those notions, which are framed by the minds of men, considered either
        Collectively; WORLD. VI
        Distributively; according to several kinds of Beings. whether such as do belong to
            Substance;
                Inanimate; ELEMENT. VII
                Animate; considered according to their several
                    Species; whether
                        Vegetative

Imperfect; as Minerals,
    STONE. VIII
    METAL. IX
Perfect; as Plant,
    HERB consid. accord. to the
        LEAF. X
        FLOWER. XI.
        SEED-VESSEL. XII
    SHRUB. XIII
    TREE. XIV
Sensitive;
    EXANGUIOUS. XV
Sanguineous;
    FISH. XVI
    BIRD. XVII
    BEAST. XVIII
Parts;
    PECULIAR. XIX
    GENERAL. XX
Accident;
  Quantity;
    MAGNITUDE. XXI
    SPACE. XXII
    MEASURE. XXIII
  Quality; whether
    NATURAL POWER. XXIV
    HABIT. XXV
    MANNERS. XXVI
    SENSIBLE QUALITY. XXVII
    SICKNESS. XXVIII
  Action
    SPIRITUAL. XXIX
    CORPOREAL. XXX
    MOTION. XXXI
    OPERATION. XXXII

Relation; whether more
    Private
        OECONOMICAL. XXXIII
        POSSESSIONS. XXXIV
        PROVISIONS. XXXV
    Publick
        JUDICIAL. XXXVII
        MILITARY. XXXVIII
        NAVAL. XXXIX
        ECCLESIASTICAL. XL.

Appendix B

Thomas Jefferson's 1783 Catalog of Books

Books may be classed from the Faculties of the mind, which being

I. Memory. II. Reason. III. Imagination
are applied respectively to
I. History. II. Philosphy. III. Fine Arts.

History.	Civil.	Civil proper.	Antient [Ancient].	Antient hist.
			Modern.	Foreign
				British.
				American.
		Ecclesiastical.		Ecclesiastical.
	Natural.	Physics.		Natl. Philosy.
				Agriculture.
				Chemistry.
				Medecine.
		Natl. histy. propr.	Animals.	
				Zoology.
			Vegetables.	
			Minerals.	
		Occupations of Man.		Technical arts.

Philosophy.	Moral.	Ethics.		Moral Philosy.
				Law Nature & nations.
		Jurisprudence.	Religious.	Religion.
			Municipal.	Equity.
			Domestic.	Common Law.
				L. Merchant.
				L. Maritime.
				L. Merchant.
				L. Ecclesiastl.
			Foreign.	Foreign Law.
			Oeconomical.	Politics.
				Commerce.
	Mathematical.	Pure.		Arithmetic.
				Geometry.
		Physico-Mathematical.		Mechanics.
				~~St.~~ Statics.
				[illegible]
				Dynamics.
				Penumatics.
				Phonics.
				Optics.
				Astronomy.
				Geography.
Fine Arts.	Gardening.			Gardening.
	Architecture.			Architecture.
	Sculpture.			Sculpture.
	Painting.			Painting.
	Music.	Theoretical.		Music Theory.
		Practical.		Music. Vocal.
				Music.
				Instrumentl.
	Poetry.	Narrative.		Epic.
				Romance.
		Dramatic.		Tragedy.
				Comedy.
				Pastorals.

	Odes.
	Elegies.
	Dialogue.
Didactic.	Satire.
	Epigram.
	Epistles.
Oratory.	Logic.
	Rhetoric.
	Oration.
Criticism.	Criticism.
Authors who have written in various branches.	Polygraphical.

Appendix C

The Dewey Decimal System

0	GENERAL	200	THEOLOGY
10	Bibliography	210	Natural Theology
20	Book Rarities	220	Bible
30	General Cyclopedias	230	Doctrinal Theology
40	Polygraphy	240	Practical and Devotional
50	General Periodicals	250	Homiletical and Pastoral
60	General Societies	260	Institutions and Missions
70		270	Ecclesiastical History
80		280	Christian Sects
90		290	Non-Christian Religions
100	PHILOSOPHY	300	SOCIOLOGY
110	Metaphysics	310	Statistics
120		320	Political Science
130	Anthropology	330	Political Economy
140	Schools of Psychology	340	Law
150	Mental Faculties	350	Administration
160	Logic	360	Associations and Institutions
170	Ethics	370	Education
180	Ancient Philosophies	380	Commerce and Communication
190	Modern Philosophies	390	Customs and Costumes

400 PHILOLOGY	700 FINE ARTS
410 Comparative	710 Landscape Gardening
420 English	720 Architecture
430 German	730 Sculpture
440 French	740 Drawing and Design
450 Italian	750 Painting
460 Spanish	760 Engraving
470 Latin	770 Photography
480 Greek	780 Music
490 Other Languages	790 Amusements
500 NATURAL SCIENCE	800 LITERATURE
510 Mathematics	810 Treatises and Collections
520 Astronomy	820 English
530 Physics	830 German
540 Chemistry	840 French
550 Geology	850 Italian
560 Paleontology	860 Spanish
570 Biology	870 Latin
580 Botany	880 Greek
590 Zoology	890 Other Languages
600 USEFUL ARTS	900 HISTORY
610 Medicine	910 Geography and Description
620 Engineering	920 Biography
630 Agriculture	930 Ancient History
640 Domestic Economy	940 Modern Europe
650 Communication and Commerce	950 Modern Asia
660 Chemical Technology	960 Modern Africa
670 Manufactures	970 Modern North America
680 Mechanic Trades	980 Modern South America
690 Building	990 Modern Oceanica and Polar

Appendix D

S. R. Ranganathan's
Colon Classification

(Selected facets for each class shown in brackets.)

1-9 Generalia

Sciences

A Science (General)

B Mathematics
[Number] [Problem] [Method] [Equation] [Form] [Degree]
[Transformation] [Order] [Variable] [Space] [Matter] [Body]

C Physics
[State] [Problem] [Wave Length] [Electricity] [Magnetism]

D Engineering
[Work] [Part] [Secondary Work] [Engineering]

E Chemistry
[Problem] [Substance]

F Technology
[Substance] [Problem]

G Biology
[Organ] [Problem]

H Geology
[Substance] [Problem]

I Botany
[Natural Group] [Problem] [Organ]

J Agriculture
[Utility] [Part] [Crops] [Farming] [Substance] [Operation]
[Disease]

K Zoology
[Natural Group] [Problem]

L Medicine
[Organ] [Problem]

M Useful Arts
[Material] [Work] [Subject Device] [Utility] [Part] [Substance]
[Handling] [Organ] [Operation]

Δ Spiritual Experience and Mysticism
[Religion] [Problem] [Entity]

Humanities

N Fine Arts
[Style] [Utility] [Part] [Material] [Figure] [Instrument] [Music]

O Literature
[Language] [Form] [Author] [Work]

P Linguistics
[Language] [Substance] [Problem] [Entity]

Q Religion
[Religion] [Problem]

R Philosophy
[View] [Subject] [Problem] [Controlling]

S Psychology
[Entity] [Problem]

T Education
[Educand] [Problem] [Subject]

U Geography
[Problem] [Geographical] [Controlling]

V History
[Geographical] [Problem] [Controlling]

W Political Science
[Type of State] [Problem]

X Economics
[Business] [Problem] [Geographical] [Controlling]

Y (Other) Social Sciences Including Sociology
[Group] [Problem] [Geographical] [Controlling]

Z Law
[Community] [Law] [Problem]

Acknowledgments

In a medieval scriptorium, it would have been considered the height of arrogance for a writer to put his name on the cover of a book. Making books was properly understood to be a collaborative effort, involving the combined talents of scholars, scribes, binders, and artists. While book production has long since evolved from a monastic craft to an industrial enterprise—and while we may now agree on the convenient fiction of an "author"—a book is still the product of many minds.

This book would not exist in its present form without the efforts of my editor Jeff Robbins, my agent Jeanne Fredericks, and the able team at the Joseph Henry Press. This book is also immeasurably better for the thoughtful criticism of several people who commented on various draft versions of the manuscript. For their intellectual generosity, I am especially indebted to Whit Andrews, Brent Berlin, Ed Costello, Eugene Garfield, Paul Kahn, George P. Landow, Rhodri Lewis, Peter Merholz, Thomas J. Misa, Mike Myers, Dave Pell, Nadav Savio, Rosemary Michelle Simpson, Andries van Dam, Edward O. Wilson, and Nicole Yankelovich.

During the final year I spent writing this book, I relied on the good graces of people who furnished me with places to work, and the gifts of both solitude and companionship. For their friendship and hospitality, thanks to Ann and Preston Browning, Judy DeMocker, Jennifer Kilian, Bill and Jocelyn Powning, Chris and Kassia Scott, and John Woodward.

As a onetime library worker, I would be remiss in failing to acknowledge the librarians who made it possible for me to research this book. Librarians are the anonymous heroes of scholarship, and they rarely get the praise they deserve. I am especially grateful to the staff at the Library of Congress, the San Francisco Public Library, and the University of Richmond. I also owe a debt of gratitude to my former colleagues at the Harvard College Library, who introduced me to a noble profession and helped me start asking the questions that would eventually lead me to write this book.

I would also like to thank the many dharma teachers and fellow students with whom I have had the good fortune to study over the past few years. For their encouragement, I would especially like to thank Acharya Lama Dawa and Lama Kalsang Rinpoche.

Finally, my greatest thanks go to my parents, Sarah Bird Wright and Lewis Wright, for their love.

Notes

INTRODUCTION

1 Tom Wolfe, *The Electric Kool-Aid Acid Test* (New York: Bantam, 1999).

2 Tom Wolfe, "Digibabble, Fairy Dust and the Human Anthill," *Forbes ASAP*, vol. 164, no. 8 (1999), 212.

3 Steven Johnson, *Interface Culture: How New Technology Transforms the Way We Create and Communicate* (San Francisco, CA: HarperEdge, 1997), 240.

4 Danny Hillis, "The Big Picture," *Wired* 6.01, January 1998, http://www.wired.com/wired/archive/6.01/hillis.html; accessed 7 December 2006.

5 Ray Kurzweil, "The Law of Accelerating Returns," 2001, http://www.kurzweilai.net/articles/art0134.html; accessed 7 December 2006.

6 H. G. Wells, "World Brain: The Idea of a Permanent World Encyclopedia" in *Encyclopédie Française,* August 1937, http://sherlock.berkeley.edu/wells/world_brain.html; accessed 7 December 2006.

7 Teilhard de Chardin, *The Future of Man*, trans. Norman Denny (New York: Image Books/Doubleday, 2004), 162.

8 Sven Birkerts, *The Gutenberg Elegies: The Fate of Reading in an Electronic Age* (New York: Ballantine, 1995), 130-131.

9   Werner Künzel, quoted in Lovink, "The Archaeology of Computer As-
    semblage," *Mediamatic*, vol. 7 no. 1, 1992, http://www.mediamatic.net/
    article-8664-en.html; accessed 7 December 2006.

10 Birkerts, op. cit., 123.

CHAPTER 1

1   Emile Durkheim and Marcel Mauss, *Primitive Classification* (Chicago,
    IL: University of Chicago Press, 1963), 43-44.

2   Peter Lyman and Hal R. Varian, "How Much Information," 2003, http:
    //www.sims.berkeley.edu/how-much-info-2003; accessed 7 December
    2006.

3   Christopher Locke, Rick Levine, Doc Searls, and David Weinberger,
    The Cluetrain Manifesto, 1999, http://www.cluetrain.com; accessed 7
    December 2006.

4   Jeff Hawkins with Sandra Blakeslee, *On Intelligence: How a New Under-
    standing of the Brain Will Lead to the Creation of Truly Intelligent Ma-
    chines* (New York: Owl Books, 2004).

5   Howard K. Bloom, *Global Brain: The Evolution of Mass Mind from the
    Big Bang to the 21st Century* (New York: Wiley, 2000).

6   Stephen Jay Gould, *Full House: The Spread of Excellence from Plato to
    Darwin* (New York: Harmony Books, 1996), 219-220.

7   John Alcock, *The Triumph of Sociobiology* (Oxford, England; New York:
    Oxford University Press, 2003), 223.

8   Bloom, op. cit., 31.

9   Edward O. Wilson initially proposed an alternate neologism,
    "culturgen," but has since embraced the now overwhelmingly popular
    "meme." Wilson argues in favor of a narrow definition of meme, how-
    ever, as a unit of "semantic memory" available exclusively to humans.
    Other biologists have embraced a wider definition that includes be-
    havioral "implicit memes"—roughly, social customs—stretching as
    far back as 720-million-year-old prehistoric clams. Other scientists
    have sought a middle ground, suggesting the presence of memes in
    smaller numbers of species, including hominids, dolphins, and a few
    other mammals.

10 Bloom, op. cit.

11 Kevin Kelly, *Out of Control: The New Biology of Machines, Social Systems and the Economic World* (New York: Perseus Books Group, 1995), 12.

12 Wilson prefers the term "sematectonic" over "stigmergy," arguing that the latter is too clumsy a term.

13 McClamrock, quoted in Andy Clark, *Being There: Putting Brain, Body, and World Together Again* (Cambridge, MA: MIT Press, 1997), 201.

14 Robert Wright, *Nonzero: The Logic of Human Destiny* (New York: Vintage, 2001), 292.

15 Carel Van Schaik, "Why Are Some Animals So Smart?" *Scientific American*, April 2006, http://www.sciam.com/article.cfm?articleID=000C1E5D-B9BA-1422-B9BA83414B7F0103&ref=sciam&chanID=sa006; accessed 7 December 2006.

16 Ibid.

17 Stanley I. Greenspan and Stuart G. Shanker, *The First Idea: How Symbols, Language, and Intelligence Evolved from Our Primate Ancestors to Modern Humans* (Cambridge, MA: Da Capo Press, 2004), 92.

18 Ibid., 340-341.

19 Edward O. Wilson, *Consilience: The Unity of Knowledge* (New York: Vintage, 1999), 138.

20 Ibid., 223-224.

21 Ibid., 128.

22 Donald Brown, cited in Steven Pinker, *The Blank Slate: The Modern Denial of Human Nature* (New York: Viking, 2002), 435.

CHAPTER 2

1 Brent Berlin, *Ethnobiological Classification: Principles of Categorization of Plants and Animals in Traditional Societies* (Princeton, NJ: Princeton University Press, 1992), 7.

2 Stephen Jay Gould, foreword to Lynn Margulis and Karlene V. Schwartz, *Five Kingdoms: An Illustrated Guide to the Phyla of Life on Earth* (New York: W.H. Freeman & Company, 1998).

3 Brent Berlin, personal correspondence with Alex Wright, 30 March 2006.

4   Conklin, quoted in Berlin, op. cit., 13.

5   Roger Brown, "How Shall a Thing Be Called?" *Psychology Review*, 65 (1958), 14-21.

6   Eleanor Rosch, quoted in George Lakoff, *Women, Fire, and Dangerous Things: What Categories Reveal About the Mind* (Chicago, IL: University of Chicago Press, 1987), 44.

7   Lakoff, op. cit., 8.

8   Emile Durkheim and Marcel Mauss, *Primitive Classification* (Chicago, IL: University of Chicago Press, 1963), 14.

9   Michael E. Hobart and Zachary Sayre Schiffman, *Information Ages: Literacy, Numeracy, and the Computer Revolution* (Baltimore, MD: Johns Hopkins University Press, 1998), 71.

10   Durkheim and Mauss, op. cit., 82-83.

11   Ibid., 85-86.

12   Brent Berlin, personal correspondence with Alex Wright, 30 March 2006.

13   Durkheim and Mauss, op. cit., 69.

14   Ibid., 73.

15   Ibid., 78.

16   Ibid., 79.

CHAPTER 3

1   Louis Baudin, *A Socialist Empire: The Incas of Peru*, quoted in "The Quipucamayu," http://www.spanish.sbc.edu/MMLatAm/Quipus.html; accessed 7 December 2006.

2   John McCrone, *Going Inside: A Tour Round a Single Moment of Consciousness* (London: Faber and Faber, 1999).

3   Steven Kuhn et al., "Ornaments of the Earliest Upper Paleolithic," *Proceedings of the National Academy of Sciences*, 98 (2001), 7641-7646.

4   Randall White, quoted in William F. Allman, *The Stone Age Present: How Evolution Has Shaped Modern Life: From Sex, Violence, and Language to Emotions, Morals, and Communities* (New York: Simon and Schuster, 1994), 215.

5   Ibid., 209.

6   Scholars have variously speculated that cave paintings were used for hunting rituals or religious ceremonies; more recently, some scholars have suggested they may be the ancient equivalent of teenage graffiti.

7   Wilson, op. cit., 142.

CHAPTER 4

1   Perhaps not coincidentally, the earliest known examples of Chinese writing have been discovered on a 6,000-year-old turtle shell.

2   Thomas Cahill, *The Gifts of the Jews: How a Tribe of Desert Nomads Changed the Way Everyone Thinks and Feels* (New York: Nan A. Talese, 1998), 11.

3   While Sumerians pioneered the notion of keeping time, they did not understand time the same way we do. Sumerian "hours" varied by season, depending on the availability of sunlight (a Sumerian hour was about one-sixth of a day's sunlight). The Babylonians later introduced the notion of 24 uniform hours in a day.

4   While traditional Western histories have situated Mesopotamia as the birthplace of writing, many historians now believe that writing emerged independently in at least three locations: Sumer, China, and the ancient Mayan civilization.

5   V. Gordon Childe, *Man Makes Himself* (New York: New American Library, 1951).

6   Wayne A. Wiegand and Donald G. Davis, *Encyclopedia of Library History* (New York: Garland Pub, 1994), 24.

7   Walter J. Ong, *Orality and Literacy: The Technologizing of the Word* (London: Methuen, 1982), 94.

8   Anonymous, quoted in Lionel Casson, *Libraries in the Ancient World* (New Haven, CT: Yale University Press, 2001), 5.

9   Melvil Dewey was the inventor of the Dewey Decimal System, still used in most U.S. public libraries (see Chapter 10).

10   Michael H. Harris and Elmer D. Johnson, *History of Libraries in the Western World* (Metuchen, NJ: Scarecrow Press, 1984), 7.

11   Matthew Battles, *Library: An Unquiet History* (New York: W. W. Norton, 2003), 7.

12   A. C. Moorhouse, "The Historical Influence of Writing," in *Writing and the Alphabet* (London: Cobbett Press, 1946), 68-74.

13   Wiegand, op. cit., 27.

14   Battles, op. cit., 12.

15   Foster Stockwell, *A History of Information Storage and Retrieval* (Jefferson, NC: McFarland, 2001), 11.

16   Robert Lamberton, *Hesiod* (New Haven, CT: Yale University Press, 1988), 64.

17   Ibid., 39.

18   This phrase was coined by librarian and classicist H. Curtis Wright.

19   Lamberton, op. cit., 41.

20   Merlin Donald, *Origins of the Modern Mind: Three Stages in the Evolution of Culture and Cognition* (Cambridge, MA: Harvard University Press, 1991), 275.

21   Plato, *Phaedrus*, trans. Benjamin Jowett (Champaign, IL: Project Gutenberg, 1999), http://www.gutenberg.org/dirs/etext99/phdrs10.txt; accessed 7 December 2006.

22   Donald, op. cit., 273.

23   Karl Popper draws much the same distinction between scientific and "pre-scientific" thought.

24   Donald, op. cit., 343.

25   Ibid., 274.

26   Strabo, quoted in Lionel Casson, *Libraries in the Ancient World* (New Haven, CT: Yale University Press, 2001), 29.

27   Aristotle, *The Categories*, trans. E. M. Edghill (Champaign, IL: Project Gutenberg, 2000), http://www.gutenberg.org/dirs/etext00/arist10.txt; accessed 7 December 2006.

28   Leslie W. Dunlap, *Readings in Library History* (New York: R. R. Bowker, 1972), 20.

29   Amr, quoted in Matthew Battles, *Library: An Unquiet History* (New York: W. W. Norton, 2003), 22-23.

30   Ausonius, *The Origins of the English Library,* trans. John Evelyn, quoted in Raymond Irwin (Westport, CT: Greenwood Press, 1981), 133.

31   Martial, quoted in Dunlap, op. cit., 32.

32   Ammanius, quoted in Dunlap, op. cit., 34.

CHAPTER 5

1   Christopher De Hamel, *A History of Illuminated Manuscripts* (London: Phaidon Press, 1994), 22.

2   Michael E. Hobart and Zachary Sayre Schiffman, *Information Ages: Literacy, Numeracy, and the Computer Revolution* (Baltimore, MD: Johns Hopkins University Press, 1998), 91.

3   Thomas Cahill, *How the Irish Saved Civilization: The Untold Story of Ireland's Heroic Role from the Fall of Rome to the Rise of Medieval Europe* (New York: Nan A. Talese, Doubleday, 1995), 163.

4   De Hamel, op. cit., 11.

5   Bede, quoted in De Hamel, op. cit., 40.

6   Cambrensis, quoted in Celtic Network, "The Book of Kells: Celtic Art's Most Magnificent Masterpiece," http://www.celticnetwork.com/culture/celtic-art/book-of-kells.html; accessed 7 December 2006.

7   Cassiodorus, quoted in Leslie W. Dunlap, *Readings in Library History* (New York: R. R. Bowker, 1972), 68.

8   Matthew Battles, *Library: An Unquiet History* (New York: W. W. Norton, 2003), 60.

9   James J. O'Donnell, *Cassiodorus* (Berkeley, CA: University of California Press, 1979). "Postprint," 1995, Chapter 5, http://ccat.sas.upenn.edu/jod/texts/cassbook/toc.html; accessed 7 December 2006.

10 Ivan Illich, *In the Vineyard of the Text: A Commentary to Hugh's Didascalion* (Chicago, IL: University of Chicago Press, 1996), 54.

11 Ong, op. cit., 119.

12 Saint Benedict, quoted in Karl Christ, *The Handbook of Medieval Library History* (Metuchen, NJ: Scarecrow Press, 1984), 17.

13 Alcuin unwittingly anticipated use of the term "walled garden" by modern-day software developers—that is, as a sealed information environment (AOL, for example, is a classic example of a networked "walled garden").

14 J. J. O'Connor and E. F. Robertson, "Alcuin of York," 1999, http://www-groups.dcs.st-and.ac.uk/~history/Mathematicians/Alcuin.html; accessed 7 December 2006.

15 Battles, op. cit., 79.

16 James Westfall Thompson, *The Medieval Library* (New York: Hafner, 1957), 348-350.

17   Ibid., 357.

18   Gibbon, *The Decline and Fall of the Roman Empire* (New York: Modern Library, 2005), 1139.

CHAPTER 6

1   Whit Andrews, personal correspondence with Alex Wright, 7 April 2006.

2   Samuel A. Ives and Hellmut Lehmann-Haupt, *An English 13th Century Bestiary, a New Discovery in the Technique of Medieval Illumination* (New York: H. P. Kraus, 1942).

3   Brian Stock, *The Implications of Literacy: Written Language and Models of Interpretation in the Eleventh and Twelfth Centuries* (Princeton, NJ: Princeton University Press, 1983), 32.

4   Ibid., 18.

5   Ibid., 62.

6   "Social fact" is a term coined by Emile Durkheim.

7   Stock, op. cit., 88.

8   "Document nation" is a term coined by Brian Stock.

9   Not to be confused with the modern stationer, the medieval stationer performed a complicated role involving taxation, quality assurance, and distribution of master copies of important texts.

10   Lucien Paul Victor Febvre and Henri-Jean Martin, *The Coming of the Book: The Impact of Printing, 1450-1800* (London: Verso, 1990), 167.

11   Johann Koelhoff, quoted in Ibid., 171.

12   Indulgences were remittances granted by the church to allay punishment for sins. The practice of selling indulgences was eventually banned by Pope Pius VI in 1567.

13   Febvre and Martin, op. cit., 173.

14   Ibid., 79.

15   Ibid., 96.

16   Xylography was a popular printing technique using wood-cut engravings.

17   Febvre and Martin, op. cit., 97.

18   John Henry Newman Newman, *Idea of a University*, quoted in George P. Landow, *Hypertext 2.0* (Baltimore, MD: Johns Hopkins University Press, 1997), 26.

19   Febvre and Martin, op. cit., 261.

20   Stockwell, op. cit., 47.

21   Landow, op. cit., 21.

22   Elizabeth Eisenstein, *The Printing Press as an Agent of Change* (Cambridge, England: Cambridge University Press, 1980), 303.

23   Ibid., 304.

24   Leonard Shlain, *The Alphabet Versus the Goddess: The Conflict Between Word and Image* (New York: Penguin, 1999), 325.

25   Ibid., 331.

26   John Lothrop Motley, "The Rise of the Dutch Republic," in *The History of the Netherlands, Complete*, 1855, http://www.literaturemania.com/jm00v10/page86.asp; accessed 7 December 2006.

27   Shlain, op. cit., 345.

28   Ibid., 372.

29   Ibid., 375.

CHAPTER 7

1   Frances Amelia Yates, *The Art of Memory* (London: Routledge, 1999), 137.

2   Rhodri Lewis, "From Athens to Elsinore: The Early Modern Art of Memory, Reconsidered" (Preprint, Berlin: Max-Planck-Institut für Wissenschaftsgeschichte, 2006), 5-7.

3   Thomas Aquinas, *De anima*, quoted in Yates, op. cit., 32.

4   Willis, quoted in Lewis, op. cit.,19.

5   Yates, op. cit., 121.

6   Yates, op. cit., 80.

7   Ibid., 113.

8   Ibid., 123.

9   Ibid., 172.

10   Lewis, op. cit., 10-12.

11   Ibid., 158.

12   Ibid., 127.

13   Bruno, quoted in Ibid., 200.

14   Bruno, quoted in Ibid., 228.

15   Yates, op. cit., 223.

16 Like the Gnostics, Bruno believed that 30 was a mystical number (representing, for example, the number of disciples of John the Baptist and the number of eons). Thirty is also deeply associated with magical practices like those of Simon Magus.

17 Yates, op. cit., 212-213.

18 Bruno, quoted in Yates, op. cit., 217.

19 See Chapter 1.

20 Lewis, op. cit., 14.

21 Aubrey, quoted in Yates, op. cit., 370.

22 Bacon, quoted in Yates, op. cit., 371.

23 Francis Bacon, *Novum Organum*, 2.26 in Graham Rees and Lisa Jardine, eds., *The Oxford Francis Bacon*, 15 vols. (Oxford, England: Oxford University Press, 1996-), 11, 285-287.

24 Francis Bacon, quoted in John Henry, *Knowledge Is Power: How Magic, the Government and an Apocalyptic Vision Helped Francis Bacon to Create Modern Science* (Cambridge, England: Totem Books, 2004), 43.

25 Bacon, *Novum Organum*, quoted in Ibid., 49.

26 The title is play on Aristotle's *Organon*.

27 Bacon, quoted in William Sessions, *Francis Bacon Revisited* (New York: Twayne, 1996), 79.

28 Bacon, *Great Instauration*, quoted in Stephen Jay Gould, "Bacon, Brought Home," *Natural History* 108(1999), 28-32, 72-78.

29 Bacon, quoted in Matthew Battles, *Library: An Unquiet History* (New York: W. W. Norton, 2003), 84.

30 Bacon, quoted in Sessions, op. cit., 78.

31 Rhodri Lewis, *Language, Mind and Nature: Artificial Languages in England from Bacon to Locke* (Cambridge, England: Cambridge University Press, 2007), Chapter 5.

32 Ibid., 224.

33 Wilkins, quoted in Lewis, op. cit., 230.

34 Ibid., 237.

35 "John Wilkins," *BBC History*, http://www.bbc.co.uk/history/historic_figures/wilkins_john.shtml; accessed 5 February 2004.

36 Jorge Luis Borges, "The Analytical Language of John Wilkins," in *Other Inquisitions: 1937-1952*, trans. Ruth L. C. Simms (Austin, TX: University of Texas Press, 1964).

CHAPTER 8

1   Lucien Paul Victor Febvre and Henri Jean Martin, *The Coming of the Book: The Impact of Printing, 1450-1800* (London: Verso, 1990), 262.

2   Thomas Heywood, *Gunaikeion*, quoted in Nona Crook and Neil Rhodes, "The Daughters of Memory," in Neil Rhode, ed., *The Renaissance Computer* (London: Routledge, 2000), 135-147.

3   Ibid.

4   Ibid.

5   Crook and Rhodes, op. cit., 143.

6   Heywood, quoted in Ibid.

7   Ibid.

8   Crook and Rhodes, op. cit., 145.

9   Stockwell, op. cit., 89-90.

10 Stock, op. cit.

CHAPTER 9

1   David G. Post, "Mr. Jefferson's Moose and the Law of Cyberspace," *FindLaw,* http://writ.news.findlaw.com/commentary/20000807_post. html; accessed 7 December 2006.

2   Harriet Ritvo, *The Platypus and the Mermaid: And Other Figments of the Classifying Imagination* (Cambridge, MA: Harvard University Press, 1997), 53.

3   Cf. Durkheim's work on primitive classification (see Chapter 2).

4   Buffon's "American Degeneracy" (Philadelphia, PA: Academy of Natural Sciences), http://www.acnatsci.org/museum/jefferson/otherPages/ degeneracy-03.php; accessed 7 December 2006.

5   Georges-Louis Leclerc, Comte de Buffon, *Histoire Naturelle*, quoted in Ibid.

6   Thomas Jefferson, Letter to Dr. John Manners, February 22, 1814.

7   Ibid.

CHAPTER 10

1   Edmund Lester Pearson, quoted in Matthew Battles, *Library: An Unquiet History* (New York: W. W. Norton, 2003), 14.

2   Battles, op. cit., 121-122.

3   Louis Fagan, quoted in Teresa Negrucci, "Historiography of Antonio Panizzi," 2001, http://www.gseis.ucla.edu/faculty/maack/Panizzi.doc; accessed 7 December 2006.

4   Elaine Svenonius, *The Intellectual Foundation of Information Organization* (Cambridge, MA: MIT Press, 2000), 3.

5   A. Wilson, quoted in Shirley Hyatt, "Developments in Cataloging and Metadata," in G. E. Gorman and Daniel G. Dorner, eds., *International Yearbook of Library and Information Management 2003-2004: Metadata Applications and Management* (London: Facet Publishing, 2003), http://www.oclc.org/research/publications/archive/2003/hyatt.pdf; accessed 7 December 2006.

6   Seymour Lubetzky, "The Vicissitudes of Ideology and Technology in Anglo-American Cataloging Since Panizzi and a Prospective Reformation of the Catalog for the Next Century," in Elaine Svenonius and Dorothy McGarry, eds., *Seymour Lubetzky: Writings on the Classical Art of Cataloging* (Englewood, CO: Libraries Unlimited, 2001), 423.

7   Panizzi, quoted in Battles, op. cit., 131.

8   Cutter, quoted in "Charles Ammi Cutter: A Biographical Sketch," 2003, http://us.geocities.com/curmudgeony_librarian/articles/cutter.html; accessed 7 December 2006.

9   One of the first known card catalogs belonged to Edward Gibbon, who recorded the contents of his considerable private library on the backs of playing cards. French librarians developed the first institutional card catalogs in the 1700s. Smithsonian librarian Charles Jewett also envisioned a large distributed catalog with cards that could be shared between libraries.

10 Melvil Dewey, "Classification and Subject Index for Cataloguing and Arranging the Books and Pamphlets of a Library" (1876).

11 Ibid.

12 Cutter, quoted in http://www.libsci.sc.edu/hoerman/clis702/classi2doc.html; accessed 20 December 2006.

13   Ethel Johnson, quoted in Robert V. Williams, "The Documentation and
      Special Libraries Movements in the United States, 1910-1960," in T. B.
      Hahn and M. Buckland, eds., *Historical Studies in Information Science*
      (Medford, NJ: ASIS/Information Today, Inc., 1997), 174.
14   Aksel G. S. Josephson, quoted in Ibid., 173.
15   Guy E. Marion, quoted in Ibid., 174.
16   Charles Ammi Cutter, "The Buffalo Public Library in 1983," *Library
      Journal* 9-10(1883), 211-217.

CHAPTER 11

1   W. Boyd Rayward, "The Case of Paul Otlet, Pioneer of Information
      Science, Internationalist, Visionary: Reflections on Biography," *Journal
      of Librarianship and Information Science* 23 (September 1991),
      135-145.
2   Paul Otlet, quoted in translation by Francoise Levy, *The Man Who
      Wanted to Classify the World* [video] (Brussels: Sofidoc, 2002).
3   Universal Decimal Classification Consortium, "About Universal Deci-
      mal Classification and the UDC Consortium," 2003, http://www.udcc.
      org/about.htm; accessed 7 December 2006.
4   Otlet, quoted in translation by Ron Day, "Paul Otlet's Book and the
      Writing of Social Space," *Journal of the American Society for Informa-
      tion Science* 48(4) (1997), 310-317.
5   Bush's prodigious resume included the invention of an early analog
      computer, stints as a vice president at MIT, president of the Carnegie
      Institution, chairman of the National Defense Council, founder of the
      National Science Foundation, and co-founder of Raytheon. During
      World War II, he served as a close advisor to President Roosevelt and
      played an instrumental role in the Manhattan Project.
6   *Life,* 19 (September 10, 1945), 117.
7   Ted Nelson, "As We Will Think," in James M. Nyce and Paul Kahn, *From
      Memex to Hypertext: Vannevar Bush and the Mind's Machine* (San
      Diego, CA: Academic Press, 1991), 148.
8   James M. Nyce and Paul Kahn, "A Machine for the Mind: Vannevar
      Bush's Memex," in Nyce and Kahn, op. cit., 45-46.

9   Vannevar Bush, "The Inscrutable 'Thirties," in Nyce and Kahn, op. cit., 67.

10 Vannevar Bush, "Memex Revisited," in Nyce and Kahn, op. cit., 201.

11 Michael Buckland, *Emanuel Goldberg and His Knowledge Machine: Information, Invention, and Political Forces* (Westport, CT: Libraries Unlimited, 2006).

12 Bush, quoted in Nyce and Kahn, "A Machine for the Mind," in Nyce and Kahn, op. cit., 42.

13 Vannevar Bush, "As We May Think," *The Atlantic Monthly*, July 1945, http://www.theatlantic.com/doc/194507/bush; accessed 7 December 2006.

14 Michael Buckland has suggested that the now-famous display depicted in Alfred D. Cimi's drawing of the Memex in *Life* draws its inspiration from a real-life workstation already developed by Leonard G. Townsend in 1938.

15 Bush, "As We May Think," op. cit.

16 Ibid.

17 Ibid.

18 Stigmergy is the process of altering external environments to introduce constraints on social behavior (see Chapter 1).

19 Microsoft's MyLifeBits program and Texas A&M's Walden's Path project both attempt to apply Bush's vision of path-based navigation to digital environments.

20 Bush, quoted in Nyce and Kahn, op. cit., 61.

21 Nelson, "As We Will Think," op. cit., 148.

22 Bush, "Memex Revisited," op. cit., 201.

23 Bush, quoted in Nyce and Kahn, op. cit., 62.

24 Bush, quoted in Nyce and Kahn, "The Idea of a Machine: The Later Memex Essays," in Nyce and Kahn, op. cit., 135.

25 "Memex II" was originally slated to appear in *The Atlantic Monthly*, but a series of editorial disagreements and convoluted contractual disputes involving *Life* and *Fortune* ultimately precluded its publication. Bush himself felt that the essay was never quite complete. He later resurrected some of its themes in a subsequent essay, "Memex Revisited," published in his 1967 book *Science Is Not Enough*.

26 Sergey Brin and Larry Page, "The Anatomy of a Large-Scale Hyper-textual Web Search Engine," 1998, http://www-db.stanford.edu/~backrub/google.html; accessed 7 December 2006.

27 Paul Kahn, personal correspondence with Alex Wright, 6 April 2006.

28 Douglas Engelbart, *Augmenting Human Intellect*, http://www.bootstrap.org/augdocs/friedewald030402/augmentinghumanintellect/ahi62index.html; accessed 7 December 2006.

29 Ibid.

30 Ibid.

31 Ibid.

32 Theodor Holm Nelson, *Literary Machines 93.1* (Sausalito, CA: Mindful Press, 1992), 0/3.

33 James Gillies and Robert Cailliau, *How the Web Was Born: The Story of the World Wide Web* (Oxford, England: Oxford University Press, 2000), 100.

34 Paul Kahn, personal correspondence, op. cit.

35 Nelson, quoted in Gillies and Cailliau, op. cit., 101.

36 Ted Nelson, speech at 1995 Vannevar Bush Symposium, quoted in Gillies and Cailliau, op. cit., 100.

37 Nelson, *Literary Machines 93.1*, op. cit., 1/24.

38 Ibid., 1/20.

39 Ibid., 1/11.

40 Theodor Holm Nelson, *Computer Lib/Dream Machines* (Chicago, IL: Nelson, 1974).

41 Nelson, *Literary Machines 93.1*, op. cit., 0/6.

42 Steven Carmody, Walter Gross, Theodor H. Nelson, David Rice, and Andries van Dam, "A Hypertext Editing System for the /360" in Faiman and Nievergelt, eds., *Pertinent Concepts in Computer Graphics: Proceedings of the Second University of Illinois Conference on Computer Graphics* (Champaign, IL: University of Illinois Press, 1969), 291-330.

43 Steven J. DeRose and Andries van Dam, "Document Structure and Markup in the FRESS Hypertext System" in *Markup Languages* 1(1), 7-32.

44 James V. Catano, "Poetry and Computers: Experimenting with the Communal Text," in *Computers and the Humanities*, 13 (1979), 269-275.

45   Nicole Yankelovich, personal correspondence with Alex Wright, 7 April 2006.

46   George P. Landow, personal correspondence with Alex Wright, 19 March 2006.

47   George P. Landow, *Hypertext 2.0* (Baltimore, MD: Johns Hopkins University Press, 1997), 55.

48   Ibid., 2.

49   Ibid., 73.

50   Ibid., 85.

51   Gregory Ulmer, quoted in Ibid., 59.

52   George P. Landow, personal correspondence with Alex Wright, 19 March 2006.

53   Ibid.

54   *Enquire Within Upon Everything,* quoted in Gillies and Cailliau, op. cit., 169.

55   Theodor Holm Nelson, "I Don't Buy In," http://ted.hyperland.com/buyin.txt; accessed 8 January 2003.

56   MacKenzie Wark, quoted in Ben Vershbow, "Small Steps Toward an N-dimensional Reading/Writing Space," Institute for the Future of the Book, 2006, http://www.futureofthebook.org/blog/archives/2006/12/small_ steps_toward_an_n-dimensional.html; accessed 19 December 2006.

CHAPTER 12

1   One Laptop per Child, http://www.laptop.org/; accessed 20 December 2006.

2   Steven Pinker, *The Language Instinct* (New York: HarperPerennial, 1995).

3   UNESCO Education, 2003, "World Literacy in Brief," http://portal.unesco.org/education/en/ev.php-URL_ID=12874&URL_DO=DO_TOPIC&URL_SECTION=201.html; accessed 13 March 2006.

4   Ong, op. cit., 8-9.

5   Ibid., 9.

6   Ibid., 87.

7   "Folksonomy" is a term coined by Thomas Vander Wal, 2004, http:// atomiq.org/archives/2004/08/folksonomy_social_classification.html; accessed 21 December 2006.

8   Davis S. Alberts and Richard E. Hayes, *Power to the Edge: Command . . . Control . . . in the Information Age* (Washington, DC: CCRP Publication Series, 2003).

9   John Seely Brown and Paul Duguid, *The Social Life of Information* (Boston: Harvard Business School Press, 2000), 170.

10   Kelly, op. cit., 45.

11   Francis Fukuyama, *The Great Disruption* (New York: Touchstone, 2000).

12   John Markoff, *What the Doormouse Said: How the 60s Counterculture Shaped the Personal Computer* (New York: Viking, 2005).

Index

A

Abbott, Edward, 3
Aeschylus, 66, 72
Aesop, 105
Age of Enlightenment, 150
Age of Reason, 133, 141
Agrippa, Cornelius, 127
Aguaruna tribe, 22
Alchemy, 63, 133
Alcock, John, 11
Alcuin of York, 93, 259n.13,14
Alexander the Great, 66, 71
Alto personal computer, 216
Amazon.com, 233–234
American Library Association, 173
American Philosophical Society, 161
Ammianus, 77
Amr, 74
"An Anatomy of the World," 230
Andrews, Whit, 102
Anklesaria, Farhad, 224
Annenberg Foundation, 220

Ants, pheromone trails, 13, 14–15, 199
Apollo mission, 218
Apple Hypercard environment, 223
Arab culture, 48, 95–98
Aristophanes, 64–65, 66
Aristophanes of Byzantium, 73
Aristotle, 25, 27, 30, 32, 65, 66–70, 71, 100, 113, 124, 128, 136, 156, 160, 164
ARPANET project, 224
Artificial languages, 123, 137–141, 142, 239–241
ASCII type, 113
As Fine as Melanctha, 22
Ashurbanipal, 54, 55, 93
Assyrians, 48, 54–55
Astrology, 35, 36–37, 63
Astronomy, 35, 63
Augustine, Saint, 113
Aurelian, 74–75
Ausonius, 75
Australian aborigines, 33–34, 36

Authoring/authorship
    collaborative tools, 220
    networked hypermedia model,
        221–223
Autodesk, 214
Aztecs, 57, 161

B

Babbage, Charles, 194
Babylonians, 53–54, 55, 59
Bacon, Francis, 131–137, 139, 148, 163,
    186
Bacteria, 11
Battles, Matthew, 88, 94
Bees, waggle dance, 13, 14
Berlin, Brent, 22, 25, 35
Berners-Lee, Tim, 183, 190–191, 225,
    226, 228
Bestiaries, 100–105, 114
Bestiary, 100–103, 105
Bible, 84–86, 91, 111, 114, 115, 120,
    162
Big Bang, 9
Birds, information sharing, 15–16
Birkerts, Sven, 3
Blogs and bloggers, 2, 83, 228
Bloom, Howard, 9, 12, 13, 131, 210
Boethius, 113
Book of Hours, 109, 115, 147
Book of Kells, 82, 84
Books and bookmaking. *See also*
        Printing, automated
    annotated texts, 89
    binding, 88
    black market, 119
    burning of, 57, 98
    Canon Tables, 84, 85
    codex format, 79
    and cultural change, 104–105,
        109–110
    digitization, 3, 6

dissemination, 103
illuminated manuscripts, 80–86, 99,
    113
illustrated texts, 114–115
K manuscript, 104
manuscript copying, 76, 82, 87–88,
    89–90, 92, 93, 103
market for and proliferation of, 75,
    96, 103–104, 105, 109, 110, 113,
    114, 115, 119, 143, 147–148, 165,
    167, 175
meta-books, 147; *see also*
    Encyclopedias
model books, 104
paper technology, 109–110
papyrus scrolls, 79, 81
popular/secular literature, 100–105,
    109, 113, 115–116, 143, 157
power of, 84–85, 150–151
reading aloud, 90
reproduction technologies, 87–88,
    103–104, 109, 110
scholarly texts, 105, 116
translations, 97, 103, 115
travel books, 116
type styles, 83, 84, 93, 113–114
woodblock printing, 110, 111
a "work" distinguished from, 168–
    169
Borges, Jorge Luis, 140–141, 191
Boston Athenæum, 166, 171, 173
Brand, Stewart, 207–208
Brin, Sergey, 204
Britannia, 80
Brown, Cecil, 25
Brown, John Seely, 234, 235
Brown, Roger, 29
Brown University, 217, 219–220, 221
Bruno, Giordano, 128–131, 262n.16
Buckland, Michael, 266n.14
Buffon, Georges-Louis Leclerc, Comte
        de, 103, 148, 157–161, 164
Bullae, 49

Bush, Vannevar, 185, 190, 192–203,
204, 205, 208, 209, 210, 265n.5,
266n.19

C

Cahill, Thomas, 48
Cailliau, Robert, 209, 218
Callimachus, 73–74, 168
Calvinists, 119
Camillo, Giulio, 122–124, 127, 141
Canon Tables, 84
Carlyle, Thomas, 170
Carolingian Renaissance, 93–94
Cassiodorus, 86–89, 94, 95
Catholic Church. *See* Roman Church
Cato, 105
Catullus, 75
Celtic Church, 81–84
Celts, 80
Cerf, Vinton G., 224
CERN laboratory, 225
Charlemagne, 92–93, 106
Charles V, 98
Chemistry, 63
Cheng Moe, 57
Childe, V. Gordon, 49
Chimpanzees, 16
Chinese
    astrological calendar, 36–37
    folk classification system, 35–36
    Heavenly Archives, 56
    libraries, 56–57, 161
    written language, 48, 56, 257n.1
Christianity, 77. *See also* Celtic Church;
    Protestant Reformation; Roman
    Church
    allegorical literature, 100–101
    cultural bias in classifications, 176
    iconography, 105
    literacy and, 80–81
Cicero, 75, 93, 124

Classification. *See also* Library catalogs
    and classification systems;
    Taxonomies
    faceted, 178–180, 187, 188, 247–249
    folksonomy, 234, 269n.7
    of historical events, 145
    and scientific method, 130–131
    universal schemes, 123, 147, 154,
    186
Claudian, 93
Clement XIII, 150
Climate change, 41–48
Cluetrain Manifesto, The, 7
Coleridge, Samuel Taylor, 213
Collective intelligence, 13
Columbus, Christopher, 116
Communism, 18
Comparator, 197
Computer Lib, 211
Computer science, 193
    biological approach, 194, 202
    commercial impetus, 195, 200, 201,
    215–216
    mathematical and logical models,
    194
Computer theory, 3, 221
Computers
    analog, 194–200, 203, 265n.5
    biological memory, 203
    bit-map displays, 207
    digital, 203
    hierarchical structure, 201
    interactive systems, 217
    interfaces, 205–208, 216
    mainframes, 216, 217
    mouse, 205, 218
    PC revolution, 200–201, 202–203,
    205, 207–208, 216, 237
    windows-style graphical desktop,
    207
Consciousness Explained, 78
Continents of Knowledge project, 221
Copernicus, Nicolaus, 116

Cortés, Hernando, 57
Cosmology, 128
Crook, Nona, 144, 145, 147
Cultural change. *See also individual
      cultures*; Oral culture and
      traditions
   biological evolution and, 9–21, 28,
      32
   books and bookmaking and, 104–
      105, 109–110
   craft literacy, 50
   demythologization, 63–64, 65, 66
   digital revolution and, 6–7, 230–
      238
   epigenetic rules, 20–21, 25, 28, 29
   literacy and, 50–51, 63–65, 78, 83,
      235
   meme exchanges, 13, 14, 16
   multidirectionality, 236–237
   narrative archetypes, 20
   printing press and, 99, 117–121,
      183
Cultural relativism, 11
Currency, 49
Cutter, Charles Ammi, 171–173, 177,
      181–182

D

Dark Ages
   Carolingian Renaissance, 93–94
   illuminated manuscripts, 80–86
   and innovation, 79, 81
   Islamic libraries, 95–98
   and literacy, 78–79, 92–93
   monastic libraries, 91–95
   oral traditions and culture, 78–79,
      92, 96–97, 102, 105, 231
Darwin, Charles, 5, 27
Dawkins, Richard, 12
de Carrara, Giovanni, 126
de Chardin, Teilhard, 2

de Hamel, Christopher, 84
de Landa, Diego, 57
de Montaigne, Michel, 127
de Rohan, Jean, 113
Declaration of Independence, 117, 161
Demetrius, 72
Democracy, 7
Deneubourg, Jean-Louis, 14–15
Dennett, Daniel C., 78
Derrida, Jacques, 221, 223
Dewey Decimal System, 136, 173–178,
      180, 186, 187, 245–246, 257n.9
Dewey, Melvil, 52, 136, 173–175, 186,
      257n.9
Diderot, Denis, 136, 147–151, 169, 186
Difference Engine, 194
Differential Analyzer, 194
Digerati, 1
Digital culture, 4, 230–238
Digital revolution. *See also* Computers;
      Hypertext; Information
      technology
   dark side of, 3
   documentalist movement, 180–181
   Engelbart's demo, 206–208
   and libraries, 177
   mystical beliefs about, 1–3
   social, cultural, and political
      transformations, 6–7, 183–184,
      230–238
Distributed information systems, 144
Divination, 35
"Document nation," 109, 151
Documentalist movement, 180–181
Donald, Merlin, 62, 63, 64
Donne, John, 230
Dot-com boom, 1
Dream Machines, 211–212, 214–215
Druidism, 80
Duguid, Paul, 234, 235
Dunlap, Leslie W., 73
Durkheim, Emile, 33–35, 36, 37, 38,
      260n.6

E

E-mail, 220, 224
Eco, Umberto, vi
Educational institutions and
    curriculum, 51, 53, 105, 173. *See
    also* Public education
Egyptians, 56, 70–75, 128, 129
Eisenstein, Elizabeth, 118
Elizabeth I, 132, 145
Encyclopedias
    Bacon's influence, 136, 148
    Camillo's Theater of Memory, 122–
        124, 141
    Diderot's *Encyclopédie*, 148–151
    folk knowledge, 148–151
    Gunaikeion, 144–147
    and political upheavals, 148–151
    preliterate equivalent, 46
    structure, 144
    Wikipedia project, 150–151
    Wilkins's universal categories, 137–
        141, 239–241
Endeca, 179
Engelbart, Doug, 185, 205–208, 209,
    210, 216, 218, 237
Enquire, 225
Epigenetic rules, 20–21, 25, 28, 29, 43–
    44, 52, 59, 65, 68, 155–156, 180
Erasmus, Desiderius, 115, 119, 122,
    127, 132
Ethernet protocol, 207, 216
Etymologies, 103
Euclid, 71
Eukaryotes, 11
Euripides, 66, 72
Evolution, biological. *See also* Natural
    selection
    gene-culture coevolution, 19–21,
        28, 32
    and hierarchical thinking, 22–28,
        30–31

and information management, 9–
    10, 12, 24–25, 28, 183
meme exchanges and, 13, 14, 16
social cooperation and, 11–12, 43–
    44
and symbolic expression, 18–19,
    43–44

F

Facets, theory of, 179
Fagan, Louis, 167
Family and kinship relationships, 18,
    33, 34–35, 37, 59, 156–157. *See
    also* Genealogies
Febvre, Lucien Paul Victor, 114, 115
Federal Bureau of Investigation, 197
File Retrieving and Editing SyStem
    (FRESS), 218–219, 220
Flamenco, 179
Flatland (Abbott), 3
Fludd, Robert, 131
Folksonomy, 234, 269n.7
Free University, 189
Freemasons, 131
French Revolution, 150, 151
Fuller, Thomas, 127
Fulwood, William, 128

G

Galen, 97
Garfield, Eugene, 203, 204
Genealogies, 34–35, 37, 55
Geomancy, 35
George III, 150
Gesner, Conrad, 154
Gibbon, Edward, 97, 264n.9
Gilgamesh, 55
Gillies, James, 209, 218
Global village, theory of, 2

Gnostics, 130, 262n.16
Goldberg, Emanuel, 196
Google, 191, 204
Gopher system, 224
Goths, 78
Gould, Stephen Jay, 10–11, 23
Government bureaucracies, 51, 109,
      197, 234
Graphical user interface, 205, 216
Grassé, Pierre-Paul, 14
Gratoroli, Guigliemo, 126
Greeks, ancient
      Christian community, 100
      Epicurianism, 76–77
      influence on other cultures, 69–70,
            76–77, 105
      libraries, 55, 57–58, 64, 66, 76
      literate culture, 58, 61–64, 66, 97
      Mycenaean Age, 58
      mythology, 59–61, 62–64
      oral traditions, 58, 59, 61, 64, 67
      taxonomies, 66–68
Greenspan, Stanley, 17–18, 35
Groupware, 206
Gunaikeion, 144–147
Gutenberg, Johannes, 86, 99, 184, 229

H

Hamlet, 122
Harvard University, 208
Hawkins, Jeff, 7
Hermetic man, 127
Hesiod, 59, 60, 61, 62, 66
Hewlett-Packard, 15
Heywood, Thomas, 144–147
Hibernia. *See* Ireland
Hierarchical thinking
      evolution and, 22–28, 30–31
      folk taxonomies, 22–28, 29
      gradation capacity, 30–31

human–computer interactions, 29–
      30
      printed books and, 223
      prototype theory, 30–31
      social networks and, 29, 42–43
Hierarchies. *See also* Library catalogs
      and classification systems;
      Taxonomies
      Aristotle's Great Chain of Being,
            69–70, 136, 156
      defined, 7
      institutional and political, 56–57,
            65, 109, 117
      natural selection and, 11
      of needs, 45
      networks and, 6–9, 7, 11–12, 29,
            42–43, 50, 65, 206, 215
      process, 206
      self-directed biological, 12
Hillis, Danny, 1
Hippocrates, 97
Hittites, 51, 52
Hobart, Michael E., 34, 79
Homer, 61, 66, 88
Horace, 75, 93
Hugo, Victor, 99
Human–computer interfaces, 29–30,
      205–208
Human–machine symbiosis, 194, 202,
      203
Humanism, 127, 132, 210, 215
Hyperbooks, 212–213
Hyperlinks, 201–201, 212, 222–223,
      225
Hypertext, 84, 121, 144, 147, 185, 201,
      208–209, 210, 212, 214, 217,
      219–222, 228
Hypertext (Landow), 221
Hypertext Editing System (HES), 217–
      218, 220
Hyper/Text/Theory (Landow), 221

I

IBM, 217, 218, 220
Ice age, 40–47, 230–231
Illich, Ivan, 90, 94
Illuminated manuscripts, 80–86, 99, 113
Indexes/indexing, 6
  manual, 197, 198–199, 201, 204, 226
India, libraries, 56, 57
Industrial Revolution, 151, 165
Information age, 3
Information clearinghouses, 181
Information ecology, 3–4, 147, 180
Information overload, 3, 9
Information processing, 205–206
Information retrieval
  associative trails, 190–191, 192, 199, 201, 202, 204, 219
  automated systems, 192–203
  bidirectional links, 218–219, 220, 228
  citation ranking, 203–204
  document links, 186, 199–200, 201–202
  graphical user interface, 205, 216
  interactive environment, 219–220
  link-node models, 204
  mouse, 205
  remote file sharing, 224
  tagging, 218, 219
  Web search engines, 6–7, 177, 179, 191, 204
Information science
  Jefferson's legacy, 164
  Ranganathan and, 186
  special libraries, 180–181
Information systems
  biological evolution of, 9–21
  birds, 15–16
  Bloom's model of collective intelligence, 13
  emotional expression as, 17–18, 19, 35
  insect societies, 13–15
  management tools, 6, 12–14, 52
  meme encoding, 12–13, 14, 16, 17, 19
  pooling strategies, 10, 13–14, 19
  social contracts and, 107
  social imitation as, 12–13, 16, 19
  stigmergy, 14–15, 46, 255n.12
  symbolic expression, 17–19, 45–46
Information technology. *See also* Technological innovation; *specific technologies*
  administrative, 215–216
  ancient, 52
  medieval, 104, 117–121
Insect societies, 13–15
Instauratio Magna (Bacon), 136
Institute for Research on Institutions (IRIS), 220
Institutions
  government bureaucracies, 51, 109, 197, 234
  hierarchical nature of, 56–57, 65, 109, 117, 234, 238
  literacy and, 50–58
Intellectual freedom, 71, 72–73
Internet, 3, 7. *See also* World Wide Web
  client–server network, 214
  distributed networking protocols, 224
  interface design, 1, 8
Intertwinglers, 83, 212
Ireland
  illuminated manuscripts, 80–86
  literacy, 80–81
  preliterate culture, 80, 81
  Saint Patrick and, 80–81
IRIS Intermedia, 220–221, 222
Isidore of Seville, 103
Islam, 83, 95, 97
Itzcóatl, 57
Ives, Samuel A., 104

J

James I, 137
Jefferson, Thomas, 117, 136, 152, 159–160, 161–164, 165
Jewett, Charles, 263
Jews, 97, 115
Jobs, Steve, 207
Johnson, Ethel, 180
Johnson, Samuel, 49
Johnson, Steven, 1
Josephson, Aksel G. S., 180
Julius Caesar, 71, 74, 75
Justinian, 97
Juvenal, 93

K

Kahn, Paul, 195, 204, 221
Kahn, Robert B., 224
Kelly, Kevin, 208, 235
King, Cyrus, 162
Knowledge workers. *See* Librarians; Scribes
Kodak, 196
Koran, 96, 162
Kuhn, Steven, 42
Künsel, Werner, 3
Kurzweil, Ray, 2

L

La Fontaine, Henri, 186, 188
Lakoff, George, 31–32
Lamberton, Robert, 59, 61, 62
Landow, George P., 116, 221–222
Lao Tzu, 56
Lateral sequencing, 27, 52
League of Nations, 185, 188, 189
Lehmann-Haupt, Hellmut, 104
Lewis, C. S., 105
Lewis, Rhodri, 131, 139

Librarians, 76, 94, 165–166, 174, 181
Libraries
    academic, 109, 138, 166, 173, 176
    American, 6, 136, 162–164, 166, 169, 171–178
    Arabian legacy, 95–98
    Aztec, 57, 161
    biblioclasms, 56, 57, 71, 74–75, 78, 87, 97, 98, 161, 183
    British Museum library, 166, 167–171, 186
    Chinese, 56–57, 161
    Christian, 76, 88
    democratic access to, 169–173
    digital, 195–196
    government archives, 52–53, 78
    Great Library at Alexandria, 55, 66, 70–75, 76, 79, 89, 161
    Greek, 55, 57–58, 64, 66, 76
    guidelines for book collecting, 94
    Indian, 56
    Jefferson's, 161–164, 242–244
    lending practices, 76
    limitations of, 195–196
    monastic, 80, 88, 89–90, 91–95
    networks, 94, 182, 264n.9
    political potency, 56–57, 72, 75, 93
    private book collections, 66, 77, 147, 162–164, 166, 264n.9
    public, 70–77, 96, 147, 166, 173, 176
    Roman, 75–77, 82, 87, 88
    Royal Library at Nineveh, 54–55
    special, 180-181
    temple, 51, 52, 55, 57
    at Thebes, 56
    Vatican, 88, 95, 121
    virtual, 181–182
Library catalogs and classification systems
    ancient bibliographic records and systems, 51–52, 76–77
    Anglo-American Cataloging Rules, 169

Aristotelian, 66
author-based, 74
Bacon's framework, 136, 163
bicameral, 76–77, 87–88, 94–95, 121
Bliss system, 177
books distinguished from works, 168–169, 180
call numbers, 52, 170, 172, 173, 182
card catalog, 165, 173, 174, 176, 264n.9
Chinese classification schemes, 56–57
Colon Classification, 145, 178–180, 247–249
colophons, 51–52
cultural bias in, 176
Cutter's Expansive Classification System, 171–173, 180
Dewey Decimal System, 136, 173–178, 180, 186, 187, 245–246, 257n.9
Library of Congress system, 162–163, 173, 176, 177, 179, 197, 242–244
meta information, 168
monastic scrutinium, 94–95
online catalogs, 176, 181–182
Panizzi's rules, 167–171, 186
subject-based, 73, 88, 168, 171–178
textual analysis–based, 88–89
Universal Decimal Classification, 177, 187, 188, 190
value-based, 91
Web displacement of, 6, 176–177, 226
Library of Congress, 6, 136, 162–164, 169, 173, 176, 177, 179, 197
Library schools, 173
Library science, 178
Lindisfarne Gospel, 82, 84
Lindisfarne monastery, 84
Links, 186, 199, 218

Linnaeus, Carolus, 4, 25, 30, 103, 153
Literacy
and cognitive conflict, 120–121
craft, 50, 106
Dark Ages and, 78–79, 92–93
entertainment-based, 61
and mythic thought, 62–63
oral culture distinguished from, 232–234
and political power, 50, 51, 54, 56–57, 58, 62, 77, 84–85, 108
printing innovations and, 166
public education and, 165
reading books, 90, 91–92, 108
and social organization, 51, 58, 65, 76, 78–79, 80–81, 83, 90, 97, 107–110, 117
spread of, 105–110, 117
Literary Machines, 211, 213, 214
"Living in the New Middle Ages," vi
Lloyd, William, 137
Locke, John, 9
Louis XV, 150
Lubetzky, Seymour, 169
Lucian, 93
Luther, Martin, 117, 118, 151

M

Macbeth, 152
Machiavelli, Niccolò, 115
Macintosh, 207
Madras University, 178
Magic, 128–129, 133
Margulis, Lynn, 11, 13
Marion, Guy F., 181
Martial, 76, 93
Martin, Henri-Jean, 114, 115
Maslow, Abraham, 45
Mauss, Marcel, 33, 35, 36, 38
Mayans, 48, 257n.4
McCahill, Mark, 224

McClamrock, Ron, 15
McCrone, John, 41
McLuhan, Marshall, 2, 4
Melanchthon, Philipp, 127
Memes, 12–13, 14, 16, 19, 254n.9
Memex, 185, 192–194, 197–198, 199, 200, 201, 202, 203, 266n.25
Memory
    association, 125
    Camillo's Theater of Memory, 122–124, 141, 142
    feats of, 126
    human, 7
    insect and hive, 14
    monastic art of, 123–132
    Novum Organum (Bacon), 132
    ordering, 124
    wheel, 129–130, 142
Meyrowitz, Norm, 220
Microfilm, 181, 192, 194, 196, 197, 200, 203
Microsoft Windows, 207
Middle Ages, 53, 69–70
    Islamic expansion, 83
    literacy, 105–110
    oral traditions, 105
Milton, John, 162
Minoans, 58
Mohammed, 48, 96
Monasteries and monacticism
    armarius, 91
    art of memory, 123–127
    Cassiodurus's Vivarium, 87–88
    Celtic bookmaking, 79, 80–86
    English scriptoria, 84, 85, 104
    libraries, 91–95
    popular literature from, 103–105, 109
    reading books, 90, 91–92
    Rule of Saint Benedict, 91–92
Money. *See* Currency
Mongol invasions, 97
Moorehouse, A. C., 53–54

Moors, 97–98
More, Thomas, 162
Morison, Robert, 137
Motley, John Lothrop, 119–120
Mouse, 205, 206–207
Mundaneum, 188–190, 192, 200
Muslim culture, 95–98
Mycenaeans, 58
Mystical beliefs about technology, 1–3
Mystical memory wheels, 123
Mythic thought, 62–63, 64, 65
Mythology, 4, 6, 135
    epigenetic rules and, 20–21, 59
    genealogical relationships, 37, 55, 59–61
    literacy and, 54, 55, 62–66, 81
    metaphorical relationships among natural phenomena, 59–60
    oral culture and, 59, 61
    symbolism in, 41
    taxonomic roots, 33, 35–36, 37–38, 61

N

NASA, 218
National Endowment for the Humanities, 221
National Science Foundation, 224, 265n.5
Natural selection, 11, 13, 24–25, 45–46
NCR, 196
Nelson, Ted, 185, 190, 193, 201, 208–215, 217, 221, 222, 225, 226–227, 237
Newton, Isaac, 162
Networks
    associative, 79, 190–191, 192, 199, 201, 202, 204
    computer, 6, 15, 43
    cultural, social, and political, 5–6, 7, 11–12, 43

defined, 7
and hierarchies, 6–9, 7, 11–12, 29,
    42–43, 50, 65, 215, 234–238
neural, 7
Otlet's vision, 190
scholarly, 134, 153
self-organizing, 11–12, 65, 147, 191,
    235, 237
superorganisms, 12, 13–14
swarm intelligence, 15
walled garden, 259n.13
New York University, 45
Newman, John Henry, 115
Newspapers, 117–118, 165
Nicolas, Nicholas Harris, 169, 170
Nigerians, 48
Novum Organum (Bacon), 132,
    133–134
NSFNet, 224
Nyce, James M., 195

O

Occultism, 128–129, 130, 131
Ong, Walter J., 50, 90, 232–233
oN-Line System (NLS), 206, 207, 218
Oral culture and traditions
    Dark Ages, 78–79, 92, 96–97, 102,
        105
    durability of, 18–19, 47, 58–59, 78–
        79, 105
    electronic media and, 231–234
    in encyclopedias, 148–151
    folk taxonomies, 46, 52, 61, 102
    Greek, 58, 59, 61, 64, 67
    literacy's threat to, 64, 84
    monastic art of memory, 125
    and mythology, 46, 59, 61, 62–63, 64
    popular literature from, 53, 62, 100,
        102, 116–117
    printing press and, 116–117, 120–121
    and social networks, 65

Oratory, 124
Organizational charts, 6
Ornament technology, 42
Otlet, Paul, 185–192, 199, 200
Oxford Internet Institute, 214

P

Page, Larry, 204
Pagerank, 204
Panizzi, Anthony, 167–171, 180, 186
Paper technology, 109–110
Pearson, Edmund Lester, 165
Pepys, Samuel, 137
Perseus environment, 223
Peter of Ravenna, 126
Phoenicians, 61
Physiologus, 100, 102–103, 105
Pinakes, 73–74
Pinker, Steven, 231
Pius VI, 260n.12
Plato, 63–64, 71
Pliny, 100, 157, 160
Poetry, 61, 62
Political changes, 43, 50, 54
    digital revolution and, 6–7, 151
    encyclopedias and, 148–151
    library catalogs and, 169–171
    printing press and, 99, 117–121,
        151, 183
Pope, Alexander, 162
Popper, Karl, 258n.23
Population density, and innovation,
    17–18, 48–49
Populist ethos, 148, 150, 169, 171, 230–
    231
Primates, nonhuman, social
    networking, 16–17, 19
Printing, automated, 86
    Gutenberg press, 99, 104, 105, 108,
        110–117, 151, 184
    laser printers, 216

and literacy, 166
and Protestant Reformation, 117–121, 151
and social and political change, 99, 117–121, 151, 184
steam-driven presses, 165, 166
Privacy issues, 3
Prosperus, 105
Protestant Reformation, 117–121
Prototype theory, 30–32
Ptolemy I, 55, 71, 72, 93, 97
Ptolemy III, 72
Public education, 165
Punch cards, 181
Punch transfer technique, 104, 110

Q

Quintilian, 124

R

Rabelais, François, 115
Rameses II, 56
Random access, 79, 81
Ranganathan, Shiyali Ramamrita, 145, 178–180, 186–187, 247–249
Rapid Selector, 196, 197, 198
Ray, John, 137, 154
Rayward, Boyd, 184–185, 189–190
Relational databases, 179
Religious wars, 118–121
Renaissance
    Arabic texts and, 98
    Gutenberg revolution, 99, 110–117
    secular scholarship, 106, 109, 115, 127, 138, 141, 143, 157
Rheingold, Howard, 208
Rhodes, Neil, 144, 145, 147
Roman Church, 2, 82
    erosion of authority of, 111–113, 118–121, 130, 132–133, 141, 151

Gutenburg press and, 111–113, 118–121, 151
indulgences, 112, 260n.12
Inquisition, 128
and scientific inquiry, 139–140
Roman Empire, 54, 75–77, 78, 80, 81, 82, 90, 124
Romberch, Johannes, 126
Rosch, Eleanor, 30, 31
Rosicrucians, 131
Rosselli, Cosimo, 126
Rousseau, 148
Royal Commission, 170
Royal Society, 137, 140

S

Saccath, 80
Saint Albans Abbey, 85
Saint Columba, 78
Saint Finnian, 78
Saint Jerome, 94
Saint Patrick, 80–81, 86
Saint Riquier Abbey, 94
Salvatorberg cloister, 94
Schiffman, Zachary Sayre, 34, 79
Schlain, Leonard, 118, 120
Scholarly publishing, 153, 196–197
    citation ranking, 203–204
Scholastic methods, 132
Science Citation Index, 204
Scientific method
    Bacon's empiricism, 133–137, 164
    classical view of categories and, 32
    emergence of, 123, 130–131, 141–142, 143
    and religious doctrine, 139–140
    and scholarly publishing, 153
Scribes, 49, 50, 53, 76, 81, 82–83, 89, 106
Secular scholarship, 106, 109, 115, 127, 138, 141, 143

Selfish Gene, The (Dawkins), 12
Semantic scaffolding, 19
Semiramis, 145
Servius, 93
Sextus, 76
Shadunu, 54–55
Shakespeare, William, 105, 122, 152
Shi Huangdi, 56, 161
Simon Magus, 262n.16
Simonides of Ceos, 124
Sixtus IV, 95
Smith, Samuel H., 162
Smithsonian, 264n.9
Social behaviors, 14–17
    and evolution, 11–12
    human universal, 20–21
Social collectivization, 3
Social contracts, 106–110
Social fact, 107, 260n.6
Social networks
    family and kinship, 33, 34–35, 156–157
    and hierarchical thinking, 29, 42–43
    self-organizing, 65, 116
    and symbolic communication, 41–42, 43, 45, 46, 50
    and taxonomies, 29, 32–38, 156–157
    textual communities, 117
    written communication and, 50–51, 62, 65
Social systems, 6. *See also* Cultural change
    caste distinctions, 51, 58
    consensual rule sets, 106
    digital revolution and, 6–7, 234–238
    evolution of, 11–12, 106–107
Social tagging, 234
Socrates, 65, 71
Solomon, 100
Sophists, 63

Sophocles, 66, 72
Sorbonne, 94
Special Libraries Association, 180
Spenser, Edmund, 105
Spiritual beliefs, 1–3, 6
Spoken language, 17, 28
Stanford Research Institute, 206
Stanford University, 204
Statius, 93
Stein, Gertrude, 22
Stigmergy, 14–15, 108, 199, 266n.18
Stock, Brian, 106, 108, 117, 260n.8
Strabo, 66
Stretchtext, 212
Subjectivity, 135, 139
Sumerians, 48–49, 52, 53, 55, 57, 59, 231, 257n.3
Superstitious belief, 135–136, 140
Svenonius, Elaine, 168
Swarthmore College, 217
Swedish Royal Society of Science, 153
Symbols and symbolic language
    adaptive value of, 43–44, 45–46
    allegorical literature, 100–101, 105
    beads and pendants, 42–43, 44, 107
    cave paintings, 43, 45–46, 257n.6 (Chapter 3)
    Christian iconography, 105, 118–119
    emotional meaning, 17–19, 43–44
    epigenetic rules, 43–44
    evolutionary progression of, 18–19
    Incan *Quipu*, 39
    illuminated manuscripts, 80–86, 99, 113
    in myths, 41
    origins, 40–41
    social documents, 107–108
    and social relationships,, 41–42 43, 45, 46, 50, 52, 107, 231
    stigmergy of, 46, 108
    totems, 42, 106

T

Tabulating devices, 49
Tarquin, 54
Taxonomies
  and adaptive advantage, 24–25
  Aristotolian, 67–68, 70, 156
  binomial naming, 67, 156
  Buffonian, 152, 157–161, 164
  classical view of categories, 32, 145
  cultural parallels, 25–28, 30–31, 33–
    38
  defined, 23
  as encyclopedic framework, 34
  epigenetic basis, 20–21, 25, 28, 29,
    30, 52, 65, 67, 155–156
  ethnobiological rank model, 25, 29,
    34
  folk, 5–6, 22–27, 28–29, 30–38, 47,
    52, 61, 68, 100, 154–156, 164
  genealogies, 34, 59, 61
  Jefferson's legacy, 152–153, 159–
    160, 161
  Linnaean, 22, 23–24, 25, 29, 32, 70,
    103, 153, 154–157, 158–159,
    160, 164
  matter distinguished from form,
    68–69
  mythologies as, 33, 35–36, 37–38,
    59, 61
  New World plants and animals,
    154, 159–160
  popular literature, 100, 102–105
  prototype theory, 30–32
  recognition of "real names," 27, 28–
    29, 156
  social role, 32–38
  and superstitious beliefs, 38
  Wilkins's universal categories, 137–
    141, 239–241
  Zuni system, 5–6, 33–34, 36
Technological innovation
  Dark Ages and, 79, 81
  disruptive, 99, 117–121, 150–151,
    183, 223
  population density and, 17–18, 48–
    49
Technological transcendentalism, 1–3
Television, 236
Temple archives, 6
Terence, 93
Termite nest building, 14
Text editing tools, 216
Textual communities, 117
Thomas Aquinas, Saint, 113, 124–125,
  126
Thompson, James Westfall, 95
Thoth, 130
Thucydides, 66
Tibetan Buddhism, 130
Tibullus, 93
Time keeping, 49, 257n.3
Timon of Philius, 73
Tournefot, Joseph Pitton de, 154
Townsend, Leonard G., 266n.14
Trade networks, 43–44, 49–50
Transcendentalism, 128
Transmission Control Protocol/
  Internet Protocol (TCI/IP), 224

U

Unicorns, 4
Universal Decimal Classification
  Consortium, 188
University of California at Berkeley,
  179
University of Leyden, 138
University of Minnesota, 224
Unix, 216
Upper Paleolithic period, 42
U.S. Department of Defense, 224
U.S. Patent Office, 197

V

van Dam, Andries, 217
van Schaik, Carel, 16–17
Vandals, 77, 78
Venerable Bede, 86
Viglius, 122, 127
Virgil, 75
Virginia Statute of Religious Freedom, 161
Voltaire, 148
von Frisch, Karl, 14

W

Wallace, A. R., 5
Walled garden, 93, 259n.13
Wark, McKenzie, 229
Watterston, George, 163
Wei Dynasty, 57
Wells, H. G., 2, 232
White, Randall, 45
Whitehead, Alfred North, 13
Whole Earth Catalog, 207–208
Whole Earth Review, 207–208
Wide Area Information Server, 223
Wikipedia project, 150–151, 238
Wilkins, John, 137–141, 186, 239–241
William of Ockham, 113
Willis, John, 124
Willughby, Francis, 137
Wilson, David Sloan, 13
Wilson, E. O., 19–21, 28, 32, 46, 254n.9, 255n.12
Wired era, 210
Witch burnings, 120–121
Wolfe, Tom, 1
Women, Fire and Dangerous Things (Lakoff), 31–32
Woodblock printing, 110, 111
Women
   encyclopedia on, 144–147
   librarians, 174

World Brain, 2
World Wide Web, 2, 147
   browsers, 8, 179, 201, 214, 220, 228–229
   Bush's legacy, 193–194
   coexistence of oral and written culture, 233–238
   commercial impetus, 215
   document control, 191
   limitations, 226–229
   Nelson's vision, 213–214, 226–228
   on NEXT platform, 226
   as oral culture, 231–234
   Otlet's réseau, 185–192
   prototypes, 223–229
   search engines, 6–7, 177, 179, 191, 204
   and social and political change, 151, 183–184, 225–226, 238
   social context, 43, 191–192, 228, 234
   symbolic communication, 44
Wright, H. Curtis, 258n.18
Writing, 4, 19. *See also* Books and bookmaking; Libraries; Literacy; *specific cultures*
   alphabets, 61–62
   chronological records, 53
   clay tablets, 49–50, 51, 81
   colophons, 51–52
   commercial origins and implications, 49–50, 106–107, 183, 215
   copying, 55, 76, 78
   craft literacy, 50, 106
   Ebla tablets, 51
   emergence of, 46, 48–50, 257n.4
   Hattusas tablets, 51
   knowledge bureaus (ancient), 50–58
   linear format, 81
   list making, 51, 52

mythological significance, 48, 54,
    56
narrative, 52, 53, 62, 64, 183
numbers, 49
phonetic system, 61–62
preservation, 53, 55
process, 206
random access form, 81, 83–84
scribes, 49–50, 51, 53, 64, 80–86,
    106
secularization, 92–93, 106, 139
self-directed, 83
social contracts, 106–110
and social transformation, 50, 62–
    63, 99, 106–110, 118
Wurman, Richard Saul, 6
WYSIWIG, 216

X

Xanadu system, 209, 213–214, 217, 227
Xerox PARC, 207, 216
Xylography, 114, 260n.16

Y

Yahoo!, 191
Yankelovich, Nicole, 220
Yates, Frances A., 126, 127, 128, 129,
    131

Z

Zenodotus, 73
Zuni people, 5–6, 33–34, 36